Teaching Cues for Sport Skills for Secondary School Students

THIRD EDITION

Hilda Ann Fronske

UTAH STATE UNIVERSITY

PEARSON

Benjamin
Cummings

San Francisco   Boston   New York
Cape Town   Hong Kong   London   Madrid   Mexico City
Montreal   Munich   Paris   Singapore   Sydney   Tokyo   Toronto

Publisher: Daryl Fox
Acquisitions Editor: Deirdre Espinoza
Development Manager: Claire Alexander
Project Editor: Susan Malloy
Assistant Editor: Christina Pierson
Production Supervisor: Steven Anderson
Manufacturing Buyer: Stacey Weinberger
Cover Designer: Yvo Riezebos Design
Text Designer: The Left Coast Group
Production and Composition: The Left Coast Group
Copy Editor: Gary Morris
Proofreader: Joan Wai
Cover Printer: Phoenix Book Tech
Text Printer: Malloy

Cover Photos: from Getty Images, basketball by Ryan McVay, shuttlecock by
C Squared Studios, football helmet by Ryan McVay, tennis racket by Steve Cole.

ISBN 0-8053-5454-9

Library of Congress Cataloging-in-Publication Data
Fronske, Hilda Ann.
   Teaching cues for sport skills for secondary school students / Hilda Anna
   Fronske.—
3rd ed.
     p. cm.
   2nd ed. published under title: Teaching cues for sport skills.
   ISBN 0-8053-5454-9 (pbk. : alk. paper)
   1. Sports—Study and teaching (Secondary) 2. School sports—Coaching. I. Title.
   GV361.F66 2005
   796'.7'7—dc22   2004007739

1 2 3 4 5—MAL—07 06 05 04
www.aw-bc.com

To my late grandfather Dr. Martin George Fronske,
who challenged me throughout my career.

Contents

Preface

Have you ever dreamed of a book that would cover teaching cues, drill progressions, and mini-games for a variety of sport skills and activities for secondary and high school students? The wait is over! Featured in this unique and exciting book are teaching cues and activities for 30 sports and physical activities.

This book also features live-action pictures of athletes executing the cues. This book will save you hours of planning time by providing you with a user-friendly format. The cues will establish credibility with your students faster because you can tell them why a particular cue works and analyze a skill better to speed up their learning.

ACKNOWLEDGMENTS

I would like to thank the awesome crew at Benjamin Cummings, especially Deirdre Espinoza, Acquisitions Editor, and Christina Pierson, Assistant Editor, for their incredible energy, inspiration, wit, enthusiasm, and editing ideas for the third edition. I also appreciate the time, effort, and suggestions of the reviewers for this edition: Tim Barrett, Ohio State University; Sheri Brock, Auburn University; Ang Chen, University of Maryland, College Park; Xiaofen Keating, California State University, Los Angeles; Anne Larson, California State University, Los Angeles; John Todorovich, University of Florida, Gainesville; Doris Watson, University of Utah.

Additionally, I would like to thank all the athletes at Utah State University and Brigham Young University who posed for the photographs for this book.

Sport Consultants

Thank you to Dr. Art Jones, Debbie Tidwell, Jennifer Holt, Beth Allen, and Rolayne Wilson for their support and assistance with the book. Thank you to Ralph and Marlene Meikle for their support and friendship. Thanks to all of the sport consultants who generously shared their time, knowledge, and expertise in their specific sports with me.

Aerobic Kickboxing: Chris Erickson, certified aerobic kickboxing instructor, second-degree black belt, elementary physical education teacher, Adams Elementary School, Logan, Utah.

Archery: Joyce Harrison, associate dean, Brigham Young University, Provo, Utah. Derek Lindley, archery manager at pro shop, Al's Sporting Goods, Logan, Utah. Val Spillet, vice president of Al's Sporting Inc., Logan, Utah.

Badminton: Peggy Savosik, Jim Leete, and Jim Stabler, USA Badminton, Colorado Springs, Colorado. Gord Smith, Badminton Canada, Gloucester, Ontario, Canada. Richard Jones, Brigham Young University, Provo, Utah.

Baseball: Justin Jensen, associate scout for Milwaukee Brewers, Rocky Mountain School of Baseball, Logan, Utah. Jonathan Howell, Health, Physical Education, and Recreation Department, Utah State University, Logan, Utah. Rick Thorne, Skyview High School head baseball coach, Smithfield, Utah.

Basketball: Coach Al Brown, assistant basketball coach for Lady Volunteers, University of Tennessee, Knoxville. Shanna Stevens, Utah State University club basketball coach, Logan, Utah.

Bowling: Richard Jones, professor in pedagogy and sports, Brigham Young University, Provo, Utah. Russell Boyer, undergraduate student, Utah State University, Logan, Utah.

Cycling—Mountain Biking: Quinn Bingham, bicycle technician, Al's Sporting Goods, Logan, Utah. Jeff Keller, Sunrise Cycle, Logan, Utah. Steven Gudmundson, graduate student, Utah State University, Logan, Utah. Emily Watkins, graduate student, Utah State University, Logan, Utah.

Cycling—Road Biking: Jeff Keller, Sunrise Cycle, Logan, Utah. Steven Gudmunson, graduate student, Utah State University, Logan, Utah. State Stowers, bicycle technician, Al's Sporting Goods, Logan, Utah. Emily Watking, undergraduate student, Utah State University, Logan, Utah.

Field Hockey: Laura Darling, United States Field Hockey Association, Colorado Springs, Colorado. Katie Harris and Deanie Stetson, Falmouth High School, Falmouth, Maine.

Flag Football: Bill Bauer, facility coordinator, Utah State University, Logan, Utah. Jeff Berg, football player, Utah State University, Logan, Utah. Art Erickson, player and coach, Utah State University, Logan, Utah.

Floor Hockey: Ross Keys, physical education undergraduate student, and Michael Burggraf, physical education undergraduate student, Utah State University, Logan, Utah. Gianni Maddalozzo, instructor in physical education, Department of Exercise and Sport Science, Oregon State University, Corvallis, Oregon.

Golf: Robert Fronske, amateur golf player, Tempe, Arizona. Dan Roskelley, golf professional, Logan Golf and Country Club, Logan, Utah. Brett Wayment, assistant professional, Logan Golf and Country Club, Logan, Utah.

In-Line Skating: Lisa Klarich Davis, teacher, Ecker Hill Middle School, Park City, Utah. Margot Willett, program director, Skate in School, Edina, Minnesota.

Lacrosse: Roger Allen, lacrosse coach, Logan, Utah. Mason Goodhand, Utah Lacrosse Association, Salt Lake City, Utah. Heriberto "Eddie" Vega, head lacrosse coach, Utah State University, Logan, Utah.

Pickle-Ball: Sarah Lowe, Angela Kimball, Amy Thatcher and Jackie Ellis, tennis team at Utah State University, Logan, Utah. Tedi Searle, physical education undergraduate student, Utah State University, Logan, Utah. Doug Smith, general manager, Pickle-Ball Inc., Seattle, Washington.

Racquetball: Chris Atkins, head racquetball club coach, Utah State University, Logan, Utah. Jim Hiser, American Amateur Racquetball Association, Colorado Springs, Colorado. Susan Hill, graduate student, Health Department, Southern Illinois University, Carbondale, Illinois.

Recreational Running and Walking: Patrick Shane, head women's cross-country/distance coach, Brigham Young University, Provo, Utah. Kevin Prusak, assistant professor, elementary physical education, Brigham Young University, Provo, Utah. Sue Vincent, assistant professor, elementary physical education, Brigham Young University, Provo, Utah.

Soccer: Chris Agnello, men's soccer coach, Department of Exercise and Sport Science, University of Utah, Salt Lake City, Utah. Brent Anderson, assistant soccer coach, Heather Carins, head women's soccer coach, Utah State University, Logan, Utah. Charles Dudschus, Health, Physical Education, and Recreation Department, Utah State University, Logan, Utah. Kelli Brooke Parsons, undergraduate physical education student, Utah State University, Logan, Utah. Jin Wang, men's soccer coach, Rockford College, Rockford, Illinois.

Softball: Lloydene Searle, women's fast-pitch head softball coach, Utah State University, Logan, Utah. Ann Schulz, softball coach, Sandridge Junior High School, Layton, Utah. Emily Watkins, graduate student, Stephanie Vasarhely, graduate teaching assistant, Nicole Downs, physical education undergraduate student, Kelly Warner, physical education undergraduate student, Utah State University, Logan, Utah.

Strength Training: Art Erickson and Don Gowans, Health, Physical Education and Recreation Department, Utah State University, Logan, Utah. Nicole Anastasia McKenzie, North Dakota State University, Fargo, North Dakota. Jamie Bennion, heptathlete, graduate student, Utah State University, Logan, Utah. Peter Mathesius, fitness specialist, Utah State University, Logan, Utah.

Swimming: Katrina Bingham, swimming and water aerobics instructor, Utah State University, Logan, Utah. Lisa Klarich and Steven Dunn, Health, Physical Education and Recreation Department, Utah State University, Logan, Utah.

Team Handball: Mary Phyl Dwight, cochair, Coaching and Methods Committee, United States Team Handball Federation, Kansas City, Missouri. Reita Clanton, assistant coach for women's team handball, Atlanta, Georgia. Peter Mathesius, physical education instructor, Utah State University, Logan, Utah.

Tennis: Janet Carey, tennis professional, Neversink, New York. Dan Clifton, tennis instructor for campus recreation instructional program, Utah State University, Logan, Utah. Steven Dunn, former assistant professor in physical education, Rolayne Wilson, associate professor of physical education, Joy Hartung, tennis athlete and undergraduate student, Tedi Searle, physical education undergraduate student, and Clay Stevens, former graduate student, Utah State University, Logan, Utah. Sarah Lowe, Angela Kimball, Amy Thatcher, and Jackie Ellis, tennis team at Utah State University, Logan, Utah.

Touch Rugby: Peter Mathesius, physical education instructor, Utah State University, Logan, Utah. Michelle Olphi, undergraduate rugby player, Utah State University, Logan, Utah.

Track and Field: Curtis Collier, track technician, Utah State University, Logan, Utah. Dayna Barrett, track and field heptathlete, and Jamie Bennion, heptathlete and graduate student, Utah State University, Logan, Utah.

Tumbling: Tana Davis and Kim Autenrieb, Ten-O-Gymnastics Academy, Logan, Utah. Ben Nilson, undergraduate assistant gymnastics coach, Utah State University, Logan, Utah.

Ultimate Frisbee: Ann Asbell, activity specialist, Department of Exercise and Sport Science, Oregon State University, Corvallis, Oregon. Janenne Graff, player/coach, Ultimate Frisbee Club, Utah State University, Logan, Utah.

Volleyball: Carl McGown, Department of Physical Education, Brigham Young University, Provo, Utah. Lana Moser, head volleyball coach, Preston High School, Preston, Idaho.

Yoga: Rachel Hebert, yoga practitioner and model, San Francisco, California. Denise "Deni" Preston, certified group exercise fitness instructor for American Council on Exercise, Brigham Young University, Provo, Utah. Photography: Christina Pierson.

Teaching Physical Education Is Fun with the Right Tools

Have you ever found yourself asking these questions: How can I do a good job teaching physical education and have fun at the same time? What is the quickest and most efficient way to teach sport skills in the time I have been allotted? What tools do I have available to provide a positive learning environment in the sports arena and to build lasting relationships with my students?

This book answers these questions and provides a wealth of teaching cues for physical education activities in your curriculum. The benefits of this book are distinct from the skills text.

- The text answers *why* a cue is appropriate for a skill.
- The text includes photographs of students and athletes, each cue labeled.
- The text provides cues for successfully teaching fundamental sport skills that are developmentally appropriate.
- The text reinforces the National Standard for Physical Education (NASPE, 1995).
- The text provides a resource for enrichment of the state core curriculums.
- Using teaching cues addresses the three learning domains: psychomotor, cognitive, and affective.
- The cues are broken down by components and are easily modified for students with disabilities.
- The cues provide a framework for authentic assessment by teachers and students.
- The cues provide an opportunity to integrate other curricular areas.

TOOL 1: WHAT AM I SUPPOSED TO TEACH?

The National Association for Sport and Physical Education (NASPE) established seven content standards and numerous benchmarks that provide curricular objectives for a physically educated person. The content standards are:

1. Demonstrates competency in many movement forms and proficiency in a few movement forms.
2. Applies movement concepts and principles to the learning and development of motor skills.
3. Exhibits a physically active lifestyle.
4. Achieves and maintains a health-enhancing level of physical fitness.
5. Demonstrates responsible personal and social behavior in physical activity settings.
6. Demonstrates understanding of and respect for differences among people in physical activity settings.
7. Understands that physical activity provides opportunities for enjoyment, challenge, self-expression, and social interaction.

The NASPE (1995) content standards and your state core curriculum provide a curricular foundation for teaching physical education.

TOOL 2: WHAT ARE TEACHING CUES?

A *cue* is defined as a guiding suggestion or a stimulus that excites the imagination to action. Cues are short, catchy phrases that call the student's attention to key components of a skill. A cue projects a clear description of a skill component into the mind's eye of the student.

Cues may be verbal, serving as a short reminder of more complete information presented about a skill. A cue developed around rich visual imagery, or related to the student's previous experience, remains in cognition much longer than a lengthy dissertation on the fine points of technique. A mind cluttered with many technical concepts cannot direct the muscles to achieve flawless coordination. At best, a mind concentrating on one visual or kinesthetic prompt may direct that one body part to obey the command. For example, a verbal cue for shooting a basketball is "palm up." Phrases may be more visual, with the intent of creating a picture in the learner's mind that results in correct skill performance. The "palm up" cue could be followed by "like holding a waiter's tray." These are prompts that provide a rich visual imagery for students to identify the skill component. By visualizing these familiar patterns, students are able to develop skill patterns, and if they begin to show poor form, a cue serves as a quick reminder of proper form.

Too often when teaching sport skills, the teacher overloads the student with too much information and technical jargon, which may make little sense to the student. Motor learning specialists have long noted that the simpler the instructions, the easier it is for the student to concentrate on the skill at hand. The KISS principle, "keep it short and simple," is applied.

TOOL 3: WHY DO STUDENTS NEED TO GET A CUE?

Cues are used to motivate students. Research has found that students who receive cues appear to be more motivated to improve their performance than students who do not receive them. The self-confidence of the cued students seems to increase steadily with improved skill ability, as they work to improve each day. Students who do not receive cues appear to be frustrated and bored

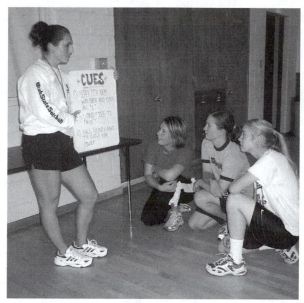

FIGURE 1.1 Cues Poster

and have a difficult time staying on task (Fronske, Abendroth-Smith, & Blakemore, 1997).

Cues can help students set higher goals in skill performance. Cues arouse students to direct their efforts toward improving their performance and provide a foundation for setting goals. When students feel the success of learning one cue at a time, other cues can be introduced without intimidation until they become proficient at the complete skill component. Mastering one cue at a time gives students very specific goals to work for. By providing a cue, or a few alternative cues, students are able to choose one and work at their own pace. Create cues posters and display them in your facility for your students to refer to as they practice the skills (Figure 1.1). Cues help all students experience success with sport skills.

Physical education teachers have students for a short period of time during the week. It is imperative that this time be utilized to the fullest. The use of short, accurate, qualitative teaching cues can save teachers hours of preparation. Research indicates that the combination of accurate, qualitative cues; appropriate numbers of cues; and use of visual demonstrations along with verbal explanations seems to produce greater skill development gains (Rink, 1993). The cues in this book have been developed by experts in their respective areas to help teachers give accurate, qualitative cues regarding a specific sport skill. These cues *work!*

Cues also address the psychomotor, cognitive, and affective learning domains. They

- Enhance the learner's memory. (cognitive)
- Compress information and reduce words. (cognitive)
- Encourage focus on one specific component of a skill. (psychomotor)
- Help teachers and students analyze a skill performance by helping them focus on a particular component of the skill. (psychomotor)
- Strengthen correct performance. (psychomotor)
- Help teachers give positive, corrective feedback. (affective and cognitive)
- Help peers give positive, corrective feedback. (affective and cognitive)
- Motivate students to develop and refine skills. (affective and cognitive)

TOOL 4: HOW DO STUDENTS GET A CUE?

Students are visual learners and need three to five demonstrations. The use of demonstrations is the best way to teach with cues. Cues used with demonstrations help students develop a strong visual image of the skill. When demonstrating a skill, the teacher focuses the students' attention on one specific component of the skill through the use of a good verbal or visual cue. To avoid confusing students, it is important to keep verbalization to a minimum. For example, having students make an upside down L when performing skipping A's gives them a picture upon which to base their skill. By picturing the correct pattern, they are able to develop the correct skipping patterns. If they begin to show improper form, a cue, a demonstration, or both serves as a quick reminder of proper form.

Do not overload students with too many cues. Here are some helpful tips when teaching with cues:

- Research in motor learning indicates that students can learn only on a limited amount of new material.
- Giving students too much information or progressing to new information before students have grasped a concept may hinder the learning process.
- Too much information is worse than providing no information at all.
- For each component of a skill, practice the whole skill, but focus on each part in turn.
- No more than one to three cues at a time should be given to students.
- Following the acquisition of the motor pattern targeted to the first cue (e.g., in the football punt, "kick the fish in the belly"), teachers then move to the next phase of the motor skill.
- Additional cues should build on the previously learned skills, with no more than three cues for each teaching episode.
- Students need short bits of information that they can quickly apply to their skill.
- Practice, practice, practice; repetition, repetition, repetition.

Provide students with lots of opportunities to respond (OTRs), such as touching the ball. You want maximum activity with minimum wait time. Each student or partners are provided with a piece of equipment. This increases a student's OTRs. We provide great drill progressions and mini-games in this book to assist you when teaching sport skills, and games that offer lots of OTRs.

Providing feedback to your students is a critical tool to help them learn sport skills. To earn your credibility as an educator, you must work hard during each class session. Giving appropriate feedback is the "heartbeat" of the class. Is it tough to give feedback in each class session? Yes. Why? Because it takes focus, intensity, time, work, and effort to pay attention to the performance of the students. When teachers are in tune and give corrective feedback, it helps to maintain the supportive climate. Why? Because, as Thomas Dewey states, "The deepest urge in human nature is the desire to be important" (Carnegie, 1981, p. 18). William James states, "The deepest principle in human nature is the craving to be appreciated" (Carnegie, 1981, p. 18). When teachers pay attention to students, students feel important, and when teachers give feedback, students feel appreciated.

Teachers need to notice details about their students. "What kind of details?" you might ask. Start with the effort the individual is giving when performing a skill of participating in a game. Study each student's face and body language. This takes hard work on your part, but if the students know you are paying attention to them and that you notice the small details, they will develop trust in you, because they sense you care about them as individuals.

But this tool is not enough for you to earn credibility with your students. You must know the correct movement patterns to analyze the skills of your students and give technical feedback. Using cues in this book will give you a jump start in earning credibility with your students. Teaching sport skills is easier and more effective when focusing on one to three cues and then giving feedback on those cues.

Just as important as technical feedback is positive communication between you and a student. Eighty percent of what a teacher communicates to students is through nonverbal behaviors, such as body language: for example, thumbs up or down, clapping, the "yes" arm pump, the raise-the-roof motion, the OK sign, facial expressions, "The Look," raising the eyebrow, a wink, the with-it-ness body stance, hands in pockets, or folded arms.

The smile is a very powerful nonverbal tool in teaching. Why? Dale Carnegie states, "Actions speak louder than words and a smile says, 'I like you, you make me happy, I am glad to see you'" (Carnegie, 1981, p. 66). People who smile, he said, "tend to manage, teach and sell more effectively and to raise happier children." There is far more information in a smile than a frown. That's why encouragement is a much more effective teaching device than punishment of other people. People rarely succeed unless you are having fun doing it" (p. 66). "The smile enriches those who receive it without impoverishing those who give it, happens in a flash and the memory of it sometimes lasts forever" (p. 70).

Another communication technique is appropriate touch, such as high fives, low fives, side fives, backward fives, and a jump with two-handed fives. Appropriate places to touch students may be the arms, shoulders, and back. Be sensitive to other cultural customs regarding appropriate touch.

There is one more tool that works when giving feedback: The Challenge. This tool is rarely discussed in the literature. The best coaches in the United States—John Wooden, Pat Summit, Phil Jackson, and many others—challenge their athletes. A Challenge is stimulating, thought provoking, something that incites or quickens actions, feelings, and thoughts, and arouses to action or effort by encouragement. The Challenge is usually disguised. It comes with risk, but it can become a major tool for taking your students beyond what they think is their potential.

The Challenge happens only after you have built positive relationships with your students. To issue a challenge, you must know the student's backgrounds, dreams, and goals. Then and only then will The Challenge be effective.

To review, the following are five examples of feedback:

- *Effort:* "Abby, great effort on trying to throw the ball left-handed. Try making a better L for me." Or "Great effort running the bases."

- *Technical:* Give positive, specific feedback on a cue, and then correct an error. "Amanda, great L throwing on the ball. Now try to take a longer step on the target." (Figure 1.2, page 6).

- *Nonverbal:* Clear across the gym you notice that Abby is practicing making an L with her left arm. Give her a thumbs-up and a big smile. (Figure 1.3, page 6).

- *Appropriate touch:* "Amanda, I like your long step to the target." A high five is given to Amanda (Figure 1.4, page 7).

- *Challenge:* John already knows how to throw. You say to John, "Is that the hardest or farthest you can throw that ball?" Another example might be found in a game situation. You notice John jogging around the bases. You might say, "John, is that the fastest you can go around the bases? I noticed you are quite a sprinter and you outrun all the boys. Show me how fast you can run."

FIGURE 1.2 Technical Feedback

FIGURE 1.3 Nonverbal Feedback

Carnegie (1981) sums up the importance of providing feedback: "You want the approval of those with whom you come in contact. You want recognition of your true worth. You want a feeling that you are important in your little world. You don't want to listen to cheap, insincere flattery but you do crave sincere appreciation. How? When? Where? The answer is: All the time, everywhere" (p. 101).

If you use these specific feedback tools, will it help you become a better teacher? Absolutely! Start today.

Mini-Games Increase Feedback Opportunities

Mini-games with three to six students on each team are recommended so that students have an opportunity to respond. Feedback is easier to give when your class is divided into smaller groups. More is better! More students with their own equipment. More opportunities to practice. More feedback gives the students more skill development and more confidence to succeed (Figure 1.5).

Feedback on the cues should be given during these games. Teachers usually do not give technical feedback in the game situation but get caught up watching the game, or if they do give feedback, it is in the form of nags (negative feedback). Mini-games provide a great opportunity to gain credibility with your students. Remember: it takes effort, hard work, observation, focus, and timing to give precisely the right feedback. Try to use a variety of feedback techniques, and always give the students something to work on. Your class will be full of exciting options to help your students learn skills, have fun playing games, and develop lifetime sport skills. You will also be so absorbed in the class that time will pass very quickly, and your passion for your work will increase. The students will feel your fervor, enthusiasm, and passion when you teach. Watch the best teachers and see what *they* do.

Customizing Teaching Cues for Your Students

After reading this book, you may want to design your own cues. Connie Blakemore (personal communication, January 1997) offers suggestions on how to begin the process:

FIGURE 1.4 Appropriate Touch

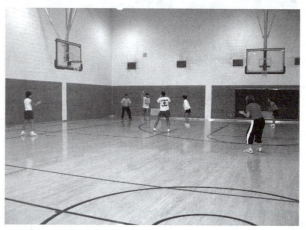

FIGURE 1.5 Mini-Game

- Go to various sources—skill books, skill videos, workshops, experts, and so on—to make sure the cue is accurate.
- Condense the skill analysis to a few effective words. Find the catchy words, metaphors, short phrases, and key words in the resources. Avoid long sentences.
- Sequence the cues properly.
- Determine, for example, what is critical to the task with three to five cues. Decide which is the most important cue for the skill, then the second, then the third, and so on.
- Design the cues for the appropriate age and learning stage.
- Cut pictures out of a sports section in the newspaper or a sports magazine, or use sports photographs of your students. Type one to three cues and place them directly onto the pictures of photos and make photocopies. Display these pictures in the gym, the locker room, or a recreation center, or at athletic events.
- Listen to your students. There are times when they come up with creative cues. However, make sure their cues are accurate.
- If you're not already there, shift to the right side of your brain and develop your own creative cues.

TOOL 5: HOW DO I ORGANIZE A SUCCESSFUL CLASS?

Develop a Supportive Climate on the First Day

On the first day of class, the teacher needs to get to know each student and the students need to get to know each other before anything else is done (Figure 1.6, page 8). How do you set the stage for the first hour of class? The first protocol, or rule, is that no one talks when a student or teacher is "on stage." Ask each student to stand and talk about something they carry with them each day, or perhaps some piece of sports equipment they would like to be. Why is this activity critical on the first day? It breaks the ice between the students and the teacher. The students begin to feel comfortable with each other. They begin relating to each other's experiences. First impressions and

FIGURE 1.6 Supportive Climate on the First Day

FIGURE 1.7 Building Relationships

judgments—good or bad—are replaced by feelings of warmth for the individual. The students feel more comfortable talking with each other, and they learn specific facts about their classmates. They can use this information to open a conversation. Walls come down. Relationships start to form. The teacher also benefits and has information with which to spark a later conversation.

Another reason this activity is so effective is that all students must be quiet. This teaches respect for each other, and the teacher can begin to work on management skills, which sets the tone for the rest of the year.

On the second day, have students network with a partner for about five minutes. Each student stands with the partner, and they share what they have learned about each other. Once again, emphasize the rule that no one else is to talk when partners are sharing their experiences about their new friend. Respect is reinforced. You will be amazed at how well the students listen during this time. Perform this type of activity throughout the year whenever you feel a need to bond with your class. The benefits of a supportive climate (Griffin & Patton, 1981) include the following:

- Group members accept more easily other's influence.
- Members of the group are less suspicious of the motives of others.
- A greater degree of tolerance of deviant behavior occurs.
- When conflicts arise, the group is able to focus on the group goals rather than on defending egos.
- The group develops trust, which allows more freedom for group risk taking.
- Members of the group feel better about themselves.
- Remember, the first few days are critical in terms of what you will do the rest of your year.

Supportive Climate Needed When Teaching Sport Skills

Teachers need to establish a framework of support in order to implement teaching cues successfully. Students need to feel safe in order to reach out and try new behaviors. Creating a supportive climate creates a safe learning environment for students. The supportive climate happens verbally, with positive, clear cues and reinforcing phrases. It also happens in a safe, nonverbal physical environment.

Nonverbal behaviors, which accompany verbal cues, also communicate to students. A teacher who says, "Nice dive," accompanied by a harsh tone of voice and disapproving facial expression, communicates, "Bad dive." The way teachers present cues—the tone of their voice, their body language, their manner of touch, or dress (such as a teacher not wearing a swimsuit)—can enhance or detract from a positive comment.

Great teachers and coaches are skillful at giving the most appropriate cue at the appropriate time, using verbal and/or nonverbal signals. Combining verbal cues and positive nonverbal cues becomes a powerful tool for providing feedback from the teacher. By creating a supportive climate, you can help students feel comfortable and become motivated to explore and learn a variety of sports.

Build Relationships and Still Get the Work Done

How does a teacher continue to build relationships (Figure 1.7) and still get the work done? Theodore Roosevelt (as all leaders know) said that "the royal road to a person's heart is to talk about things he or she treasures most" (Carnegie, 1981, p. 94). Teachers have many opportunities to learn each day about students' lives and what they treasure. Here are some options to think about: Take time before school, at lunch, and after school to visit with your students. Interview them about their interests, dreams, and goals. Attend school functions to let them know you care about them. Let them talk about what they did over the weekend, on spring break, or during their summer vacations.

Expending the effort to build relationships with your students develops their respect and trust. They will be more willing to work for you, so work on building relationships daily. The best teachers do, and the work gets done in a supportive climate.

Protocols and Management Skills

Protocols are necessary to provide a safe learning environment and to provide structure for your students. Just like any other sport skill, the protocols need to be practiced repeatedly. For further information, refer to Graham, Holt/Hale, and Parker (2000) and Pangrazi (2001). The following protocols are just a few to get you started.

1. Establish start and stop signals. The signals need to be different from each other. They can be auditory or visual, or a combination of both—for example, one whistle blow to start and two whistle blows to stop.

2. Establish protocols, for example: (Figure 1.8, page 10)
   - Proper dress: tee shirt, shorts, tennis shoes, and socks
   - No talking while others are talking
   - A gathering place for giving instruction and talking to the entire class
   - Distributing and collecting of equipment
   - Grouping students: partners, teams, and so forth
   - Off-task behavior; for example, three strikes, you're out—one strike is a warning; second strike, the student sits out for five minutes and observes the class; third strike, the student sits out for the entire class

3. Provide a piece of developmentally appropriate equipment for each student; this is the key so students have many opportunities to practice sport skills. Teachers (Figure 1.9, page 10) need to be creative in finding ways to work their budget to buy safe, age-appropriate equipment. For example, good, inexpensive leather volleyballs can be purchased from college volleyball teams. Old tennis balls can be purchased from tennis teams or

FIGURE 1.8 Establishing Protocols

FIGURE 1.9 Everyone Has a Piece of Equipment

tennis clubs. Send home a letter with students at the beginning of the school year indicating your equipment needs. Enlist the help of the high school shop or an applied technology school to make equipment. Use your creativity to find solutions.

4. Establish a "home" for the equipment when giving directions: for example, a basketball or softball between the feet. (Figure 1.10).

5. Move around the perimeter of the area, with your back to the wall. You can observe the entire class, give instruction, and offer feedback to students.

6. Maximize activity time and minimize wait time. Mini-games are very effective in increasing OTRs and minimizing wait time.

7. Avoid having lines of students wait for their turn.

8. Use caution about circle formations. See Wood and Langley's concerns (1997, pp. 8–9)

- Lack of practice time
- Requirement of complex use of the skill
- Organizational pattern that does not match game requirements
- Potential to embarrass and discourage
- No clear goals for success
- Potential to increase management problems

They then list six suggestions for effective student learning:

- Adequate practice time
- Requirement of less complex use of skill
- Organizational patterns that match game requirements
- Development of student self-confidence
- Clear goals for success
- Effective management of student practice

FIGURE 1.10 Establish a Home for the Equipment

FIGURE 1.11 Demonstrate So All Can See and Hear

Use a Successful Teaching Model

How does a teacher teach a motor skill correctly? What is a correct and successful teaching model? How do teaching cues fit into this model? The following are components of a good teaching model and how cues are implemented.

- Get the students' attention! Use anticipatory sets (attention getters). This motivates the students to want to perform the skill. Make sure they pay attention to the instructions. Be enthusiastic!

- Organize the group so that everyone can see and hear. State the lesson objective by describing what is to be learned and why it is important. Your objective should be brief, simple, and direct. This should lead to a demonstration (Figure 1.11).

- Preassess your students by asking how many of them know how to perform the skill, or ask the students to perform the skill if it is relatively safe.

- Demonstrate the entire skill three to five times. Show the skill from front, side, and back angles. Demonstrations should be performed as they would appear in a game situation. Move the class around so they can see the demonstration from different angles. The students should see a correct demonstration of the skill. Remember, a picture is worth a thousand words when learning a sport skill.

- After the demonstration, have the students practice the skill. This will give you time to assess their proficiency.

- Use one teaching cue at a time. This directs the students' attention to the specific area of focus.

- Have the students practice the skill. You provide feedback on the cue words used in the demonstration. Use a systematic approach to giving feedback to all of your students during the class.

- Provide additional demonstrations and new cues when students have mastered the previous ones.

- Review and/or demonstrate the cues during class closure. Provide the students with an opportunity to ask questions.

- Have students repeat aloud the cues for the skill. The cues will be fresh in their memories.

Students with Disabilities

You might have the opportunity to teach students with disabilities. Be creative in developing cues and activities for these students. For example, you should put a bell around a ball for a blind student, integrate brightly colored equipment for the hearing impaired, and use balloons for the student in a wheelchair. Include all of the other students. Let them participate on their own levels, see their excitement in being able to participate, and feel the emotional bonding with your students.

TOOL 6: AUTHENTIC ASSESSMENT: HOW DO I KNOW IT IS WORKING?

Cues Help Instructors Analyze a Skill

Some physical education teachers tend to analyze skills excessively and tell all they know (Lockhart, 1996). Cues are short and to the point, and they focus the assessment process on giving specific feedback.

Teaching cues provide students with valuable information to accompany demonstrations. Cues aid you in focusing on correct skill performance so that appropriate feedback can be given. Incorporating cues in the teaching process makes it possible for you to identify major errors quickly. For example, when the students are performing the forehand stroke in tennis, and the cue is "swing racket low to high," it is easy to observe whether the racket head is high at the end of the stroke. It is also important to provide a reason why it is necessary to perform a particular cue accurately.

Cues Strengthen Correct Performance

A critical component of skill acquisition is identifying the parts of the skill that are being performed correctly. You can have the students work in pairs or in small groups; in this way, they can analyze their performance and give feedback to each other on one specific cue. For example, the following three cues for throwing a ball are used: (1) Take the ball straight down and graze your shorts, (2) stretch your arm way back, and (3) make an L. Student responses might include the following:

- "Hey, I like the way you brought your arm down and grazed your shorts. That action will give you more distance."

- "Way to make an L shape with your arm! You're keeping the ball away from your head."

- "Wow! Way to stretch your arm way back! That was a great stretch. It looks like Barry Bond's or Dale Murphy's."

This type of specific feedback increases the likelihood that the student will repeat the correct response in the near future.

Cues Help Correct Errors in Technique

"Coach, how can I get over the hurdles faster?" "How do I improve my sprint time?" "What is the best way to exchange the baton?" These are questions students might ask about track skills. Are you ready to answer these questions without criticizing or giving the student too much information?

Your challenge is to identify the cause of the problem and look for solutions. The effective use of cues avoids judgment and criticism. Cues are used to correct errors constructively. Cues help you identify the problem and provide accurate feedback to the student: for example, "Stacie, I really liked how you made a 'banana shape' when performing the long jump. This time, work on the 'jackknife position' when you land."

Cues Help Peers Correct Errors in Technique

When students are provided with correct teaching cues, they can help give feedback to other peers. Pair students and have them observe their partner's performance. For example, if the cue given on throwing is, "Stand sideways and take a long step toward the target," a student can watch her partner and assess whether she is standing sideways and taking the long step. If her partner steps too high or takes a short step, but is standing sideways, she can provide her partner with the following feedback: "Hey, Stacie, you stood sideways. Now remember to take a long step with your foot toward the target." This feedback emphasizes a student's correct performance, notifies her of the error, and suggests a specific way to correct it, providing a more positive interaction.

Using Cues to Assess Students' Performance

By using cues, you have a valuable tool for assessing your students. You can assess them specifically on the cues you have taught. Your students know specific components of the skill they need to practice and how they will be assessed. This gives them an opportunity to practice the important cues. For example, a rubric can be designed with a four-point checklist. A rubric on the overhand throw might include the following:

- Stands sideways to the target
- Makes an L with the throwing arm
- Takes a long step with the leg closest to the target
- Throws hard

Decide how you want to mark the checklist. You might choose a yes-or-no format or a scale ranging from proficiency to almost there to needs more practice.

CONCLUSION

The tools outlined in this chapter help make teaching fun and exciting. Students will appreciate your expertise and retain knowledge in a fun and caring environment. We hope this book widens your vision about teaching. We have found the cues in this book to be effective, motivating, and life altering when students are successful. To establish credibility quickly, incorporate the teaching cues in subsequent chapters to obtain the edge that is necessary to connect with your students. Have fun!

FYI

PUBLICATIONS

Carnegie, D. (1981). *How to win friends and influence people.* New York: Pocket Books.

Fronske, H., Abendroth-Smith, J. & Blakemore, C. (1997). The effect of critical cues on throwing efficiency of elementary school children. *The physical educator, 54*(2), 88–95.

Graham, G., Holt/Hale S., & Parker, M., (2000). *Children moving: A reflective approach to teaching physical education* (5th ed.). Mountain View, CA: Mayfield.

Patton, B. R., & Giffin, K. (1981). *Interpersonal communication in action: basic text and readings* (3rd ed.). New York: Harper & Row.

Lockhart, A. (1966, May). Communicating with the learner. *Quest, VI,* 57–67.

NASPE. (1995). *Moving into the future: National standards for physical education.* St. Louis: Mosby.

Pangrazi, R. (2001). *Dynamic physical education for elementary school children.* Boston: Allyn & Bacon.

Pangrazi, R. (2001). *Dynamic physical education for elementary school children. Lesson Plans.* Boston: Allyn & Bacon.

Rink, J. (1993). *Teaching physical education for learning.* St. Louis: Times Mirror/Mosby.

Woods, A., & Langley, D. (1997). Circle drills: Do they accomplish your goals? *Journal of physical education, recreation, and dance, 68*(3), 8–9.

Aerobic Kickboxing

INTRODUCTION

Taebo, CardioKarate, Karabo, Cardio Kickboxing, or even kickboxercise all refer to the same thing, the rhythmic repetitions of traditional fighting techniques combined with elements from aerobic dance. This blending of martial-arts-based techniques, such as punches, kicks, and knee and elbow strikes, with aerobic dance music and choreography produces aerobic kickboxing.

Currently, aerobic kickboxing is the fastest growing new addition to the health and fitness craze in the United States. As its name implies, aerobic kickboxing is really a type of cross-training workout. An aerobic kickboxing workout incorporates all the muscles of the body and can include anaerobic components through the use of burnout drills: muscular endurance with prolonged repetition of techniques. Although aerobic kickboxing works quite well as a solo activity, it is a good supplement for other sports or physical activities.

Why Should Physical Educators Teach Aerobic Kickboxing?

In an effort to motivate more kids to participate in physical education classes (particularly in school districts where PE is an elective), some schools are currently experimenting with activities that high school students already choose to do in their free time. The current huge success of aerobic kickboxing in the health and fitness clubs and the massive media hype on aerobic kickboxing due to the success of Billy Blank's Taebo video series has made it an obvious choice as just such an activity. Aerobic kickboxing is already now being offered either as a unit or as a regular class in some public schools. In both cases it is generally the regular physical education staff that ends up teaching it. It is for you, the physical education teachers of the third millennium, who will very likely find yourselves teaching aerobic kickboxing at some point in your career, that this chapter has been written.

What Do I Need to Get Started?

Contrary to what many current fitness clubs and martial-arts studios advertise, you don't need experience with either, just a basic knowledge of the techniques you plan to incorporate, an ability to keep a steady beat, and tons of energy and enthusiasm. Nevertheless, expertise with either simple martial arts techniques or aerobics would enhance the quality of your program.

SKILLS LISTED WITH CUES

Aerobic kickboxing has a plethora of skills that can be used and therefore taught, which makes it impossible to cover all of them in just a few short pages. But wait! Don't panic just yet. There are a few basic skills that, once learned and performed correctly, can make any instructor look good in front of a class regardless of a lack of experience with aerobic kickboxing. What's more exciting is that not only will your class get an incredible workout, but they will more than likely have fun doing it! . . . and you will too. The techniques covered in this chapter along with their cues are the "boxer's" stance, center position, Roc Hop step, step-and-touch step, bob and weave, jab punch, cross punch, uppercut punch, aerobic uppercut punch, hook punch, speed bag punch, back fist strike, front kick, side kick, roundhouse kick, and back kick. Once learned, these techniques can be used as a strong backbone of any aerobic kickboxing program for all experience levels.

TIPS

1. The best way to learn to teach any aerobic class, including aerobic kickboxing, is to attend classes taught by a variety of instructors to get a feel for their teaching styles until you can develop your own.

2. If you find particular instructors or teaching formats you like, imitate them (not directly copy them) for a while until you feel comfortable teaching with your own style.

3. Videos can be an invaluable resource for new ideas. Remember though, many of your students may also have the same video, so you'll still need your own creativity to keep the combinations from the videos fresh. Re-arranging combinations and entire routines found on videos is always a good idea and will help avoid copyright problems, since many routines found on videos are copyrighted.

4. A good rule of thumb to use when preparing an aerobic kickboxing class is to mirror your routine on both sides of the body (i.e., what you do on one side you have to do on the other side). This will keep your classes feeling balanced.

5. A good idea, especially for beginning aerobic kickboxing instructors, is to write out the entire workout from warm-ups to cooldowns. List the specific techniques you want, in the order you want, with the approximate amount of time needed for each activity. Remember, if you do jab punches with the left hand, you'll have to do them on the right side as well.

6. It is *never* a good idea when teaching aerobic kickboxing (or any other type of aerobics class) to just roll in the video cart, plug in an aerobics video, and expect the class to follow along. Watching a video for class is very boring and looks very unprofessional. Either make up a routine using techniques you know or find someone else with more experience to teach that unit.

EQUIPMENT TIPS

1. Equipment needed to teach aerobic kickboxing includes a good stereo system, kickboxing targets or punching bags, bag gloves or hand wraps to protect the knuckles and wrists from injury, jump ropes, regular hand weights, and music. Good, clean, high-energy music and a decent sound system are critical to the overall quality of the class. Nothing destroys an aerobic kickboxing class faster than music that is too slow, too fast, too loud, too soft, or just plain inappropriate for the activity. If the music flops, so will your class.

2. Aerobic kickboxing does not require any special clothes or equipment—just a pair of secure shorts (remember you will be bouncing on the balls of your feet a lot, so things can fall off) and a cool tee shirt.

3. Hand wraps, if used, should secure the wrist enough so that the range of motion is limited but should not restrict blood flow in the hand or forearm. A lot of boxing and marital arts supplies now include wrap instructions.

4. Equipment such as bags, jump ropes, and hand weights should be in place before class begins so that students can get to it in a matter of seconds, but it should also be out of the way so that it doesn't become a safety hazard.

5. If you decide to incorporate bags into your class, it is suggested that a portable heavy bag, such as the Century Wave Master bag, be used rather than smaller bags like handheld focus mitts or kicking shields. This way students can work alone if need be, and time will not be wasted showing new students how to hold the smaller bags.

6. When focus mitts are used, be sure everyone knows how to hold the bag correctly for the partner. If students don't know how to hold a bag, safety problems can arise.

7. Be sure to match students of equal size and power when using focus mitts and kicking shields in order to reduce the chance that a student will be blasted by a technique too powerful for the pad holder.

8. Smaller pads can be a lot of fun. Use some creativity on how you have the class hold the smaller bags so both students are getting a great workout. For example, to keep students' heart rates up, have one student punch the focus mitts as many times as he or she can until tired, then have the pad holder do squat thrusts until tired while the puncher bounces in place. This can be done several times in two-minute periods, with students exchanging pads.

TEACHING IDEAS

1. Teaching aerobic kickboxing is slightly different from aerobic dance classes. Aerobic kickboxing classes do not have to be taught using the standard 32-count system used in dance aerobic. (The 32-count system has students performing combinations in exactly 32 counts of music.) Aerobic kickboxing techniques are different from the dance techniques used in dance aerobics, and therefore timing is less of a factor. If you know how to stay on count, this ability will help your classes. However, simply staying on beat (listen to the bass for help) with correct technique, lots of energy, and enthusiasm is sufficient for aerobic kickboxing.

2. Do not shortcut techniques to stay on beat with the music. If the music seems too fast, either simplify the combinations or pick slower music.

3. If you're familiar with professionally produced aerobics music, step music works really well for aerobic kickboxing. It's about a 128 count.

4. Write your entire routine on a 3 × 5 index card so that it can be taped to a mirror, a nearby desk, or some other convenient place. If you should forget a combination, you can glance at your note card.

5. Aerobic kickboxing is aerobic in nature, meaning it is continuous. Keep the class in their target heart rate range of about 70–80 percent of their maximum heart rate. *All feedback and corrections should be done while the class stays moving.*

6. The old adage "Fake it until you make it" definitely applies to aerobic kickboxing. If you forget what comes next in your routine, fake it until you remember. Doing so will keep the class on task and heart rate up.

A Warning

One of the scariest things about the current media push for aerobic kickboxing is the notion that aerobic kickboxing teaches self-defense. Aerobic kickboxing does not teach self-defense. While the techniques may be the same, and even technically correct, aerobic kickboxing is intended more to improve overall fitness than to teach self-defense. Techniques such as hook punches or roundhouse kicks may be the same as in self-defense class, but aerobic kickboxing does not teach students how or when to use these techniques. It would be just as fair to say that by shooting free throws a person can learn how to play basketball. Aerobic kickboxing instructors should explain this principle to students right from the beginning.

FYI

For further information about aerobic kickboxing, consult the following organizations and resources.

ORGANIZATIONS

Chris Erickson
1615 Dana Way
Roseville, CA 95661

Promise Enterprises
P.O. Box 7654
Jackson, MS 39284
Phone: (601) 372-8313

EQUIPMENT SUPPLIES

Century Martial Supply
1705 National Boulevard
Midwest City, OK 73110-7942
Phone: (800) 626-2787
Website: www.centuryma.com

Asian World of Martial Arts
917 Arch Street
Philadelphia, PA 19154-2117
Phone: (215) 969-3500
Website: www.awma.com

PROFESSIONAL MIXED AEROBIC WORKOUT MUSIC

Aerobic and Fitness Association of America
15250 Ventura Blvd., #200
Sherman Oaks, CA 91403

Power Music
P.O. Box 27927
Salt Lake City, UT 84127-0927

Dynamix: (800) 843-6499
In-Lytes Productions: (800) 243-7867
Muscle Mixes Music: (800) 52-Mixes
Musicflex: (718) 738-6839
Sports Music, Inc.: (800) 391-7692
The Work Out Source: (800) 552-4552

PUBLICATION

Thiboutot, F., Croteau, K. (2001, January 1). *Cardio kickboxing elite.*
Roslindale, MA: YMAA Publications.

WEBSITES

www.aerobickick.com
www.artofcombat.com/aerobic2.htm
www.iboxaaka.com

STANCES AND STEPS

SKILL	CUE	WHY	COMMON ERROR
Boxer's Stance	Shoulders and hips face straight ahead	Allows boxer to hit target with maximum power and reach	Shoulders turn inward
Boxer's Shuffle (Figure 2.1)	Dominant leg steps back		Hands drop below chin
			Feet flat on floor
	Fists by cheeks; knuckles scrape cheeks	Develops good technique that protects face and ribs	Shoulders turn inward
	On balls of feet	Keeps body moving and light on feet	
		Allows boxer to move quickly	
	Shoulders and hips face straight ahead		
Center Boxing Stance Position (Figure 2.2)	Feet shoulder-width apart with slight bend in knees	Allows for maximum movement laterally	Feet too close or wide
	Fists by cheeks— knuckles scrape cheeks, shoulders square	Protects face	Hands drop below chin

continued

SKILL	CUE	WHY	COMMON ERROR
Roc Hop Step	Bring lead leg knee up (or kick)		
	Feet return to side by side		
Roc Hop Step	Rear leg steps back		
	Feet return to side by side	Step is more of a dance step that is used in conjunction with punches and kicks	Not returning feet to side by side
Step and Touch	Move point foot of trailing leg laterally		
	Step and touch		
Bob and Weave	Drop body bending at knees	Allows the boxer to drop under a punch, come up chambered to center a punch	Bending over at the waist
		Can be used with or without a partner	
	Move upper body side to side		Whole body rising up all at once
	Lead with shoulder coming up		
	Keep hands and eyes up		Looking down during bob

FIGURE 2.1 Boxer's Shuffle or Fighting Stance

Hands up
Fingers tight

Knuckles scrape cheeks

Feet facing forward on balls of feet

FIGURE 2.2 Center Position

Hands up

Shoulders square

Feet shoulder-width apart

Note: Cues for all punches except one are to be executed while in the boxer's stance. The one exception is the aerobic uppercut punch, which is always done from the center position. This punch is not intended to create any power. It is used as a burnout exercise for the arms and shoulders and should not be practiced on pads.

There are a couple of cues to remember that apply to any punch. Hands always start and end by the cheeks, the wrists should always be locked straight out, and the nonpunching hand should be kept up by the cheek at all times. A common error that many people make while learning to punch is that they use just their arms and shoulders to punch. A correct punch actually uses the entire body beginning with a slight turn of the pivot foot, continued by a slight turn of the hips and shoulder, until the force is finally released through the arm and fist to the target.

PUNCHES			
SKILL	**CUE**	**WHY**	**COMMON ERROR**
Jab	Extend lead arm straight out		Arm not fully extended
	Fist tight with wrist straight		Fingers loose Wrist bent
Cross Reverse	Extend rear arm straight out		Arm not fully extended
	Rear leg pivots onto ball of foot	Pivot creates power and distance for punch	Foot stays flat on ground
	Shoulders turn inward leading with punching shoulder		Shoulders stay square
Uppercut Punch	Knees dip	Power for punch comes from hip as knees push on return back	Punch uses only shoulders
	Punching hand chambers back held in tight 45° angle		Arm kept too vertical
	Explode off feet pushing fist and navel through target		Punch stops at target Shoulders stay squared
Aerobic Uppercut Flutter Punch	Feet and shoulders square up		One leg stays back
	Both arms held in tight 45° angle		
	Rapid punch using just the shoulders and arms	Rapid punches are designed to burn out arms and shoulders	Arm kept too vertical
	With elbows brushing sides		Elbows point outward

continued

SKILL	CUE	WHY	COMMON ERROR
Lead Arm Hook	Lead arm drops to make a tight L between shoulder, elbow, arms, and wrist	Arm drops to be able to strike to sides of bag or partners	Wrist slightly bent
	Generally at rib or head level		
	Lead foot lifts up onto ball of foot		Foot stays flat
	Lead foot, hips, and lead shoulder pivot inward through target	Creates power punch	Only leg turns Punch stops at target
Back Fist Strike	1. Lead arm drops to make a tight L between shoulder, elbow, and wrist with palms facing you		Wrist slightly bent
	2. "Open the gate"	Arm extended for open gate in order to align back of hand with target	
	3. Extend arm and shoulder through target	Push through target with fist to create power	
Speed Bag Punch	One or both arms turn inward 45° so elbows point out		Arm(s) drop to make L
	Move arms in circling motion		
	First 2 knuckles should lead punch		Pinkie finger leads punch
	"Hit the back of the hand"		

Note: All kicks can be broken down into four basic parts. These parts are the *chamber* when the knee lifts up, the *extension* or kick, the *recoil* where the knee returns to the chambered position, and the *recovery* when the kicking leg returns to the ground. Be sure to watch for all four parts in your students' kicks.

As beginning kickers get excited, they tend to kick faster by shortcutting one or more of these four parts. By shortcutting a kick, students develop poor technique and will not be able to generate much power. They may also injure themselves in classes that incorporate the use of kicking bags. So watch for it!

Kicking leg
chambered at knee

Fists
by cheeks

Bottom foot planted
Toes pivoted

FIGURE 2.3   Chamber for Roundhouse Kick

KICKS			
SKILL	**CUE**	**WHY**	**COMMON ERROR**
Front Kick	Bring kicking leg knee up	Tight chamber and recoil creates power	Kicking with foot dorsiflexed
	Flex the ankle	Flex ankle to allow kick to make contact with ball of foot	
	Extend kick out		
Side Kick	Bring knee to chest, heel pointed out	Tight chamber creates power	Kick not locked out
	Extend kick straight out		Kicking with entire bottom of foot
	Push heel through target	Power for kick is maintained when sent through target rather than bouncing off target	
	Stomp your target		

continued

SKILL	CUE	WHY	COMMON ERROR
Roundhouse (Figure 2.3)	Bring kicking knee up at 45° angle		
	Planted foot pivots 180°	Power from kick is created when hips are in line with target; by pivoting the hips they will turn to align with target	Foot doesn't pivot
	Extend kick with toes pointed		Kicking with foot dorsiflexed
Back Kick	Pick up kicking knee		Kicking with entire bottom of foot
			Knee points out
	Kick straight back, hit with heel		
	Brush knees together "like a cricket"		

3

Archery

INTRODUCTION

Are you looking for a new way to have fun or a new sport to add to your curriculum? Archery is one of the oldest sports participated in today. Why is archery still being enjoyed by many? Young and old alike enjoy the challenge of hitting a target. Archery can be enjoyed year-round: indoors during inclement weather and outdoors in the fresh air. Archery provides opportunities for exercise and competition. Those who join archery clubs or leagues can participate with archers their own age and abilities. In many high schools and universities, students can join archery teams and perhaps even receive scholarships.

If students are taught the fundamental archery skills, display an interest, and experience success, teachers could then suggest they pursue related sports, which include field archery, bow hunting, bow fishing, and target archery.

By providing these archery cues teachers might incorporate archery into their curricula. Consequently, students of all ages can learn a new sport and "be on target for fun" (Parker & Bars, 1994).

SKILLS LISTED WITH CUES

In this chapter we have designed equipment cues for selecting a bow, arrows, arm guard, and finger tab. Cues are given for safety techniques and retrieving arrows from a target. The other cues cover beginning skills for the stance address, bow arm, nock, draw, anchor (target shooting), aim, release, follow-through, and adjusting the sight pin.

TIPS

1. Purchasing a peep sight (a tiny aperture the archer looks through to align the arrow with the target) and stabilizer makes the archery experience more enjoyable and successful.

2. A frequent archery error is dropping the bow arm to see where the arrow is going. This is called *peeking*. An archer gets in a hurry and peeks to see where the arrow is going, and consequently the arrow drops. Keep the arrow on the string by not peeking. Have patience and wait until the arrow is off the string.

3. If an archer has a problem with inconsistency in accuracy, go to an archery pro shop for suggestions or check for consistent anchor point and consistent draw length. If everything is done the same each time, accuracy will result.

EQUIPMENT TIPS

1. There are a variety of bows: long bows, recurve bows, and compound bows. They can be manual or automatic.

2. Carbon graphite arrows, although more expensive than aluminum arrows, are lighter, faster, stronger, and straight.

3. The peep site is a tiny aperture the archer looks through to align the arrow with the target. The peep sight will force the archer to anchor in the same place for each shot. Anchoring in the same place time after time increases accuracy.

4. The stabilizer assists the archer by quieting the bow and placing the pin on target. The stabilizer also prevents the archer from shaking.

5. An archery pro shop is the best place to purchase a bow because the personnel can set up the bow for proper shooting and give specific instruction.

6. The mechanical release is a pull trigger that releases the strings on a bow. The trigger provides a quicker, smoother, and more accurate release.

7. Field archers shoot in rough terrain, with three-dimensional targets, from a variety of distances.

8. Bow hunting requires arrows with different points—broad heads for larger game and blunt heads for smaller game. To hunt game birds such as quail, use flu flu arrows with larger and more feathers to reduce the distance the arrow travels.

9. Bow fishing is another unique option, requiring solid fiberglass arrows with fish point. A bow fishing reel is another good idea.

TEACHING IDEAS

1. Practice without shooting and to check the proper skill cues.
2. Have partners check cues.
3. Start students with large, easy to hit targets.
4. Use balloons for some fun targets and noise when they are popped.
5. Use cooperative groups and keep score in a group at first for a nonthreatening and fun learning environment.
6. Shoot at paper targets with a bull's-eye. Keep score. Should be done when fundamentals are mastered.

7. Shoot to a variety of paper targets. Target shooting during the winter months maintains correct form and technique, thus increasing the archer's ability to hit the game during hunting season.

8. Getting involved in an archery club provides an opportunity to learn from the experience of other archers and to improve techniques.

9. To hunt game, an archer needs correct equipment, an in-depth knowledge of the ethical principles and laws of hunting game, and correct techniques to harvest the game as well as camouflage scent masking and tracking skills.

FYI

For further information and special help, consult the following organizations and resources.

ORGANIZATIONS

Provides archery videos.

> National Archery Association
> One Olympic Plaza
> Colorado Springs, CO 80909
> Phone: (719) 866-4576
> Fax: (719) 866-4733
>
> The Athletic Institute
> 200 Castlewood Drive, North
> Palm Beach, FL 33408

Go to the local pro archery shop for lessons and proper equipment setup.

WEBSITES

www.encarta.msn.com
www.usarchery.org
www.BearGoldenEagle.com
www.alsport.com

SKILL	CUE	WHY	COMMON ERROR
Selecting Bow	Choose a bow that you can draw comfortably and hold for 10 seconds	Reduces straining	Bow too heavy
Selecting Arrow	Place nock against chest; reach with fingers; arrow should be 1 inch past fingertips (or draw a marked arrow)	Less chance of injury and better projectory	Arrow too short or too long
	Partner stands to the side and reads marking even with bow		
	Hunters add 1 inch		
Arm Guard	String should divide the arm guard in half; this varies with modern compound bows	Protection	
Finger Tab or Glove or Release	Protect fingers with tab or glove	Shoot longer and more comfortable	String hurts fingers
Safety	Do not draw or shoot a bow unless you are shooting on a line	Safety and common sense	Injuring students
	Do not release a bow without an arrow in it	Avoids breaking equipment	Bow splits along laminations
Retrieving Arrows	Stand to side of arrow; check position of other archers		Bending arrow Injuring students
	With one hand: fingers straddle arrow; press against target	Safety; for example, by pulling an arrow straight out, a student poked himself in the eye	
	With the other hand: grasp arrow close to target; rotate and pull straight back		
What Is the Dominant Eye?	Hold arms at arm's length, make a triangle with both hands; center a small object in the triangle keeping the object certain, move hands toward face; hands will automatically come to dominant eye	Enhances shooting skills	

SKILL	CUE	WHY	COMMON ERROR
Stance Address	Straddle the shooting line (one foot on each side)	Consistency	Standing behind the line
	Weight even		Leaning forward or backward
	Good posture		
	Feet shoulder-width apart		
Bow Arm	Grip bow like holding a soda can	More accuracy	Gripping bow too tightly
	Thumb and index finger touch	Smoother release	
	Push bow toward target		Gripping bow too lightly
	Elbow points outward at shoulder level		
Nock	Nock arrow at 90° angle to ⅛ high	Consistency	Arrow too high or low on string
	Snap nock on bowstring under nock locator		
	Index finger points away from bow		
Draw (Figure 3.1)	Make a scout sign (3 fingers up)	Consistency	More or less than 3 fingers on string
	String in first groove of index finger		String on fingertips or hand wraps around fingers
	Keep back of hand flat		
	Elbow level with hand		Elbow too low
	Squeeze shoulder blades together		Drawing with arm only

continued

SKILL	CUE	WHY	COMMON ERROR
Anchor (Target Shooting) (Figure 3.2)	Touch string to center of chin and center of nose; index finger pushes against jawbone	Consistency; doing everything the same, one is more accurate	Failing to anchor
Aim	Look through pin to center of gold		Looking at target instead of pin
	Aim 3–5 seconds prior to releasing		Releasing while drawing
	Close dominant left eye when shooting right-handed		Leaving dominant left eye open when shooting right-handed
Release	Relax fingers; string "slips" off fingers	Arrow performance; prevents left-to-right wobble	Jerking string hand back or allowing the string to "creep" forward before releasing it
Follow-Through (Hold) (Figure 3.3)	Fingers move back along side of face		Moving string hand
	Hold position until arrow hits target	Increases accuracy; prevents peeking	Moving bow arm

continued

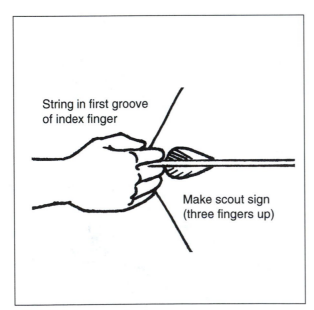

FIGURE 3.1 Draw the Arrow

FIGURE 3.2 Anchor (Target Shooting)

SKILL	CUE	WHY	COMMON ERROR
Adjust Sight Pin	Choose arrow with sight pin		Moving sight after each arrow or failing to adjust sight
	If arrows go high, move pin up		
	If arrows go low, move pin down		
	If arrows go left, move pin left		
	If arrows go right, move pin right		

Fingers move back along side of face

Hold bow like a soda can

Hold position until arrow hits target

FIGURE 3.3 Follow-Through (Hold)

4

Badminton

INTRODUCTION

Badminton is a physically demanding sport that provides players with a good measure of aerobic and anaerobic power, flexibility, strength, and speed. The skill of badminton can be relatively easy to learn, especially with the correct teaching cues. When designing these cues we consulted the USA Badminton Association in Colorado Springs, Colorado, and the Canadians for their expertise and suggestions. For example, the cue for the wrist action when teaching the badminton overhead clear is "supinate the wrist," which describes clockwise hand rotation; the thumb moves from 9 o'clock to 1 o'clock with palm facing up for a right-handed player. Snapping the wrist would be the common error. This cue and others will provide the teacher with correct teaching techniques.

Jim Stabler likes to think of the grip in terms of "shaking hands with the racquet." Hold the racquet with the racquet head perpendicular to the floor. Now shake hands with it. Hold it loosely with the index finger open along the handle. Do not grip it like you would a baseball bat. If your index finger is open, it is possible to break your wrist and twist your arm when hitting the shuttles. If you grip it like a bat, you can't break your wrist. The tendon to your index finger is all tied up in the grip, so you won't have the flexibility to break your wrist and utilize the power you can generate by breaking your wrist. How does a baseball pitcher throw a baseball at 90 miles an hour? He uses his legs, back, arm, and wrist as he hurls the ball to the catcher. If he used only his arm, he'd have very little velocity. It is the same whip of the wrist and twist of the arm that allow an advanced badminton player to hit a shuttle at 150 miles per hour or more. The shuttle weighs one-sixteenth of an ounce, so you are not hitting an object that weighs very much. You can utilize the twist of your wrist and arm to hit it very hard.

Badminton is unique in that the object you're playing with can fly at 150-plus miles an hour by hard hits or you can just dink it ever so slowly over the net at a very slow pace. No other sport employs this wide range of speeds in its game.

Jim Leete has provided this chapter with some wonderful warm-up and drill progressions for the beginner to the advanced badminton player and has called them the "nifty fifty." These drills come from years of experience teaching and coaching young and old alike.

SKILLS LISTED WITH CUES

A recommended teaching progression of skills before the strokes are taught is as follows: grips, flick up, feeding, ready position, and court position. Teachers should take extra time to teach flick up and feeding skills. The cues for the badminton skills in this chapter include this teaching progression as well as forehand/backhand underhand clear, forehand/backhand overhead clear, forehand/backhand smash, forehand/backhand drive, net shots (finesse shot), long singles serve, short doubles serve, and singles/doubles boundaries, scoring, and strategies. After each skill we have added some drills to work students' skills.

TIPS

1. Remember . . . correct grip, ready position.
2. Get into the habit of hit-move, hit-move, hit-move.
3. Move to hit the shuttle; don't wait for it.
4. Court sense for singles: after each shot the singles player should attempt to return to base position, which is midcourt. Remember to get in ready position regardless of court position.
5. Court sense for doubles is different. Partners adopt an "up-back" arrangement and, when attacking, a "sides" arrangement. Communicating with and supporting each other is the key to playing a good doubles game.

EQUIPMENT TIPS

1. Shuttles may be made from feathers or nylon. The flight of a shuttle is what makes the game unique, since it does not soar in an arc as a ball does. Very often, cheap nylon shuttles do not "catch" the air very well and are too fast. One may test the speed of a shuttle by striking it underhand as hard as possible, hitting it the length of the court fairly close to parallel to the floor. If the shuttle is the correct speed, it should gall on or near the doubles service line at the other end.
2. Use gym tape to mark a court. (It is not advisable to use a rope or a line for a net. It would be difficult to determine whether a shuttle went over or under the rope. Nets are not expensive and last for years if properly cared for.)
3. Court shoes are recommended.
4. You will need 100 to 200 shuttles for a class.
5. Shuttles also used to feed to their partner.

TEACHING IDEAS

1. Badminton is a demanding game with lots of running, stopping, starting, and lunging. Warm up before stretching. Suggested warm-up activities: light jogging, running in place, jumping jacks, running in various directions, tag games, circuits. After the warm-up, stretch out legs, ankles, arms, and so on.

2. Partner-feed drill: One partner feeds shuttle by hand to the receiver. Receiver hits and then attempts to assume ready position and base position after each return. Cue words are "feed-hit-ready position." Instructor specifies type of hand feed. This drill can be done with or without a net.

3. Racket-feed drill: same as item 2 above but the feeder racket-feeds to receiver. Feeder gradually sends shuttle to more challenging positions: "further right," "further left," "in front," and "behind" specify the type of feed and type of return.

4. Triples games are designed for large badminton classes. Six can play on a court rather than four. The game is played with three players on each side. Two players from each side are in the front half of the court. Each front player must remain on his or her respective side of the centerline. The third player plays back and may move anywhere in the back half of court. Serve is always from right front position. Team rotates clockwise each time serve is regained.

5. Badminton Advancement

"THE NIFTY FIFTY"

The Beginner 10: Getting Acquainted with the Racquet, Shuttle, and Court

1. Throw the shuttle over the net from short service line to short service line.
2. Catch the shuttle thrown over the net to you from the short service line.
3. Walk or run with the shuttle on the racquet cork up, palm down.
4. Do the same with the palm down (backhand).
5. Do the same with the shuttle on its side, palm up.
6. Do the same with the shuttle palm down.
7. Grip the racquet properly, using the handshake position, and in a ready position make figure 8's with it.
8. Raise the racquet up, cock the wrist out, swing forward, uncock wrist.
9. Raise the racquet up, cock wrist out, swing forward, uncock wrist.
10. Hold racquet arm up just below wrist, swing forward with wrist only.

Basic Novice 10

1. Bounce shuttle, a little above your head, using forehand, palm up.
2. Repeat, alternating forehand to backhand and back.
3. Repeat, alternating backhand to forehand and back.
4. Hit shuttle overhead and straight to and from short service line.
5. Drop shuttles gently over the net from midcourt area.
6. Hit shuttles straight to and from midcourt area like clears, but shorter.
7. Serve backhand fairly short and low.
8. Repeat, and then follow with high and clear.
9. Attitude and cooperation.
10. Sportsmanship . . . fair play and court manners, etc.

Warm-up Exercise and Strokes

1. Hands on shoulders, full slow circles, elbows touching in front.
2. Arm up, grasp wrist, pull over with full side bend, rotate wrist.
3. Arm up, bend elbow, scratch back, cup elbow, push down, scratch again.
4. Full hip, then body, then knee circles.
5. Feet apart, slow squat elbows on knees and hands locked, rock slowly.
6. Position foot across, outside next to other foot, bend down slowly.
7. Raise, grasp, and pull leg toward chest, rotate ankle fully.
8. In place jump, run, knees up side straddle jump rope.
9. On the court, hit clears, drops, smashes, and drives.
10. On the court, hit short and long serves and touch serves.

Moving on Court 10 Steps

1. Move up center for a short hit near T to midcourt, then run left and back.
2. Start with a long hit, then do short hit, run left and back.
3. Alternate hitting and moving for long and short shots till missing.
4. Hit in sequence from deep center, mid-right, short, mid-left.
5. Mix up by feeding longs or shorts at random.
6. Mix up by feeding longs or shorts to the four corners at random.
7. Hit from four corners in sequence as fed.
8. Hit from any corner as fed randomly, returning to midcourt each shot.
9. Move in response to a racquet pointed to any corner or spot.
10. Hit shuttle fed to any spot, any corner, or in between.

Advanced Novice or Above 10

1. Rapid midcourt drives, back and forth, low and flat.
2. Round-the-head forehand shots in preference to back hand.
3. Hit full-court, accurate high clears to middle and back alley either side.
4. Place various shots to designated corners and midcourt spots accurately.
5. Serve very low and close to T or high and deep consistently.
6. Stretch or lunge for short net shots close to net level if possible.
7. Develop a strong low and down smash, then on toes or a jump smash.
8. Develop various backhand strokes for clears, drops, drives, and smashes.
9. Perform the clear, drop, drop running stroke accurately and consistently.
10. Perform the clear, smash, drop, or block sequence as in #9 above.

A Few Important Observations to Consider

1. Practice leads to progress, and that leads toward perfection and playing better.
2. Improving stroking skills and consistency takes concentration and practice.

For further information and special help, consult the following organizations and resources.

ORGANIZATIONS

Provides information on instructor manuals, videotapes, drills, skill progressions, program materials, awards, pictures.

Badminton Canada
1600 James Naismith Drive
Gloucester, Ontario, Canada KIB 5N4
Phone: (613) 748-5605
Fax: (613) 748-5695
Telex: 053 3660

USA Badminton
One Olympic Plaza
Colorado Springs, CO 80909
Phone: (719) 866-4808
Fax: (719) 866-4507
Email: usab@usabadminton.org
Website: www.usabadminton.org

VIDEO AND MANUAL

Badminton 2000 Plus Guide to Teaching Badminton. Can be purchased through USA Badminton. $39.99 plus shipping.

PUBLICATIONS

Golds, M. (2002). *Badminton (skills of the game).* Ramsbury, Wiltshire, England: Crowood Press.

Grice, T. (1996), *Badminton: Steps to success.* Champaign, IL: Human Kinetics.

USA Badminton. *Badminton official rule book.* (2001). Colorado Springs, CO: USA Badminton.

WEBSITES

www.usabadminton.org
www.worldbadminton.net

BASIC GRIPS AND STANCE

SKILL	CUE	WHY	COMMON ERROR
Forehand Grip	Heel of hand at butt of racket		Choking up on racket
	V on top bevel		Grip too tight
	Index finger positioned to pull trigger		Incorrect placement of index finger
	Squeeze trigger finger on impact		
Backhand Grip	Turn racket clockwise		Failure to rotate grip from forehand to backhand
	Make V on left bevel		
	Knuckle on top		
Ready Position	Hold racket up	If racket is down at your ankle, it takes a good part of a second to get it back up. That part of a second is all it takes for you to be late in making a good shot sometimes	
	Knees bent		Standing upright
	Weight on balls of feet		Weight on heels
Correct Order of Play	1. Be ready to hit the shuttle 2. SEE the shuttle 3. Hit the shuttle	Make sure you do this in order. If step 2 comes before step 1, you might be late in hitting the shuttle	Fall backward/ fall away

FLICK UP AND FEEDING

SKILL	CUE	WHY	COMMON ERROR
Flick Up			
Definition	Slick move using the racket to scoop the shuttle from the floor (speeds game up); players must employ proper grip to do this move		

continued

SKILL	CUE	WHY	COMMON ERROR
Flick Up, *continued*			
Action	Side scooping action, feel snap of wrist as racket head turns		Forward and up action
	Raise shuttle to land on strings		Improper grip
Feeding			
Definition	Serving the shuttle by hand or by racket so that receiver has a good chance to return it		
Drill: Have the players serve or hit the shuttle underhand and overhand against the wall as many times as possible without missing		Provides more practice trials; beginners have a better opportunity to contact the shuttle successfully; move to court ASAP when they have made contact with the shuttle	
Hand Position	Hold cork of shuttle with thumb and forefinger		Holding plastic/feathers
	Throw it like a dart to target		Throwing it like a baseball
	Hold shuttle in open hand, cork toward target; throw to target		
	Racket-high serve and forehand underhand clear are important for feeding (*see* Serving cues on pages 42–43)		
	Take time to sharpen the feeding skills of players		
Drill: Have the players hit the wall as many times as they can—ask for scores of how many in a row without missing			
Drill: Partners feed to each other on the court			

SKILL	CUE	WHY	COMMON ERROR
Forehand Underhand Clear	Whip wrist and brush shorts	More power	Snapping wrist
	Contact shuttle below waist	Rule	Contacting too soon, lack of height
	Swing up over opposite shoulder	More distance	Not following through, lack of depth
Forehand Overhead Clear	Supinate hand; thumb rotates from 9:00 to 1:00 clockwise for a right-handed player, palm rolls up (Figure 4.1)	More distance and power	Snapping wrist Not extending elbow
	Supinate hand; thumb rotates from 3:00 to 11:00 counterclockwise for a left-handed player, palms rolls up	More power and distance	Snapping wrist
	Reach up and contact shuttle high in front of body, like throwing something on roof		
	Whip!		
	Push from back to forward foot (Figure 4.2)	More power	Weight forward

continued

FIGURE 4.1 Hand Action for Forehand Overhead Clear

FIGURE 4.2 Forehand Overhead Clear

SKILL	CUE	WHY	COMMON ERROR
Drill 1: *High/Clear Tip Drill* So often beginners hit under the shuttle. Contact the shuttle high and in front of the body. Don't let the shuttle get behind you when you hit high clear. Take a step back so that you are hitting it well in front of you. If you swing and miss it, for example, it should fall against the front of your body and not over your head			
Drill 2: *1, 2, or 3 feeders* Feeders have at least 25 shuttlecocks: One player hits underhand clears, rotate; one player hits underhand and overhead clears, rotate; spend lots of time hitting clears— 3 or 4 days can be spent having students practice feeding and clears forehand, backhand, underhand, and overhead clears			

FIGURE 4.3 Next Shot (Finesse Shot)

SKILL	CUE	WHY	COMMON ERROR
Forehand Smash	Lean into the net		
	Contact shuttle in front of body	Control	Contacting shuttle behind head
	Supinate hand; thumb rotates from 9:00 to 1:00 clockwise for a right-handed player, palm moves up	Shuttle will go downwards	Snapping wrists
	Supinate hand; thumb rotates from 3:00 to 11:00 counterclock-wise for a left-handed player, palm moves up	Power	
	Wrist starts cocked, finishes in supinated position	Power	
	Whip action	Faster	
	Swing is half-moon with faced racket pointing down at contact	Control	Swinging too long or too short
Forehand Drive	Move racket foot toward shuttle		Feet are stationary
	Contact more to the side of body, like throwing a ball sidearm	Control and accuracy	Contact too high or too low
Backhand Drive	Same as forehand; change grip		
Net Shot (Finesse Shot) (Figure 4.3)	Loosen grip	More control	Firm grip
	Be gentle; slide racket under shuttle		Swinging at shuttle
	Focus on palm of hand; lift shuttle over, use arm only, not racket		Hitting hard
	Push/lift/nudge/caress		

continued

SKILL	CUE	WHY	COMMON ERROR
Drill: *1-, 2-, or 3-feeders* Feeders hit high clears; hitter smashes shuttle. Rotate hitters. Switch to backhand smashes. Then feeders feed to forehand and backhand. Partner smashes both sides.			
Drill: *3 feeders, 1 hitter* Each feeder needs 25–30 shuttles. All 3 feeders feed 1 hitter. Feeders mix up shots: long, short, high, low, side; hitter moves all over court. Rotate hitters. Great workout.			

SERVING

SKILL	CUE	WHY	COMMON ERROR
Long Singles Service	Bend knees and swing under and up		Side swing
	Contact out in front of body		Contact behind body
	Swing under shuttle		
	Follow-through straight up to hit face with biceps		No follow-through
Short Doubles Service	Stand 12–18 inches behind T		
	Hold shuttle tip of feather		
	Gently stroke the shuttle into opponent's court with backhand motion		
	Stand up straight		Leaning over holding the shuttle close to the floor

continued

SKILL	CUE	WHY	COMMON ERROR
Serving Drill: Players serve to each other short and long serves.	You want to be as tall as you can so the shuttle starts out high. You want shuttle to go on its downward path after it goes over the net	You want player to hit up so that you and your partner have advantage on third shot; opponent can't attack if hit obtaining shot	
	The rules require that you strike the shuttle at your waist or below		
	The entire hand holding the racket must be higher than the racket head as you strike the shuttle upwards over net		
Gamelike Drill: This drill can be done with clears, clears and smashes, or all the skills of badminton; good drill to use with large classes. Assign 3–4 players per court; 1 player hits, gets off court to back; partner comes on court and plays next shot. Rotate hits.	This drill allows each player to play the full court		

The serve is a defensive shot, not an offensive shot as it is in tennis for example. Remember the quote of the great doubles champion Don Paup: "The serve and return of serve are the two most important shots in any rally."

SKILL	CUE	WHY	COMMON ERROR
Scoring	Only the server can score points		
	1 point scored when opposing player fails to return shuttle back over net		
	1 point scored when shuttle comes back over the net and lands out of bounds		
	Server serves in right court when server's score is 0 or even		
	Server serves in left court when server's score is odd		
Service Boundaries	Tall and narrow man (Figure 4.4)		
Men's Singles	Played to 15 points		Forgetting to take the option to set when score is tied
Setting	14–14, play to 17		Starting score at 13 and playing to 17
	First player to 14 has option to play 17		Starting score at 14 and playing to 17
Match Play	Player who wins 2 out of 3 games wins the match		
Women's Singles	Played to 11 points		Forgetting to take the option to set when score is tied
Setting	10–10, play to 13 points		Starting score at 9 and playing to 12
	First player to reach 10 has option to play to 13		Starting score at 10 and playing to 12
Match Play	Player who wins 2 out of 3 games wins the match		

SKILL	CUE	WHY	COMMON ERROR
Strategies	Play opponent's weak side		Playing opponent's forehand side
	Mix up shots; be unpredictable		Using same shot
	Use deception, and disguise shots		
	Use clears to force opponent deep in court and on the move		Hitting shuttle to middle of court
	After hitting, get back to the Big T		
	Mix shots, then take advantage of the weak return with a well-placed, powerful smash	Make your opponent run to weaken his or her return	
	The patient, aggressive player wins points		

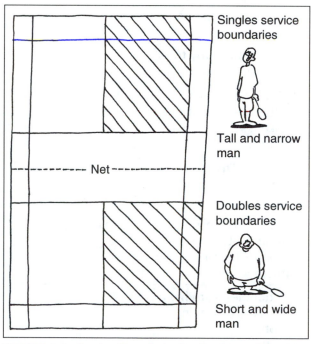

FIGURE 4.4 Service Boundaries for Singles and Doubles

SKILL	CUE	WHY	COMMON ERROR
Front/Back (Figure 4.5)	"Up/back" formation in attack mode after a smash or drop		
	Front player is halfway between service line and net		
	Back player is shadow to front player		
Side to Side (Figure 4.6)	If one partner moves to side of court, the other goes to the opposite side of court to cover court area		
	When defending or in trouble, use side position that is parallel to partner		
	Each player covers own property		
	Stay within property line		Crossing over line
Basic Guidelines	Support partner in every way possible		
	Always be ready to cover for partner		
	Don't get in each other's way; let partner take his or her own shots		
	Call for "iffy" (in-between) shots ("mine")		
	Whenever possible send shots between opponents to confuse them		
Inning	A doubles team has an "inning," meaning both players are entitled to serve		
Starting Position	Start in right-hand court		
	One hand in first inning (first server)		

continued

Starting Position, *continued*	Two hands in each inning after (two servers)		
	We like to use the term ABBA to help remember the order: A: Player A1 serves one hand, then B: Player B1 serves one hand, then B: Player B2 serves one hand, then A: Back to player A1 and then to player A2		
Server	Server alternates serving court each time point is made	AABB = Two hands in each inning after ABBA	
Receivers	Receivers do not change courts		
Scoring	Serve to score		
Points	15-point games; *see* Men's Singles, setting on page 44		
Match	Win 2 out of 3 games		
Break	5-minute rest period between second and third games		
Doubles Service Area	Short and wide man (Figure 4.4)		

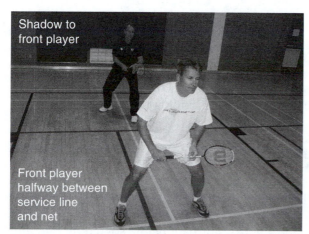

Shadow to front player

Front player halfway between service line and net

FIGURE 4.5 Doubles Formation for Attack Mode after a Smash or Drop

If one partner moves to side of court, the other goes to the opposite side to cover court area

FIGURE 4.6 Doubles Formation when Defending or in Trouble

5

Baseball

INTRODUCTION

"There is no joy in Mudville: mighty Casey has struck out."

What the fans in joyless Mudville never knew about their mighty slugger Casey is that after striking out, Casey decided to ask his coach how to improve his batting skills. Casey's coaches now face the challenge of correcting Casey's swing and restoring joy to Mudville. Was there really anything wrong with Casey's swing or was the pitcher just better that day???

Selecting critical errors and giving the right cue is not an easy task for the coach. The cues in this chapter were designed to help coaches analyze skills and provide effective cues. For example, the cue "See the ball hit the bat" helps the batter focus on the ball all the way into the hitting zone as the bat head makes contact with the ball.

SKILLS LISTED WITH CUES

This chapter presents cues for the following baseball skills: hitting, throwing, fielding ground balls and fly balls, bunting, pitching (fastball, curveball, slider, knuckleball, forkball, screwball), catching, and sliding (feet first, head first).

TIPS

1. Warm up with a fungo bat. This drill teaches quick hands, increasing bat speed. Warming up with heavy bats teaches your hands to drag the bat through the strike zone.
2. Run a couple of laps around the bases or park before stretching out and warming up the arm. This activity warms the arm up a little faster and helps circulate the blood.

3. Start with short-distance throwing and move into a long toss. A long toss is defined as throwing the ball as far as one can but still keeping it on the line. The long toss is the only true way to increase arm strength, and it also feels good.

4. Using the fungo bat in a drill with Wiffle ball golf balls is ideal. "See the ball hit the bat" helps with a quick wrist to develop bat speed.

5. Regular bats are okay for batting tees and soft toss drills.

EQUIPMENT TIPS

1. Gloves: infielders need short-pocket gloves for quick access and release, and outfielders need large-pocket gloves for flyballs and fielding ground-balls on the run.

2. Bats: pick a bat that is comfortable in the hands, one that is not too heavy or long. The key to hitting is bat speed.

3. A fungo bat is used to hit infield balls. These bats are not made for hitting pitched balls. The bat will break hitting a pitched ball.

4. Batting gloves protect the hands when hitting. They also provide protection under the mitt as well as protection when base running. The runner should hold the batting gloves in clenched fists to protect fingers when sliding.

5. Wiffle balls can be used for soft-toss drills. They can also be used for batting practice in a very small area if a cage is not available. A player can use Wiffle balls for batting practice before games. The use of Wiffle balls avoids damage to fences. Baseballs have a tendency to bend a chain-link fence.

6. Catcher equipment is needed for protection: shin guards, chest protector, helmet, cup, mask, and throat guard.

7. Baseball caps are critical to help block the sun.

8. Shoes with cleats/spikes plastic are recommended because they help with traction.

TEACHING IDEAS

1. *Batting drill stations:* To develop the necessary techniques and rhythm to hit a live pitch, many repetitions of a correct swing are necessary. The emphasis in these drills should be on hand position at setup, hand action during the swing, and hip rotation.

   a. *Soft-toss drill:* The batter hits into a fence or net. The player or partner kneels at a 45-degree angle from the batter, a short distance off the batter's front foot, and tosses underhand. The batter cocks the bat as the partner takes the ball back to tossing position and swings upon delivery.

   b. *Batting tee:* A tee is used. The ball is rotated to different positions to give the batter a variety of areas to hit.

   c. *Hip drill:* The batter places the bat behind his back, cradling it in the crook of the elbows. Now rotate back and forth and feel how the body weight is naturally transferred from back to front foot as the hips rotate. Make sure the back foot comes up at the heel (squash the bug) as the weight is transferred forward.

2. *Four-corners drill:* Four to 12 players on the four bases throw the ball around the bases. The goal is to try to catch the ball in the catching zone. (The catching zone is the top left-hand side toward the glove side, to the left of the heart for a right-handed player.) This drill teaches players to shuffle feet and have a quick ball exchange. Modifications of four-corners drill: catch, shuffle, throw; hop, chase. Go clockwise, then counterclockwise.

FYI

For further information and special help, consult the following resources.

PUBLICATIONS

Petrack, C. (1998). *Complete guide to outfield play.* Haworth, NJ: Harding Press.

Delmonico, R. (1996). *Offensive baseball drill.* Champaign, IL: Human Kinetics.

Delmonico, R. (1995). *Defensive baseball.* Chicago, IL: Masters Press.

WEBSITES

www.howtoplay.com/ht_p/baseball/essentials.html
www.educationworld.com/a_sites/sites082.shtml
www.freezone.com/sports/baseball/contents.html

SKILL	CUE	WHY	COMMON ERROR
Hitting			
Stance (Figure 5.1a)	Stand sideways with eyes focused on pitcher		Standing forward, head tilt
	Feet slightly wider than shoulder width, knees flexed/bent slightly	Proper balance	Feet too far apart or too close together
	Weight over balls of feet, heels lightly touching the ground, more weight on back leg		Weight on heels
Arm Swing	Hitter should think "shoulder to shoulder" (start with chin on front shoulder; finish swing with chin on back shoulder)	Keeps the head in proper position; head should stay still	Moving head during the swing; head too tense
Hip Rotation (Figure 5.1b)	Back hip snaps or rotates at pitcher; drive body through ball; take photograph of pitcher with belly button		No hip rotation
	Throw hands through baseball; "slow feet, quick hands"		Using arms instead of wrists
Focus of eyes	See the bat hit the ball	Gets the barrel of the bat to the ball and not the handle	Not seeing the ball hit bat
	Watch ball all the way into catcher's mitt	Helps the batter to see the ball all the way into the hitting zone	
Step	Step 3–6 inches (stride should be more of a glide)		Overstriding causes bat to drop during swing (jarring step)
			Also causes head to drop, which causes eyes to drop as well; obscures vision on the ball
	Short stride, quick swing		Hitter "steps and then hits"
Follow-Through (Figure 5.1c)	Top hand rolls over bottom hand; bat goes around the body on follow-through		

continued

SKILL	CUE	WHY	COMMON ERROR
Recommended Progression	Teach cues in order listed; when first 3 are mastered, add others		
Bunting	Pivot toward pitcher; square body to pitcher	Both eyes focused on the ball	Hitter or bunter does not get properly squared around in position to bunt
	Slide top hand up bat; keep bat head slightly above the handle; keep fingers behind bat or protect fingers from ball	Less chance to hit ball in air	Hands remain together (bat is not kept level if pitch is either high or low); wrapping hand around bat
	Catch ball with bat— imagine a net in the barrel of the bat; catch the ball in the net	Deadens the ball	Pushing bat at ball, swiping at ball

(a) Batter's Stance

(b) Hip Rotation

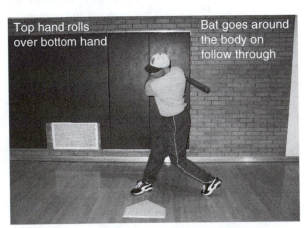

(c) Follow Through

FIGURE 5.1

SKILL	CUE	WHY	COMMON ERROR
Checkpoint for Coaches	If the batter is not gripping, standing, or holding the bat correctly, coach could correct the player individually		Don't use these cues unless a player needs assistance; give one at a time
Grip	Hold bat in base of fingers (this allows wrist to roll freely and generates bat speed)	Enables wrists to turn freely during the swing	Bat held in palm of hand, squeezing bat slows the swing
	Align knuckles "Eight middle knuckles, all in a row"		
Closed Stance	Feet are shoulder-width apart; then front foot is placed toward plate (helps untrained hitter step toward the pitcher)		Stepping back or stepping into the bucket
Bat Position	Bat held armpit high and far enough away from the body that both fists of player could fit		Bat held too close to shoulder
	Back elbow held away from body at about an 8:00 position. Front elbow should be in closer to body	Creates a shorter swing	Back elbow drops, creating an upswing and a fly ball swing
Bat Angle	Straight up in air or up and angled slightly back over shoulder	Helps make a short, quick swing	Cradling bat around head; bat is pointing back toward pitcher

SKILL	CUE	WHY	COMMON ERROR
Grip	Get a seam, either across the seams or with the seams	Makes ball spin backward, allowing it to travel further and straighter	Not getting a seam, poor control of ball
	Hold ball with fingertips: first 2 fingers on top of ball, second 2 underneath to the side, thumb opposite side		Holding baseball in palm or placing more fingers on top of ball
Stance	Stand sideways, instep of back foot faces target		Standing facing the target
Throwing Action	Point glove hand shoulder at target		Staying square to target (no shoulder or hip rotation is possible)
	Take a long step toward target		Stepping across body, no step at all, or a step that is too high
	Stretch arm way back		
	Make L shape with throwing arm		Taking the ball directly behind head with bent elbow
	Pull glove arm down, and replace glove arm with throwing arm		
	Whip the arm through, snap wrist		No wrist action, all arm
	Follow-through; wrist goes to opposite knee; slap knee		No follow-through

SKILL	CUE	WHY	COMMON ERROR
Stance	Feet shoulder-width apart, weight on balls of feet (right-handers lead slightly with left foot because the slight lead of the left foot means that less time is needed to rotate body to throw)	Proper balance	Weight on heels, feet too close or too far apart
	Create a triangle with both feet and glove; the glove is the apex (top) of the triangle		Glove inside or behind knees
	Bend at knees; slightly at waist		Bending at waist and not at knees
Catching Action	Field ball out in front		Trying to play ball behind the legs
	Keep glove close to ground		Starting with glove waist high and trying to go down at ball
	Keep the glove lower than the ball		
	Elbows inside knees act as shock absorber to cushion the impact of a ground ball	Creates soft hands	
	Put your nose on the ball; follow the ball into glove with eyes		Pulling head up; not seeing ball into glove for fear of being hit in the face
	Secure ball with both hands	Keep throwing hand close for quick release	Fielding ball with only the glove
	Read a hop; read the path of the baseball; try to field ball on big or long hop; after a big hop, ball will usually stay low		Letting ball dictate way to play it (letting ball play fielder)

FIELDING—FLY BALLS

SKILL	CUE	WHY	COMMON ERROR
Stance	Comfortable stance, weight on balls of feet	Running with weight on the heels makes it difficult to track a fly ball	Rigid, fight stance; weight on back of heels like a boxer
Catching Position	Position body underneath flight of baseball (the path should be coming down to the eyes)	Having to catch ball behind your head or below your waist	
Catching Action	Place glove slightly out from and above head; reach for the sky with fingers just before the ball arrives		Catching ball to side of body; fingers stretched out rather than up
	Always use both hands to secure ball		One-handed "showboat"
	Follow ball into glove with eyes		Not watching ball all the way into the glove

PITCHING

SKILL	CUE	WHY	COMMON ERROR
Delivery	Step directly toward home plate		Foot goes too far one way or the other
	Use normal throwing motion, nice and easy "loosey goosey"	Don't try to throw across body	Overthrowing, trying to throw the ball too hard; avoid sidearming
	Simply play catch with catcher, throw strikes		Trying to do too much, overthrowing and not throwing any strikes
	Comfortable, smooth delivery		No rhythm
	Follow-through throwing hand should come down and brush against the opposite knee		
Pitches *Fastball*	Grip with seams for a sink action; grip across seam for a rise		Wrong grip or simply grabbing ball
	Pressure on fingertips		No pressure points
	Smooth delivery		Rushed motion
	Wrist snap		No wrist action

continued

SKILL	CUE	WHY	COMMON ERROR
Pitches, *continued*			
Curveball	Grip with seams	Creates a spin on the baseball, causing it to spin or curve	Wrong grip
	Fastball motion		Motion too slow and obvious
	Reduce speed of ball		Too much speed, no rotation or spin
	Tickle ear		Not cocking wrist
	Pull down		Lazy arm action
	Snap fingers		Letting ball simply roll off fingers
Slider	Backward C		Wrong grip and placement of fingers
	Off center		Holding ball in center
	Fastball speed and motion		Slow or rushed motion
	Turn wrist over or turn doorknob		Throwing like a curveball, cocking wrist
	Second finger		First finger releases ball
Knuckleball	Fingernail grip	Lack of spin causes ball to float	Knuckles on seams
	Dig seams		Not enough pressure on seams
	Extend and push toward plate		Forcing the ball
	Stiff wrist		Snapping the wrist
Forkball	Make a fork shape with fingers	Causes the ball to dip or dive	Fingers not far enough apart
	Fingers outside seams		Fingers directly on seams
	Ball rolls away		Pressure on fingertips
	No wrist action or snap		Too much wrist
Screwball	Grip narrow seams	Causes the ball to spin and break opposite of curveball action	Simply grabbing baseball
	Overhand		Sidearm
	Inside out		Curveball motion
	Reverse snap		Not enough wrist action
	Thumb flip		No thumb

SKILL	CUE	WHY	COMMON ERROR
Catcher's Stance (Figure 5.2)	Feet outside shoulders, heels elevated	Balance	Kneeling
	Head up		Flinching, head down
	Elbows resting outside the knees		
(Figure 5.2)	Place throwing arm behind back	Placing arm directly behind or to the side of the catcher's mitt is more likely to cause injury	
	Catch the ball using both hands; elbows act as shock absorbers		Relying solely on catcher's mitt
	Move to ball laterally. Allow the ball to get through the hitting zone	Batter may make contact with mitt or hand, causing injury	Reaching for ball

FIGURE 5.2 Catcher's Stance

SLIDING			
SKILL	**CUE**	**WHY**	**COMMON ERROR**
Feet First	Sprint		Slowing up
	Slide early		Sliding too late (injuries)
	Sit down		Falling and hopping
	Curl leg under, making a figure 4		Sliding with both legs forward
	Keep hands in front of the body		
	Roller-coaster ride		Lying down completely
Head First	Sprint		Slowing down
	Sink		Upright and no balance
	Dive		Belly flopping onto base
	Outstretched arms	Prevents injury	Hands and arms too close to body
	Balance and fingers up		
	Superman in flight		

6

Basketball

INTRODUCTION

Former Assistant Coach Al Brown from the University of Tennessee states, "You need to develop three fundamental skills—dribbling, passing, and shooting—to become a good basketball player." This chapter provides teaching cues and fundamental drills to practice these skills and others. Try to provide lots of opportunities for the students to touch the ball. Have lots of basketballs and baskets available. When possible, lower baskets and have dunk contests.

SKILLS LISTED WITH CUES

Cues are provided for stationary ball handling, dribbling, passing and catching, the set shot, shooting drills, right- and left-handed lay-ups, basic ball handling, free throw, jump shot, rebounding, jumping and dunking, blocking out, the pick, offensive footwork, offensive one-on-one moves, spacing, defense, and out-of-bounds plays.

TIPS

1. Play a lot of games: half-court and full-court games.
2. Play dribble tag, relays, passing games, shooting contests (using right and left hands).
3. Be creative in your games. Use your imagination. Change and modify your rules (e.g., you must find a way to score without dribbling).
4. Time players on dribbling the length of the court, dribbling right- and left-handed.
5. Time the player rebounding and throwing a baseball pass the length of the court.

6. Direct stretching, footwork, and ball handling at the beginning of each session before activity begins.

7. All jump balls go to the defense.

EQUIPMENT TIP

Have a lot of basketballs and baskets available.

TEACHING IDEAS

1. Every player should have a basketball. A must.

2. Practice should be 90 percent dribble, pass, shoot, and handling the ball.

3. Practice—practice—practice! How many hours are you willing to practice?

4. Use two basketballs per player to dribble or pass to a partner.

5. Know the feel for the ball and what the ball can do for you.

6. The best players shoot the ball around 8 hours a day. Recruiters look for 90 percent ball-handling and shooting skills. Tell students that to be good they need the fundamentals: dribble, pass, and shoot.

7. When playing a game you must boil teaching down to the basic cues of the game, like placing your rebounder under the basket on the right-hand side of the basket. Why? Most of the balls go there.

Court Sprints

1. Diagonal sprint from under the basket on the baseline to the left hash mark to the right hash mark on the other side of the court to the other baseline; repeat.

2. Run forward from baseline to baseline.

3. Run backward from baseline to baseline.

4. Run from far baseline to far free-throw line forward, then backward, back to the baseline. Keep your balance by using your arms when running backward.

5. Conditioning your players must involve forward, backward, lateral, sprinting, and jumping gamelike movements. You can sprint while dribbling the ball.

6. Use half-court and full court for speed drills and change-of-speed crossover drills. Emphasize change of direction and change of speed. Keep head up. Ball-handling drill on the end line.

For further information and special help, consult the following organizations and resources.

ORGANIZATIONS

University of Tennessee Women's Intercollegiate Athletics, Basketball Coach Pat Summitt
207 Thompson-Boling Arena
1600 Phillip Fulmer Way
Knoxville, TN 37996-4610

Shanna Stevens
845 West Factory Rd.
Garland, UT 84312
e-mail: SLPLT@cc.usu.edu

PUBLICATION

Krause, J. V. & Meyer, D. (1999). *Basketball skills and drills*. Champaign, IL: Human Kinetics.

WEBSITES

www.basketballworldinc.com
www.prostar.com/web/northshr/bb-tips.htm
www.vyi.org/bballdrills.htm
www.encarta.msn.com

STATIONARY BALL—BALL HANDLING

SKILL	CUE	WHY	COMMON ERROR
Hand Position Drill	Slap the ball with wide fingers	This will develop a feel for the ball and control of the ball	Palm on ball
Around the World	Move the ball around the waist; change directions; then move the ball around your head; then change directions quickly	To develop quick reaction time with hands and body awareness	Dropping the ball
Figure 8 Around Legs	Move ball in figure 8 formation around the knees and then change directions quickly		
Scissor Walk with Basketball (Crab Walk)	Lunging down the court, move the basketball in and out of your legs, going from baseline to baseline and staying low	Promote basketball position and coordination in ball movement	Standing straight up

SKILL	CUE	WHY	COMMON ERROR
Hand Placement on Ball When Dribbling	Thumb out, fingers spread wide, ball touching all 5 finger pads when dribbling; look up court	Develop feel for the ball	Fingers together
Hand Action	Yo-yo action with your hand on the ball; push ball hard toward floor	Develop feel for hand on ball and force in dribbling	Slapping the ball
	Waving action with your hand		Palm touches the ball
	Hand waving down at the ball		Dribble with both hands
	Note: Use left and right hands equally when practicing		
Eyes	Eyes looking up the court for open players and for opportunities to pass, shoot, or drive; see the defenders but don't look at them	To develop court awareness and player positions	Eyes looking down at the ball
Speed Drills			
Change of speed, Crossover	Emphasize change of direction and change of speed; keep head up	To promote ball-handling skills and ability	
Five-Trip Dribble (Single Ball)	Used to change your directions on the court; protect ball with arm guard		
Speed Dribble	Quickly dribble down the court with right hand; dribble back with left hand	Control with speed	Bouncing ball too high
The Crossover	Take 3 dribbles with the right hand toward the sideline, lower the dribble and cross the ball over to the left hand knee high, then dribble toward the other sideline; repeat; use the crossover down to the baseline and back to the other baseline. In a zigzag pattern	Develop change of direction skills	High dribble

continued

SKILL	CUE	WHY	COMMON ERROR
Five-Trip Dribble (Single Ball), continued			
Around the Back	Take 3 dribbles with the right hand toward the right sideline; bring the ball around your back to the other hand, then dribble toward the other sideline; go down and back		Holding ball too long in hand
Through the Legs	Take 3 dribbles with the right hand toward the right sideline; make sure the left foot is in front when you bounce the ball between your legs to change directions, then dribble with the left hand toward the left sideline, make sure your right foot is forward to change directions; go down and back		Stepping with the wrong foot
Reverse Spin	Take 3 dribbles toward the right sideline; keep ball in your right hand and quickly spin so your back shuts out your defender; switch the ball to the left hand, take 3 dribbles and reverse spin again; go down and back; keep ball low on spin		Carrying the ball
Five-Trip Dribble (Two-Ball)	Used to change your direction; keep rhythm with balls		
Speed Dribble (Figure 6.1)	Dribble 2 balls to half-court and back		
The Crossover	Repeat the single-ball crossover drill using 2 balls, to half-court and back	Helps improve confidence, creativity, and dribbling skills	
		Develop advanced skills in dribbling	

continued

FULL- AND HALF-COURT DRIBBLING DRILLS

SKILL	CUE	WHY	COMMON ERROR
Five-Trip Dribble (Two-Ball), *continued*			
Around the Back	Repeat single-ball drill with 2 balls		
Through the Legs	Repeat single-ball drill with 2 balls		
Reverse Spin	Repeat single-ball reverse-spin drill using 2 balls, to half-court and back; keep balls low		

FIGURE 6.1 Dribbling two Balls, Ball Handling

SKILL	CUE	WHY	COMMON ERROR
Passing			
Hand Position	Two thumbs down behind the ball	For proper spin	Thumbs up
Fingers	Spread fingers wide	For control	
Eyes	Eyes focused on your target	For accuracy	
Passing Action	Extend your arms like shooting horizontally, following through with thumbs down	For proper speed and accuracy	
	Palms out at finish		
Catching			
Hand and Finger Position	Big hands, wide fingers	To develop receiving skills	
Catching Action	Reach out, pull the ball in, or suck the ball in like a vacuum, your nickname "Hoover"	Prevent defense from stealing ball	
Eyes	Smother the ball with your eyes	To assure catching	
Passing and Catching Drills			
Partner Passing	Face each other using one ball, one-hand push pass with your right hand and then your left hand; follow through each time	Like shooting a basketball, only horizontally with right hand	
		To pass around a defender; right side/left side	
Target passing	Throw to your partner's target (e.g., partner's shoulder, head, or hands); make a target on the wall when practicing by yourself	Like shooting a basketball, only horizontally with the left hand	
Chest Pass and Bounce Pass Simultaneously	Both partners have a ball; 1 partner will 2-hand chest pass while the other partner will bounce pass at the same time; then switch after a while	Develop advanced skills in passing	

continued

SKILL	CUE	WHY	COMMON ERROR
Passing and Catching Drills, *continued*			
Pass with a Figure 8	Perform a figure 8 around your knees, then pass to your partner off the figure 8; keep the ball moving	Passing while on the move	
Behind the Back Passing	Standing slightly sideways, bring ball behind the back, pass to your partner; use your right hand, then your left hand; learn through error	Alternative pass for advanced players	
Baseball Pass	Throw (as a football quarterback passes a football) to your partner	For long-distance passing with accuracy	
	Start close to your partner, then keep taking steps farther back as needed to throw farther		
	Stretch arm back and make an L at the elbow		
	Release the ball at 2:00 on your pretend clock		
One-Bounce Baseball Pass	Use strong then weak arms to throw your baseball passes with a bounce first	Alternative pass for advanced players	
	Step farther back as needed, to throw longer passes		
Buzzer Beater Baseball Pass Length of the Floor	Dribble once, then throw down court to partner at the other end of court counting to self . . . 3-2-1 BZZZZZ	Develop end-of-game confidence	
Two-Player Running and Passing Drills			
Dribbler and Trailer	Player 1 baseball passes to player 2, who is at half-court	To develop necessary skills in passing for advanced players	
Full Court	Player 2 passes to player 1, who drives to the basket		

continued

SKILL	CUE	WHY	COMMON ERROR
Two-Player Running and Passing Drills, *continued*			
Pass and cut	Partner 1 stands at half-court		
Half-Court	Partner 2 stands on free-throw line extended at the wing spot		
	Partner 1 then passes to the wing and cuts hard inside to the basket, receiving the ball from partner 2 for a layup shot		
Three-Man Player Drills			
Side Center Side	Start with 3 lines, ball in middle line		
	Pass back and forth with no weave		
	Pass back and forth down court with 1 shooter		
	Perfect execution for the layup		
Three-Man Weave	Start with 3 lines, ball in middle line	To include movement in passing as done in game situations	
	Running down court, middle passes to player on right side who passes to the player coming toward him or her		
	Pass and go behind Follow your pass Be ready to receive ball back quickly		
	Person who receives the ball at key drives in for the layup		
	Use game speed Go all out		

continued

PASSING AND CATCHING, continued

SKILL	CUE	WHY	COMMON ERROR
Three-Man Player Drills, *continued*			
Rebound Pass	Two players start in the paint, one outside the paint	To develop fast break strategy	
	Teacher tosses the ball of the rim		
	Player rebounds		
	Everyone takes off down court with no dribble		
	Pass down the floor to closest player by the basket for the layup		
	We want to move the ball up the floor as quickly as possible for a quick layup		

SET SHOT

SKILL	CUE	WHY	COMMON ERROR
Set-Up	Shooting is the most important aspect of the game	To develop a knowledge base	
	Layups and free throws are 2 shots you must make; these are freebies		
	The best 3-point shot is a layup and a free throw, not the arch shot		
Shooting Hand	Air valve between index finger and middle finger	To develop proper position for successful shooting	
	Extend thumb along seam when shooting		
	Spread fingers		Fingers close together

continued

SKILL	CUE	WHY	COMMON ERROR
Set-Up, *continued* (Figure 6.2)	Hand up; balance like a waiter's tray		Ball held in palm
	Elbow makes an L with ball sitting on a pretend serving tray of finger pads		
Nonshooting Hand (Figure 6.2)	Hand faces side of ball; fingers only touch ball		
	Hand brushes ball		
Alignment	Arm, eye, and hand line up with nail hole in floor and with basket, like throwing a dart		Elbow points to side Pushing ball sideways Arm at 45° angle
Sight	Focus on 2 inches above the rim	You have to see what you're shooting for	
	"Basket looks like big bin and the basket gets bigger on a good night," (Michael Jordan)		

continued

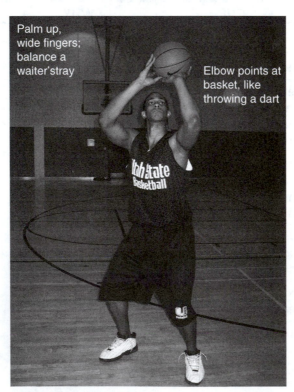

Palm up, wide fingers; balance a waiter's tray

Elbow points at basket, like throwing a dart

FIGURE 6.2 Setup

SKILL	CUE	WHY	COMMON ERROR
Set-Up, *continued*			
Legs	Slightly bend knees with buttocks out	Strength of shot comes from legs	Insufficient force from no use of legs
Footwork	Feet square to basket and balanced		
Shooting Action			
Fingers	Ball rolls off fingers for a nice, pretty backspin	To develop proper backspin	Ball is thrown
Wrist	Flip wrist, wave good-bye to ball		Inadequate wrist action
Shoot Over	Shoot up over a telephone booth	Important for arch development	Insufficient drive upward, loss of balance
Path of Ball	Make a rainbow; exaggerate your arch, your first couple of shots		Lack of follow-through and arch
Finish Position (Figure 6.3)			
Wrist	Gooseneck finish, thumb points at shoes	To ensure proper and consistent release	
	Freeze hand at the top		

(a) Side View

(b) Front View

FIGURE 6.3 Set Shot—Finish Position

SKILL	CUE	WHY	COMMON ERROR
Fundamentals			
Right Hand and Left Hand	Start close to the basket shooting 5 on the right side 1-handed, then shooting 5 on the left side 1-handed	Develop confidence and form at close distances	
Shooting Practice with No Defender	Take 5 steps back from under the basket, shoot 5 right-handed and 5 left-handed	Develop consistency and accuracy	
	Take 5 steps back until you are at the free-throw line; shoot 5 with strong hand only		
Consecutive Free Throw	Consecutive free-throw shot with no dribble and a partner	Confidence	
	Find a rhythm		
Shooter Rebounds Free Throw	Shooter rebounds ball before it touches floor and passes back to partner for the shot; so shooter rebounds own shot and passes to partner on foul line	Shoot and follow shot	
	Left hand comes off ball with the shot; thus it is a 1-handed shot		
	You want to shoot without a defender because you make more shots when you're open; when you're defended you tend to pass and not shoot	Shoot when open; more shots are made	
Body Position for the Shot	Feet and hand must be in line with the basket	Extremely important for successful shooting	

continued

SKILL	CUE	WHY	COMMON ERROR
Three-Man	You need a passer, a shooter, and a rebounder	Practice advanced skills	
	Rebounder cannot let ball hit the floor before passing it to the passer		
	The passer bounce-passes it to the shooter along the free-throw line		
	Shoot from the right side of the court and then the left side of the court, then rotate		
	Rebounder to passer to shooter to rebounder		
Three-Man	Same formations as previously, only the shooter runs along the 3-point line; s/he shoots where s/he receives the pass		
Two-Man	Need a shooter and a rebounder		To develop individual shooting skills
	The shooter rebounds, passes to the partner, and plays defense on the shooter		
	Do not block the shot		
Three-Man Weave with a Bounce Pass	Get into 3 lines along the baseline, ball in the middle line		
	While running full court, pass the ball with a bounce pass to the right side; follow the pass and go behind		
	Expect the ball back		

SKILL	CUE	WHY	COMMON ERROR
Right-Handed			
The Approach	Head up, eyes on top of square	The closer you are to the basket, the more likely you are to make it	
	Ball in outside hand with low approach		Shooting ball more likely to be blocked if approach is high
Release of Layup	Bring ball close to chin; chin ball, step, and push off foot with opposite shooting hand	Harder to block	
(Figure 6.4)	Extend arm, reach high (ball kisses backboard)		
	Release ball at peak of reach		
Left-Handed			
Foot Work	Step left, right, hop (jump)	Same as right hand	Jumping off wrong foot
Shooting Action	Left hand shoots ball		Using wrong hand on wrong side

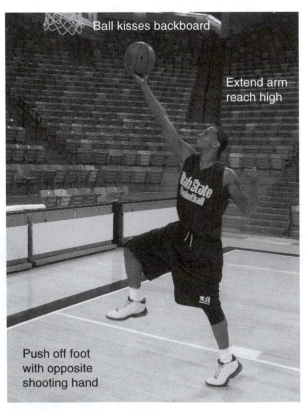

Ball kisses backboard

Extend arm reach high

Push off foot with opposite shooting hand

FIGURE 6.4 Right handed lay-up

BASIC BALL HANDLING

SKILL	CUE	WHY	COMMON ERROR
Ready Position	"Triple threat"	A position that allows player to execute all parts of the game	Not assuming the position
	Purpose: to fake out opponent with the option of shooting, passing, or dribbling		
Hand Position	Shooting position on ball		Hands not in shooting position; hands too close together
Holding Ball	Hold ball to side on hip		Ball held too high or too low
	Keep ball on hip—hold ball to side to pass, dribble, or step into shot		
	Elbows out		

FREE THROW

SKILL	CUE	WHY	COMMON ERROR
Front Toe Stays on Line	Work off the center of free-throw line with front toe in direct line with rim	It lines up the player with the center of the basket	
	Place front toe directly on center of free-throw line, find the nail hole	Shooting is a straight line function	
	Put the front toe on same place every time; toe on the line	Consistency	
Head Position	Put head down; head comes up with ball in one motion	Focuses eyes on target	
	Head level eyes up		
Balance	Get balanced on free-throw line	Important to have weight properly distributed	
Routine	University of Tennessee uses player's choice—no dribble or 1, 2, or 3 dribbles	Develop consistency	

continued

FREE THROW, continued

SKILL	CUE	WHY	COMMON ERROR
Body	Body makes a line with the basket same place every time		
Leg Action	Bend your knees, my legs compel the shot	Consistency comes from the legs	
Back Foot	Feet shoulder width apart, then place back foot slightly back	Help maintain balance	
	Back foot does not have anything to do with shot		
Fundamental Drills	Repetition and competition: dribble 3, shoot	Develops confidence and consistency	
	Rebounder passes to shooter		
	Find a rhythm		
	Example: Partner shooting: shoot 5; person with the most shots made wins		
	Group free throw; everybody shoots 1 and runs for the missed shots		
	Speed or lightning shots with eyes closed (Michael Jordan drill)	Advanced skill players only	
	More shots made off bounce shot—why?		
	Body legs are down; eyes are down—ready to go		

JUMP SHOT

SKILL	CUE	WHY	COMMON ERROR
Execution	Jump above the defense, then shoot at the top of the jump; get high	Reduce blocked shots	
	Body in a coil all ready to jump	Develop consistency	

REBOUNDING

SKILL	CUE	WHY	COMMON ERROR
Attacking Basket	Work on blocking out, then attacking the basket	To reduce chance of opponent getting ball	
One Player	Cover the weak side of basket (opposite side of shot)	70% of missed shots fall away from side shot on	
	Most shots go long off the back side		
	Rebounding involves contact		
	Move from side to side and back up into a player, keep contact		
	Be active, aggressive, and alert		
Two Players	Check the player without the ball: if he or she moves to the basket, take him or her; if not, attack the basket for the ball	To reduce chance of opponent getting ball	

JUMPING AND DUNKING

SKILL	CUE	WHY	COMMON ERROR
Jumping *Fundamentals*	Jump naturally	Forced movement reduces ability	
	Work on getting high; act like a bungee cord		
Dunking	Lower baskets for student to dunk on	Develop confidence and have fun	
	Do not hang on rims		
	Have lots of baskets to jump with		
	Use jump ropes		

SKILL	CUE	WHY	COMMON ERROR
Action of Body	Find with hands	Develop a routine to keep opponent from getting ball	
Turn Back to Opponent (Figure 6.5)	Put buttocks under opponent's hip or create a stable wall between opponent and ball		Not able to hold position
Hands (After Pivot)	Elbows out, palms wide; feel for opponent		

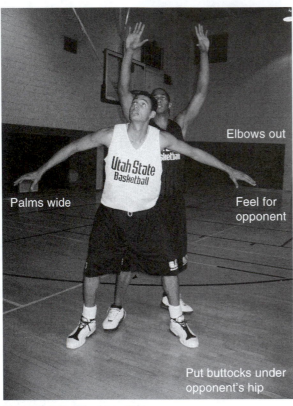

Elbows out

Palms wide

Feel for opponent

Put buttocks under opponent's hip

FIGURE 6.5 Blocking Out

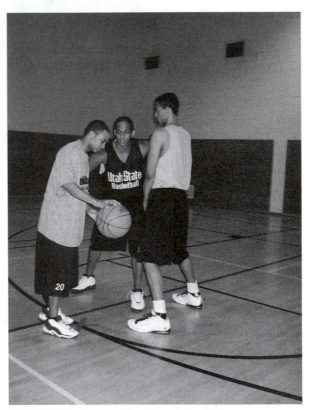

FIGURE 6.6 Player Coming off the Pick

SKILL	CUE	WHY	COMMON ERROR
Hustle	Earn your position	To avoid fouling	
Stance	Stand wide	Develop larger target, more effective	
	Weight on balls of feet		
Arms	Elbow bent and big		
Men	Hands clasped in front to protect sensitive parts of your body		
Women	Arms crossed against body to protect sensitive parts of your body		
Coming off the Pick (Figure 6.6)	Rub shoulder to shoulder	To shake off the defender with the pick	
	Right to right; left to left		
Pick and Roll	After you pick, you pivot toward basket	Gives a player more opportunity to get open	
	Hand up high, ask for ball		
	Receive pass and go in for layup or shot		
Defender Going Through a Pick	Anticipate taking a hook step around player	To beat the defender to a position	

OFFENSIVE FOOTWORK

SKILL	CUE	WHY	COMMON ERROR
Technique	Read and triple threat position	To develop advanced skills	
	Two-step stop—emphasis on heel-toe (jump stop to be used for post people only)		
	Change of speed and direction		
	Fake shot and drive—left and right (without the ball)		

OFFENSIVE ONE-ON-ONE MOVES

SKILL	CUE	WHY	COMMON ERROR
Guards and Wings	Catch and shoot	To develop confidence and advanced skills	
	Catch and drive		
	Catch and reverse		
	Catch shot fake and drive		
	Catch, swing through, and drive		
	Catch, jab, and go (emphasis on heel-toe technique)		
Posts	Front pivot shot (both ways)		
	Front pivot crossover		
	Drop step baseline/power shot		
	Drop step middle, drophook, jumphook, or power shot		
	Pull back-shot drive		
	Post people can also use perimeter drills		

SPACING

SKILL	CUE	WHY	COMMON ERROR
Teach Spacing When Passing on Offense			
Spacing Creates Open Areas	The perfect passing distance is 15 feet	Put pressure on defense to react	
	Anything beyond 15 feet is a potential stolen pass		
	Teach students to play off each other to create efficient spacing		
	Use the free throw line to gauge distance; use lines on the floor to gauge the distance of 15 feet		

DEFENSE

SKILL	CUE	WHY	COMMON ERROR
Man-to-Man Defense	Force opponents from the middle to the sideline; force them to play on one side of the floor	So teammates will know where to help	
On-Ball Defense (Figure 6.7)	One hand mirrors the ball, the other hand is in the passing lane	Prepares defender to block pass or steal ball	
	One eye on your player, the other eye on the ball one pass away		
Help Defense	Deny defense is one hand always in the passing lane, palm facing ball	Develops a team defense concept	
	One eye on your player, one eye on the ball two passes away in pistol formation		

One eye on player, other on ball

one pass away

One hand mirrors the ball, other hand in passing lane

FIGURE 6.7 On-Ball Defense

	WHAT DOES ZONE DO?		
SKILL	**CUE**	**WHY**	**COMMON ERROR**
Zone Defense	Will win more games		
	Effective because teams can't shoot over the zone		
	Teams can't pass or play against stationary defense		
Zone Movement	Defense shifts with ball movement		
	Everybody knows where the ball is at all times, including those on the bench		
The Key to a Zone	A key to zone defense: keep them out of the lanes and deny the passing lanes		
	Run an odd front when playing zone defense: If they have an offense set at a 1-2-2, you play a 2-3 zone defense; if they have 1 guard, you have 2 defenders on their point guard; if they run a 1-3-1 defense, you run a 2-3 offense (2-guard front and 3 low post)		
	The objective is to take the point guard out of the game; he or she runs the show		

SKILL	CUE	WHY	COMMON ERROR
Box Set-Box 1	Player 1 takes the ball out of bounds		
	Players 3 and 4 run to right-side elbow of key and set a double pick for player 2, who rolls off pick to receive ball from 1 guard for lay-up; player 5 is decoy		
Line Formation-Stack	Player 1 takes ball out of bounds		
	Players 2, 3, 4, and 5 make a line outside of key under basket		
	Players 3 and 4 roll toward basket after pick for possible option		
	Player 1 slaps ball, indicating teammates 2 and 4 to split to left, and teammates 3 and 5 split to the right		
	Player 1 passes to open player		
Box Set-Box 2	Player 1 takes ball out of bounds		
	Players 2 and 4 on left side of key		
	Players 3 and 5 on opposite side of key		
	Players 2 and 4 run across key to set picks for 3 and 5 away from ball, 2 and 4 set screen away from ball		
	3 and 5 come off screen		
	5 receives ball on ball side of floor, then passes to 3		
	3 passes to 2 on the wing		

continued

SKILL	CUE	WHY	COMMON ERROR
Box Set-Box 2, *continued*	2 passes to 4 on the baseline for the shot		
	1 steps in bounds to rebound		
Out-of-Bounds Defense	Man-to-man formation		
	Player 1 is on ball		
	Player 2 guards opposing guard at top of key		
	Player 3 defends guard opposite player 2		
	Player 4 guards lower post, opposite side of ball; Player 5 guards lowerpost, ball side		

7

Bowling

INTRODUCTION

"Strike!" The crashing of the pins fills the air with excitement and anticipation of bowling the perfect game of 300. Families, friends, coworkers, and peers can all join in the fun of bowling. How does one learn to bowl? Many bowlers learn by trial and error. Teachers offering bowling in their curriculum could use the cues in this chapter to explain the skills of bowling, even when a bowling alley is not available. (How do you add bowling but not a bowling alley to your curriculum? See equipment tips.)

SKILLS LISTED WITH CUES

Teachers can use simple instructional cues in this chapter to teach the following bowling skills: grip, stance, arm action and leg action on approach and delivery, delivering a straight ball and hook ball, use of arrows for spares and placement of feet, and finding an eye target for spares, splits, and adjustments. Because scoring the game of bowling can be confusing and frustrating to the beginning bowler, we have added scoring cues.

We hope that these cues will help students be more comfortable with bowling and that they will seek real bowling opportunities. Friends can go bowling and experience success together.

ETIQUETTE FOR BOWLERS

1. Remain behind the foul line at all times.
2. Never walk in front of another bowler.
3. Give the bowler to your right the right-of-way.
4. Remain quiet while other students are bowling.
5. To avoid injuries, have students cradle the ball when walking with it.

EQUIPMENT TIPS

1. Gym floor.
2. Rubber bowling balls can be ordered, or round soccer nerf balls can be used.
3. Pins can be made from two-liter pop bottles or empty tennis ball cans, or white plastic pins can be ordered.
4. Scorecards can be obtained from a local bowling alley.
5. Long ropes can be used for lane dividers, or a gym wall can be one side of a lane.
6. Use colored tape for lane arrows and x's to mark the spots where the pins stand.
7. Bowling shoes are used so dirt and other abrasive particles are not brought onto the lanes.
8. Go to a pro shop to get fitted for a ball.
9. Bowling shoes are designed with soles that allow the bowler to slide.

TEACHING IDEAS

1. Have students practice technique and scoring in gym. Have two lines back to back at center court. Pair up in partners (bowl to wall, take turns with balls).
2. Same drill as above except bowl to one pin only, progress to three pins, five pins, and all 10 pins. Work on technique. Scoring options: Set one pin up; if they knock one pin down, award one point. Set three pins up; if they knock three pins down, score one point. Set five pins up; knock five pins down to score one point. Team competition: four on a team; set three pins up; count number of pins knocked down by team, have a five-minute time limit. One student bowls; the other runs the ball down to partner; and the other two set up pins. Rotate after they finish their frame at bowling (Figure 7.1). Work on fitness and bowling skills.
3. Strength Activities: squeeze a tennis ball, pushups, swing a bowling ball.
4. Throw one frame to warm up if bowling alley permits it.
5. Teach scoring with 10 pins in gym. Get bowling cards from local bowling alleys. Even teams of four. One student bowls, one student runs the ball down to bowler, one sets up pins, one keeps score; rotate after these finish their frame at bowling. These drills and scoring system add fitness to the lesson, and the students enjoy the competition.
6. Handicapping is used in bowling to create parity between bowlers and stimulate greater competition. The following rules and formulas are used when computing a handicap.
   a. A minimum of nine games must be bowled before students can compute a handicap
   b. Handicap = (200 − Average score) × 0.8
   c. Average score = total points ÷ number of games
   d. The handicap is added to each player's total score at the end of a game during tournament play, as in the following example:

One runs ball back to bowler

One bowls

Two set pins up

Rotate counterclockwise after one bowler bowls a frame

FIGURE 7.1 Gamelike Fitness Drill

Joe bowls the following scores for nine games: 107, 113, 121, 115, 135, 101, 112, 115, 140

$$(107 + 113 + 121 + 115 + 135 + 101 + 112 + 115 + 140) \div 9 = 117.6$$

Joe's average number of pins per game is 117.6. To compute his handicap

$$(200 - 117.6) \times 0.8 = 65.87$$

Joe bowls Frank in the tournament. Joe gets a final score of 132, and Frank's score is 159.

Joe's handicap is 66, and Frank's handicap is 63. The final scores are as follows:

Joe: 132 + 66 = 198

Frank: 159 + 63 = 222

Frank wins the tournament.

7. Bowling in a gym is fun. Tournaments can be set up. However, the best place to bowl is at a bowling alley.

8. Trip to local bowling alley funded by parents.

For further information and special help, consult the following organizations and resources.

ORGANIZATIONS

American Bowling Congress (ABC) coordinator at local bowling center.

Young American Bowling Alliance (YABA)
5301 South 76th Street
Green Dale, WI 53129-1127
Phone: (414) 423-3384
Fax:(414) 421-3013
Website: www.bowl.org

PUBLICATIONS

Blassingame, C. & Cross, T. S. (1994). *Success in bowling through practical fundamentals*. Champaign, IL: Kendall/Hunt.

Harrison, M., & Maxey, R. (1987). *Bowling*. Glenview, IL: Scott, Foresman.

WEBSITES

www.nashville-schools.davidson.k12.tn.us/CurriculumAwards/tulipgrove/
    bowling.htm
www.amug.org/~a249/pinboy.html
www.encarta.msn.com

SKILL	CUE	WHY	COMMON ERROR
Conventional	Thumb on top, handshake position		
	Thumbhole at 12:00, finger holes at 6:00		
	Grip ball with second groove of 2 middle fingers		Squeezing with thumb
	Ring finger and middle finger		
Fingertip	Cradle ball in opposite arm	Helps balance the ball	
	Grip ball with first groove of 2 middle fingers		Thumb in first Squeezing with thumb
Stance	Erect, knees relaxed		Knees locked, shoulders not square to pins
	Stand tall		
	Ball supported by non-delivery arm	Helps balance the ball	Ball hanging from thumb and fingers
	Ball carried on palm of right hand		
	Ball on right side		Ball too high or low
	Ball hides right shirt pocket (good place to start); find your comfort zone		
	Lower right shoulder	Helps put bowler on plain with bowling ball	
	Tilt body slightly to right		
	Feet slightly apart		
	Three boards between feet		
	Left foot slightly advanced		
	One-half foot length ahead		
	Eyes focus on aiming spot	More ball control by looking at spot or arrows	Looking at pins
	Look at second arrow from right	Ball will hit the pocket and blow out the pins	

SKILL	CUE	WHY	COMMON ERROR
Arm Action (Figure 7.2)	First step and arm push away together		Stepping before pushing away
	Step away, push away		
	Extend ball arm straight forward horizontally		Pushing ball up or to the right too far
	Long reach but short step, like handing ball to friend		
	Use pendulum swing, like ball on end of string	Accuracy and speed	Applying too much force changing direction of ball
	Ball falls downward and backward		
(Figure 7.3)	Ball swings back, shoulder high	Power	Ball goes to high or arcs behind body
	Horizontal in front to horizontal in back		
	Extend left arm outward for balance	Balance	

continued

FIGURE 7.2 Bowling Stance

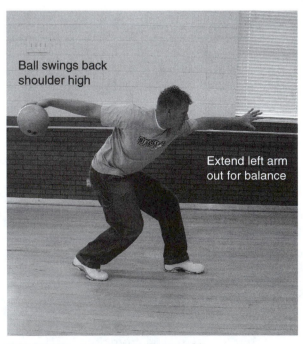

FIGURE 7.3 Arm Action (Approach)

SKILL	CUE	WHY	COMMON ERROR
Arm Action, *continued*	Keep ball swinging, arms relaxed		Trying to throw ball too fast
	Gravity and inertia provide main force		
	Release ball as arm passes vertical; ball should land 3–4 feet beyond foul line	Will drop ball and cause it to bounce	Dropping ball or setting it down on boards
Drill: *When a bowler first starts to bowl* Roll the ball and see how the ball is moving. Look to see if it goes straight down or slides. Then the bowler can start playing with arrows, dots, etc. Once you get the ball performing the way you want, you can move on.			
Leg Action	First step very short	Short steps control	First step too long
	Each step is a little longer and faster		
	Second step medium		
	Third step long		
(Figure 7.4c)	Fourth step longest	Longer steps power	
Timing	First step and push away together		Feet finishing before arm swing
	Keep ball swinging and feet walking		
	Second and third steps with down and backswing		
	Fourth step with forward swing and delivery		
How to Avoid Ball Bouncing	Bend at knees	Smooth ball delivery and higher scores	Straight legs
	Release knee high		
	Lean forward at waist		Standing up
Coordination	Push, step, swing, roll		Taking 2–3 steps

continued

APPROACH, continued			
SKILL	**CUE**	**WHY**	**COMMON ERROR**
Drill: Take a white locker-room towel or towels used to wipe hands in bowling. Fold towel and place by foul line. Make sure ball goes over towel— prevents the bowler from dropping the ball			

DELIVERY			
SKILL	**CUE**	**WHY**	**COMMON ERROR**
Straight Ball (Figure 7.4a)	Wrist straight and firm		Arm rotation right or left
	Thumb at 12:00		
	Release ball as arm passes vertical and starts upward		Dropping or setting ball on approach before foul line
	Trajectory like airplane landing 3–4 feet beyond foul line		Holding ball too long causes you to loft ball
(Figure 7.4b)	Follow-through in straight upward swing		Stopping arm action on release of ball
	Arm points in direction you want ball to go		
	Shoulders stay square (parallel) to foul line		Body rotates clockwise on ball of foot
Hook Ball	Cup the palm		
	Thumb at 10:30		
	Hand stays behind ball		Hand on side of ball
	Thumb comes out first (ball spins counterclockwise)	Control of back	Spin like a top
	Deliver ball with finger only		
	On release, flip the fingers and shake hands	Spins the ball	
	Release with the V form		
	Follow-through in straight upward swing	Power and accuracy	

continued

SKILL	CUE	WHY	COMMON ERROR
Leg Action	Lower the body during third and fourth steps		Bouncy up-and-down action
	Bend knees to smoothly lower body at end of approach		
	Decelerate fourth step		Loss of balance from too quick a stop
	Left foot steps and slides to a stop		
	Keep back foot in contact with floor		Poor timing results in picking up back foot and clockwise body rotation
	Don't spin out		
	Left knee and foot point toward pins		Body rotation
	Keep facing target		

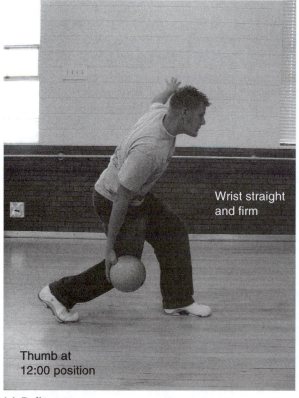

Wrist straight and firm

Thumb at 12:00 position

(a) Delivery

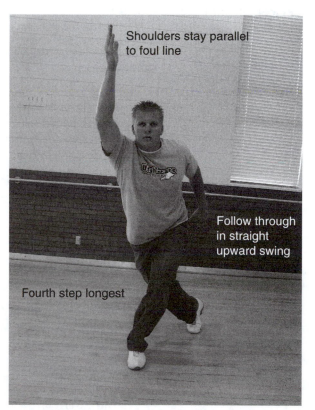

Shoulders stay parallel to foul line

Follow through in straight upward swing

Fourth step longest

(b) Follow Through

FIGURE 7.4 Straight Ball

SKILL	CUE	WHY	COMMON ERROR
Using Arrows	Easier to hit a target 15 feet away than one 60 feet away		Looking at pins
	Focus eyes and attention on aiming points (arrows)		
Three Basic Positions			
Strike	Second arrow from right (10 boards in from right edge)	More control of ball to hit correct pin	
Right-Side Spare	Third arrow from left (15 boards in from left)		
Left-Side Spare	Third arrow from right (15 boards in from right)		
Aim of Eyes (Strike)	Second arrow from right (10 boards in from right side)		Bowling down center of lane
Placement of Feet (Strike)	Left toe on second dot board from right		
	Third dot from right at foul line		
Use of Arrows (Spare)	Use 1 of 3 basic positions; move start position 1 board left to move ball contact 3 boards right; move feet 1 board right to move ball contact 3 boards left	More control of ball to hit correct pin	
	1-inch change in starting position equals 3-inch change in ball contact point		
Aim of Eyes (Spare)	Left-side spares (7 pin, etc.): same starting position as strike ball-aim over third arrow from right		Bowling down left side of lane
	Right-side spares (10 pin): third arrow from right		

continued

	USE OF ARROWS, continued		
SKILL	**CUE**	**WHY**	**COMMON ERROR**
Placement of Feet (Spare)	Left-side spares: Same as strike starting position; make slight adjustments right or left to change ball contact point		
	Left toe on second dot from right		
	Right-side spares: left foot 4 boards in from far left edge of lane		
Splits	Use same arrows as spares; adjust starting position slightly right or left to change contact point of ball	More control of ball	
Adjustments *Leaving Spares*	Are you hitting your target on arrow? If no, hit target	More control of ball hitting correct pins	Not hitting target on arrow

	SCORING		
SKILL	**CUE**	**WHY**	**COMMON ERROR**
Open Frame	Count pins you knock over		
	Pin count		
Spares (Figure 7.5)	Score 10, plus pin count from next ball		
	Maximum 20 points		
Strikes (Figure 7.5)	Score 10, plus pin count from next two balls		
	Maximum 30 points		

continued

SKILL	CUE	WHY	COMMON ERROR
Tenth Frame	There is an opportunity to score bonus points in the tenth frame by bowling a spare or a strike		
Open	Score like a regular frame		
Strike	Bowl 2 more balls		
Spare (Figure 7.5)	Bowl 1 more ball; 10 points plus score from first ball; for example: 8 points plus spare = 18		
Strike Plus Spare	Bowl 3 balls; add 20 points to total score after ninth frame		
Three Strikes	Bowl 3-ball maximum; add 30 points to total after 9 frames		
	This is a tip to scoring a 300 game: you have to get 3 strikes in the last frame		
	Note: When scoring, mark a spare with a slash (/) and a strike with an X.		

Enclosed are blank score sheets (see Figure 7.6)

Helpful Bowling Hints (see Figure 7.7)

How to Mark Score

Spare (/) Count 10 plus what you knock down on next ball.
Strike (X) Count 10 plus what you knock down on next two balls.
Immediately after each ball bowled mark results in proper frame box.

1	2	3	4	5	6	7	8	9	10
7 /	X	6 2	X	X	0 /	3 3	X	X	X X 6
20	38	46	66	86	99	105	135	165	191

FIGURE 7.5 How To Mark Score

Bowling Game Score Sheet

Name	HDCP	1	2	3	4	5	6	7	8	9	10	Total
1												
Name	HDCP	1	2	3	4	5	6	7	8	9	10	Total
2												
Name	HDCP	1	2	3	4	5	6	7	8	9	10	Total
3												
Name	HDCP	1	2	3	4	5	6	7	8	9	10	Total
4												

Bowling Game Score Sheet

Name	HDCP	1	2	3	4	5	6	7	8	9	10	Total
1												
Name	HDCP	1	2	3	4	5	6	7	8	9	10	Total
2												
Name	HDCP	1	2	3	4	5	6	7	8	9	10	Total
3												
Name	HDCP	1	2	3	4	5	6	7	8	9	10	Total
4												

Bowling Game Score Sheet

Name	HDCP	1	2	3	4	5	6	7	8	9	10	Total
1												
Name	HDCP	1	2	3	4	5	6	7	8	9	10	Total
2												
Name	HDCP	1	2	3	4	5	6	7	8	9	10	Total
3												
Name	HDCP	1	2	3	4	5	6	7	8	9	10	Total
4												

FIGURE 7.6 Bowling Game Score Sheet

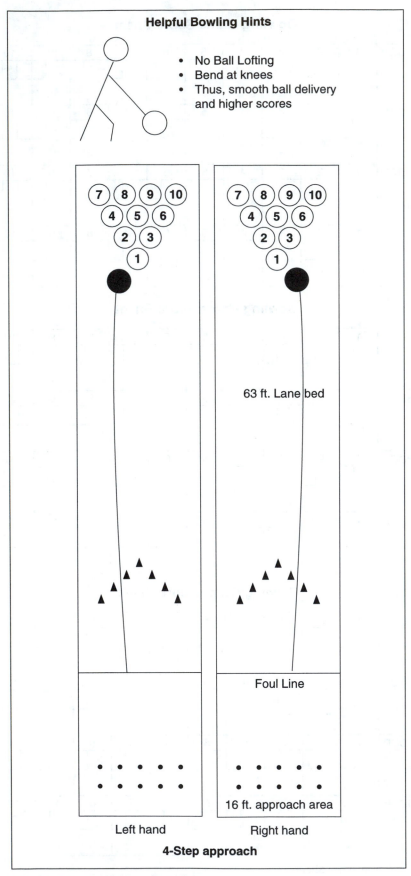

FIGURE 7.7 Helpful Bowling Hints

8

Cycling—Mountain Biking

INTRODUCTION

Mountain biking has become an increasingly popular activity since its beginning in the early 1980s. It is a great aerobic workout and at times requires anaerobic power as well. It can challenge your technical riding ability depending on where you ride, and it's also a lot of fun. However, to make it the most fun, one should take precautions to prevent personal injury, injury to other trail users (bikers, hikers, and equestrians), and damage to the bicycle or trail.

Mountain biking requires a variety of skills to cope with obstacles such as rocks, logs, switchbacks, creeks, ditches, holes, tire ruts, animal crossings, washouts, shale, and the like. The cues in this chapter are intended to help the biker ride safely, learn correct biking techniques, have more fun, and experience success more quickly.

One of the most important safety features in mountain biking is a helmet. Wearing a helmet will minimize the risk of serious head injury. Following are two examples where a helmet saved a rider from serious injury, and perhaps even death.

One was a friend of mine, Curt, who was riding a trail on his way to work at a hospital. He slid off the trail, and as he landed, he hit his head, shoulder, and ribs. He separated his shoulder and broke a couple of ribs, and his helmet had a huge crack in it. Had he not been wearing his helmet, it would have been his head with the crack in it. Curt happens to be a pediatric anesthesiologist, and he sees many children admitted to the hospital with head injuries because they weren't wearing a helmet when riding a bicycle.

The other instance in which a helmet saved the person from injury was perhaps even more serious than Curt's accident. A young woman was pulling her child in a carrier behind her bike. She was crossing a busy street during morning rush hour and was hit by a car. The wheel of the car ran over her head. Had she not been wearing a helmet, she would most likely have died.

Fortunately, her child was unharmed, and her helmet kept her alive. Some people may think helmets look silly or that it's too big a hassle to put one on, but a helmet can save one's life.

SKILLS LISTED WITH CUES

Included in this chapter are cues for the following techniques: buying the correct size bike, body position (feet/seat/upper body position), body position while climbing/ descending, bunny hop, braking (to stop fast, to corner in loose terrain, to ride in rough terrain), pedaling and shifting under a load, riding down curbs, riding up curbs, cleaning the bike, and rules of the trail.

TIPS

1. Statistics show that in the majority of bicycle accidents, the rider, for some reason, simply falls off the bicycle. The remainder of bicycle accidents are collisions with automobiles, fixed objects, and other bicyclists.

2. Check brakes and pads. There shouldn't be so much play in brakes that you have to completely squeeze them before they'll work. Check quick releases; make sure they are tight (by the way, that's what holds the wheels on).

3. Check all cables (frayed cables could cause a serious accident).

4. Check bottom bracket. Grab the crank arms, not the pedal, and move them from side to side. If there is any play, the bike needs adjustment. This procedure should be repeated with the wheels. Any play in these needs to be eliminated immediately.

5. Check lock on front brake. Rock it forward and back. If there is any play in the head set, get it adjusted immediately, or a repair can be expensive.

6. Every bike, no matter how much it is ridden, needs a checkup every year. If something is wrong with your bike, get it checked more often.

7. Check wear and tear on drivetrain: chain/crank set/cassette.

EQUIPMENT TIPS

1. The first and most important equipment needed is the *helmet.* Different brands fit different heads. The author recommends a Bell helmet (see FYI). The biggest problem with wearing a helmet is getting the correct fit. Find one that is the correct size for your head, and then use the supplied pads to make it fit comfortably without any pressure spots. It should be about a finger's width up from your eyebrows and fit squarely on your head. Buckle up the helmet and tighten the strap so that moderate forces won't allow it to slide more than about an inch. You can test the fit by grasping the helmet and moving it from side to side and front to back. It should be tight enough so that you can feel the strap slightly pressing your throat as you swallow. Some helmets have a lower retention system that cradles the lower rear portion of your head. This is the best type of helmet for mountain biking because it creates a more secure fit and will keep the helmet from rattling on a rough trail or dislodging when you have a big crash.

2. Lightweight biking components are suggested.

3. Gears are a matter of personal preference and riding terrain. Counsel with local bike dealers for area specifications.

4. Padded biking gloves are best because they provide safety and cushioning during a ride and during a wreck (the palms usually hit first in a wreck);

they also provide better friction between hand and grip, especially when hands are moist. Gloves will also keep your hands from getting too sweaty, sore, blistered, or cold.

5. Take two water bottles. Precaution: hydrate well even when you don't feel like drinking. Bikers are not aware of how much water is lost.

6. Snacks can include hard candies to keep mouth moist. Cut fruit and other foods into bite-size pieces and put in plastic sandwich bags. Carry "gorp" on long rides: raisins, peanuts, M&M's, and so on. Milky Way and 3 Musketeers bars are high in carbohydrates (two-thirds of their calories).

7. Take juice or fruit drinks in aluminum foil packets.

8. Binoculars improve view and enjoyment of outdoors.

9. Take a lightweight jacket.

10. Padded biking shorts are optional. They not only increase comfort but also improve circulation.

11. The following items should be carried on every ride in your backpack or bag: tire repair kit and chain breaker, spare tube, portable air pump, patch kit, tire levers, and spare change for phone calls or a cell phone.

12. Toe clips (clipless pedals) are optional but highly recommended. They will keep the foot in the proper position on the pedal and will allow force to be applied while both pushing down and pulling up on the same pedal, a motion known as pedaling in circles (see the body position cue for riding uphill). Toe clips are helpful especially when climbing hills and doing bunny hops.

13. Sunglasses will be helpful when it is sunny, and will also help keep bugs, rocks, and dirt from entering the eyes. If it isn't sunny, a pair of clear sport glasses will help protect your eyes from debris.

14. Suspension is a feature that adds a lot of comfort to your riding. Having front and/or rear suspension helps absorb the bumps and provides a smoother ride, making your arms and body less tired.

15. Bar ends on your handlebars allow for a change in hand position as a rest from the traditional grip, and they make it easier to lean forward when riding up hills.

RULES OF THE TRAIL

1. *Ride on open trails only.* Respect trail and road closures, private property, and requirements for permits and authorizations.

2. *Leave no trace.* Don't ride when ground will be marred such as on certain soils after it has rained. Never ride off trail or skid tires. Never discard any object; pack out more than you pack in.

3. *Control your bicycle.* Inattention for even a second can cause disaster. Excessive speed frightens and injures people.

4. *Always yield.* Make your approach well known in advance to hikers, horseback riders, and other bikers. A friendly greeting is considerate and appreciated. Stop and walk when horses are present.

5. *Never spook animals.* Give them extra room and time to adjust to you; running livestock and disturbing wild animals are serious offenses. Leave ranch and farm gates as you find them, or as marked.

6. *Plan ahead.* Know your equipment, your ability, and the area in which you are riding, and prepare accordingly. Be self-sufficient. Keep bike in good repair. Carry necessary supplies.

TEACHING IDEAS

1. Start in a parking lot and become familiar with the bike and its gears. Practice shifting; get the feel of what makes it easier and harder. Practice turns and braking, then move to wide flat dirt roads, and then to a wide dirt hill with a gradual incline to it.

2. Practice braking techniques: apply rear brake first. Practice on dirt roads so when the rider gets on the trail, it is not a drastic transition.

3. Practice smooth transitions while shifting and especially while shifting under a load such as when ascending a hill.

4. Technical riding: provide rocks or cones and ride between them. Make different trails. This drill lets riders know when they hit a rock or cone, or when they do it right. This drill will teach where the front and rear wheels are on the trail.

5. Practice braking downhill as well as riding downhill.

6. Technical skills can be practiced all the time.

7. Once you get the feel of the bike on these terrains, you can move to rougher terrains and sharper turns, with hills and other different situations.

8. Practice these basic skills on varying types of terrain.

FYI

For further information and special help, consult the following organizations and resources.

ORGANIZATIONS

U.S. Cycling Federation
One Olympic Plaza
Colorado Springs, CO 80909
Phone: (719) 578-4581
Fax: (719) 578-4956
Website: www.usacycling.org

Provides rules of the trail and a free 40-page book especially for newcomers who want to get started right on a bike.

Bicycling Magazine
New Rider Network
Box 6075
Emmaus, PA 18098

Provides information regarding helmets.

Bell Sports Customer Service
1924 County Road 3000 N.
Rantoul, IL 61866
Phone: (800)-456 Bell
Fax: (217) 893-9154

1. Bell will replace your helmet starting at $20.00 if you write and describe the crash.

2. With this information Bell can do research on actual crashes.

3. A Bell helmet has many air vents, permitting hot air to be replaced by cool air while riding. This ventilation reduces the risk of heat exhaustion.

4. A Bell helmet goes down lower and protects the occipital lobe of the brain, which is responsible for sight and other critical functions.

PUBLICATION

Sloane, E. (1988). *The complete book of cycling.* New York: Simon & Schuster.

WEBSITES

www.bicyclesuorce.com
www.kenifer.com/bikepages/traffic

BIKE SIZE			
SKILL	**CUE**	**WHY**	**COMMON ERROR**
Upper Body	Good cockpit space		If space is too small, hunchback occurs. If space is too large, you end up in a stretched-out position, causing upper back and neck to get sore or stiff
	Seat-to-handlebar distance is comfortable		
Legs	Stand over bar		Bike is too big. When riding up steep hill, front wheel comes up. Bike also corners poorly
	Ride a few sizes		A bike that is too small can be uncomfortable because you bend over too far
	Get a bike that fits you perfectly		Bike too big, high center, "ouch"
Seat Height	At bottom of stroke knees slightly bent	More efficient	Too high: knees are hyperextended, or hip rocking occurs

BODY POSITION

SKILL	CUE	WHY	COMMON ERROR
Feet	Ball of foot over axle of pedal	More efficient	Foot too far forward, pedal under arch
Seat Position	Position seat so that when knees and legs are at 3:00 and 9:00, seat is slightly behind ball of foot and pedal axle		
Upper Body	About 60% of body weight should be over rear wheel and 40% over front wheel		

UPHILL—DOWNHILL—ROUGH TERRAIN RIDING

SKILL	CUE	WHY	COMMON ERROR
Riding Uphill	Balance weight 60–70% over back wheel and 30–40% over front wheel to keep traction in back	More efficient	Not enough weight on front wheel will cause front wheel to come off ground
	Shift weight to middle to keep front wheel down so that you do not lose traction in loose dirt		
	Pedal in circles, using both a pulling and pushing action on each pedal	Less injury	Using only a pushing action
Riding Downhill	Move back on seat and down	Won't crash	Sitting too far forward on seat causes flying over handlebars
	Hold seat with upper thigh		
(Figure 8.1)	Watch ahead; pick a path	Won't fly over handlebars	

continued

SKILL	CUE	WHY	COMMON ERROR
Riding in Rough Terrain	Power through corner		
	Keep rear wheel behind you	More control of bike	
	Relax, go with the flow		Too stiff; cannot let knees, elbows, body flow to absorb bumps
	Stutter-step; get dominant foot in front toe position		
	Be like a shock absorber		
	Soak up the bumps with knees and arms like a sponge	More efficient	
	Let bike float over things		
	Straddle saddle, stand on pedals		
	Avoid hitting obstacles with pedal	Won't crash	

Watch ahead; pick a path

Move back on seat

Hold seat with upper thigh

Stay low

FIGURE 8.1 Body Position for Riding Downhill

SKILL	CUE	WHY	COMMON ERROR
Pedaling	Mountain cadence at a spin of about 80 RPM	Don't get tired as fast	Usually too slow, which lugs your motor
	Ride smarter, not harder		
Braking *To Stop Fast*	Scoot buttocks back	Very efficient in stop	Sitting too far forward, weight shifts forward
	Pedal at 3:00 and 9:00 position		
	Squeeze both brakes		Squeezing one brake
	Keep both wheels on the ground		When squeezing both brakes, body position is too far forward
	Keep tires from skidding		
To Corner in Loose Terrain	Control slide of rear wheel for faster shape cornering		Failing to make corner, slowing way down, losing control of front wheel, and turning too hard
	Move weight to inside		
	Pedal through corner		
Shifting Under a Load	Anticipate shift	Easier to shift when gears are under loaded	Waiting before cadence slows before shifting
	Shift front gear first; fine-tune with smaller gears		
	Give pedals a hard push for half-stroke; then ease off and shift		Not easing off pedal prior to shifting

SKILL	CUE	WHY	COMMON ERROR
Riding Down Curbs/ Obstacles	Make sure there is enough speed to maintain forward motion		Going too slow
	Stand up on pedals with both knees slightly bent		Sitting
	Balance weight over pedals		Weight too far forward may cause you to go over the top of handlebars
	Keep handlebars straight		Turning handlebars
	Let front tire roll off curb; back wheel will follow		
	Slightly bend elbows and knees to absorb shock		Keeping extremities stiff
Riding Up Curbs/ Obstacles	Go fast enough to maintain forward motion		Going too slow
	Stand up on pedals		Sitting
	When you're about 3–6 inches from curb, pull up on handlebars to lift front wheels on to curb		Either pulling up too soon or waiting too long
	When front wheel has landed, lean forward slightly to get weight off back of bike		Keeping weight back
	Continue to pedal through so back tire just rides right up curb		Stopping pedaling and freaking out
Bunny Hop	Use for jumping over large rocks and branches in the trail		
	Go fast enough to maintain forward motion		Going too slow

continued

SKILL	CUE	WHY	COMMON ERROR
Bunny Hop, *continued*	Stand up on pedals with knees slightly bent		Sitting
	Just before reaching the object, bend knees and elbows so back is nearly parallel with ground		Keeping extremities stiff
	Pull up on your handlebars as if you were riding up a curb		Not pulling soon enough
	When the wheel is in the air, push the handlebars out forward and down as you leap, or spring with your legs (this will bring the back wheel up)		
	Your front wheel actually goes through an arc motion as you pull up on the handlebars then push forward and down		No arc motion

CLEANING THE BIKE

SKILL	CUE	WHY	COMMON ERROR
Drivetrain	Remove dirt and grease, use oil-based lubricants	Water causes rust and ruins gears	Using water
Cleaning Steps	Turn bike upside down, balance on handlebars to clean		Resting bike on kickstand
Spraying	Spray oil-based lubricant on chain in back cassette while turning pedals backward		Turning pedals forward
	Continue to spray for 3–5 seconds		Spraying longer than 5 seconds
	Chain in middle of back gears when spraying		Chain on either end

continued

SKILL	CUE	WHY	COMMON ERROR
Cleaning Steps, *continued*			
After Spraying	Grab a rag and place it around bottom part of chain in between the two cassettes		
	Continue pedaling backward; change rag to a clean spot; continue pedaling		Pedaling forward
	Change rag until no more dirt or grease comes off on rag		Using dirty rag
	Take rag and run it between gears trying to remove any excess dirt		
Finish Coat	After removing all dirt and grease, place a finish coat of polytech or dry lube; both are dry lube-based and will protect chain from collecting dirt while riding		Not applying a finish coat
Spray	Spray dry lube-based finish coat for one to two complete backward pedal rotations		
Check Chain	Even though a chain looks clean, it usually is not		Not cleaning chain often enough

9

Cycling—Road Biking

INTRODUCTION

Accomplished riders become highly skilled through countless hours aboard a bike, for there is no substitute for time and mileage. Most have also had some coaching, both formal and informal, which has honed their skills at all levels, especially early in their experience. Remember, cycling isn't fun if you're not in shape or if you lack technique.

Oftentimes cycling skills are learned by trial and error. For example, you purchase a new road bike, strap yourself in for the first time, and feel a little uncomfortable with the new situation. You take the bike for a spin and find yourself faced with narrow roads, sand and gravel on roads, hills, different terrain, traffic, corners, new gears, trying to drink from a water bottle, and so on, not to mention rude drivers. Cyclists could benefit from cues to help them feel more successful with techniques and master the different situations. Following the rules of the road is key to increasing safety when riding in motor vehicle traffic.

SKILLS LISTED WITH CUES

The ideas and cues contained in this chapter are concerned with methods of learning to cycle properly, including buying the correct size of bike, developing correct body position on the bike, pedaling for effective energy transfer (pedaling action, revolutions per minute, and riding in a straight line), cornering (braking, anticipating turns, sharp corners), climbing hills, and the transition from climbing to descending a hill.

TIP

Practice bunny hops, corners, and turning.

EQUIPMENT TIPS

1. Purchase road bikes that weigh less than 24 pounds.

2. The first road bike should cost about $700 to $900.

3. Clipless pedals are easier to twist out of (twist sideways) and more energy efficient.

4. It is harder to get feet out of strapped pedals. Coast to 5 MPH, practice pulling feet out of pedals. Caution: the rider will tip over sideways if the foot is not pulled out in time. Adjust pedal tension as needed.

5. Purchase riding shoes that are comfortable and have stiff soles. The bottom of the foot is like a platform that gives you more energy transfer.

TEACHING IDEAS

1. Stretch before and after riding, especially the hamstrings, quadriceps, and calf muscles.

2. Start slow and progress. As your miles increase, increase the number of days. Add another day up to five or six days a week. Take Wednesday and Sunday off. Learn to listen to your body.

3. Each rider is different when he or she starts putting in mileage. Ride for fun! Ride more days rather than taking one long ride.

4. Technical skills: practice bunny hopping in a parking lot. Use lines in a parking lot to hop the bike or jump with both wheels over an obstacle. Lift up on the handlebars; jump over the line or bunny hop over the line by raising both wheels. This drill helps the rider when faced with an unexpected pothole or other obstacle in the road. Learn to ride with a group; doing so improves technical skills and enhances intensity of the workouts.

5. There are two types of spinning drills—muscle and spinning cadence. Always spin at a constant cadence.

6. Spin to win! Try to keep the same pace on long rides. For example, if you are laboring and spinning too slowly, drop from 8th gear to 6th gear for a 10-speed bike, and 16th gear to 12th gear for a 20-speed bike. Spinning faster causes less pressure on the legs, but the rider maintains the same speed.

7. Practice positioning down hills. Tuck in behind the stem. Every time you run out of pedal, practice getting very aerodynamic.

8. Practice sprinting: come up out of the saddle into a standing position, hands hanging on to brake hoods and handlebars. Rock bike side to side, keep the wheels in line, and stay in a straight line or hold your line. Avoid wheels zigzagging.

9. Hydrate your body before and after each ride.

For further information and special help, consult the following organizations and resources.

ORGANIZATIONS

U.S. Cycling Federation
One Olympic Plaza
Colorado Springs, CO 80909
Phone: (719) 578-4581
Fax: (719) 578-4956
Website: www.usacycling.org

Provides a free 40-page book especially for newcomers.

Bicycling Magazine
New Rider Network
Box 6075
Emmaus, PA 18098

Bell Helmets (see FYI, Chapter 8)

PUBLICATIONS

Burke, E. (1986). *The science of cycling.* Champaign, IL: Human Kinetics.
Doughty, T. (1983). *The complete book of competitive cycling.* New York: Simon & Schuster.

WEBSITES

www.bicyclesource.com
www.kenifer.com/bikepayes/traffic

BIKE SIZE

SKILL	CUE	WHY	COMMON ERROR
Selecting a Bike	Proper bike size is critical when purchasing a bike		
	Stand straddling bike with 2–3 inches of crotch clearance		No clearance or too high: 3–4 inches off ground
	Get fitted by qualified bike shop		

BODY POSITION

SKILL	CUE	WHY	COMMON ERROR
Become More Aerodynamic (Figure 9.1)	Decrease frontal area; keep back flat	Faster, more efficient on bike	Body is big, like a sail
	Get prone with elbows and knees in		
	Wear tight clothing		Wearing baggy clothing
	It takes practice to become comfortable; work 5–10 minutes at a time in biking position		Not holding position
	Hands should hold bar lightly		White knuckles, gripping too tight, wasting energy
	Bend at waist		Back vertical
	Eyes glance ahead		People do not look ahead, and they run into things or the head stays down

FIGURE 9.1   Correct Body Position on Bike

SKILL	CUE	WHY	COMMON ERROR
Pedaling Action	Spin, pedal in circles not squares	More efficient; less energy used	Mashing and stomping pedals
	Downstroke motion, like scraping mud off your shoes		Pushing hard at bottom of stroke will not do any good, just attempts to lengthen crank action
	Backstroke motion: pick up your feet		Many riders only push on downstroke and fail to apply pressure to pedals all the way around the circle
			Dead time at 6:00 or bottom of pedal stroke
Revolutions per Minute (RPMs)	80 RPM, adults 90–120 RPM, racers		Pedaling too slow, lugging motor, hard on your knees
Riding in a Straight Line	Keep eyes on road 10–15 yards ahead	Prevent crashing	Not looking ahead causes one leg to fight the other and creates a rocking or a bouncing motion that depletes energy
			Keeping eyes focused on front wheel
	Ride straight		Wobbling

SKILL	CUE	WHY	COMMON ERROR
Braking	Assess the speed and do all braking entering corner or curve	Prevents crashing	Applying brakes while leaning through a corner or curve will cause handling problems
Anticipating Turn	Start wide and head for inner tip or point of turn	More efficient and faster	Not turning until well into the corner, which slows you down and can be dangerous
Anticipating Turn	Visualize the line or path you will travel through the curve and follow it		Following a jerky, changing path
	Lean bike and carve your line through the turn		
(Figure 9.2)	Keep outside pedal down; stand on it to lower center of gravity	Prevent crashing	Leaning too far into curve, hitting ground with inside pedal; crash
Sharp Corner	Raise inside pedal to top of pedal stroke	Prevents pedal from making contact with ground and crashing	Making sparks while cornering with pedal
			Dragging pedal

Keep outside pedal down; stand on it

Pop inside knee out

Raise inside pedal to top of pedal stroke

FIGURE 9.2 Cornering

SKILL	CUE	WHY	COMMON ERROR
Breathing	Breathe from stomach like blowing into an instrument	Exchange of 0.2 better helps cardiac functions	Breathing in chest, short gasping breaths
Sitting Climb	Push butt into saddle and push back on handlebars (squeeze saddle with butt like a leg press)		
	Scoot back on seat; sit hunkered down; helps to use your buttocks' muscles more		Sitting on seat too hard and not standing on pedal
	Choose easy gear	Easier to go up hills	Gear too tight
	Pull up on bars, so you can push harder on the pedals like giving yourself more weight on a scale		
	50 RPM minimum; spin if you can, uphill		Low RPM makes poor recovery
	Get into *your* rhythm		Trying to match someone else's pace
Standing Climb	Stand, lean forward, pull up and down on bars, and rock the bike		
	Make sure your line stays straight		
Transition from Climbing to Descending	Accelerate near top of hill, pick up speed fast	Faster	Trying to recover at top of hill
			Decelerating at crest of hill
	Recovery occurs after descending speed is reached		

SKILL	CUE	WHY	COMMON ERROR
Position for Fast, Steep Descent	When you cannot pedal fast enough, you spin out	Faster	
Grip	Hands on end of handlebars		Grip the handlebars near the stem, hands right next to each other
Body Position (Figure 9.3)	Back flat, feet at 3:00 and 9:00 position	More streamlined, less air currents; faster	Chest up
	Weight on the pedals, knees in		Weight on arms, knees out

Back flat

Knees in

Weight on pedals, feet at 3:00 and 9:00 position

FIGURE 9.3   Body Position for Descending

SKILL	CUE	WHY	COMMON ERROR
Ride on the Right	Always ride on right; go with flow of traffic		Riding in middle of road; going against traffic
	Be predictable; maintain a straight line; change direction without swerving	Prevents crashing	Swerving back and forth
Hand Signals	Use hand signal when turning same as motorist; when making a right turn, use your right arm to point		Not using hand signal when turning
Stay Alert	Obey all traffic laws Pay attention	Prevents crashing	Breaking traffic rules Wearing headphones
	Use your eyes and ears as warning devices alerting you to potential hazards		
	Assert yourself		Letting vehicles creep by, forcing biker into parked cars or curb
	Ride defensively		
	Expect a car to pull out from side street or turn left in front of you; if you anticipate the worst, it will rarely happen		Daydreaming
What to Wear	Be visible, wear bright colors, and put reflectors and reflective tape on your bicycle	Prevents crashing	Wearing light colors in daytime
			Wearing dark clothing at night
			Not putting reflective tape on bicycles
Warning Signal from Cyclist	Shout: it's the quickest way to let motorists know you're putting them in danger or to warn inattentive pedestrians you are approaching		Not giving a warning signal
Feet Strapped or Connected to Pedal	Loosen strap, twist foot out of pedal		Leaving foot strapped or not twisting foot out of pedal

EATING AND DRINKING WHILE RIDING

SKILL	CUE	WHY	COMMON ERROR
Rule of Thumb	Drink before you're thirsty and eat before you're hungry		Not drinking or eating before ride; eating too much
Hot, Humid Weather	Take a big swig from water bottle every 15 minutes		Not drinking during ride
Most Popular Food	One banana provides 105 calories of carbohydrates and replaces potassium, an important element lost via sweating		
Storing Food	Best place: rear pocket of jersey		
5–20 Miles; Less Than 90 Minutes	Eat a preride meal with lots of carbohydrates		Eating too much and not waiting 30 minutes for food to digest
15–50 Miles; 45 Minutes–3 Hours			
Avoid Bonking	Do not allow glycogen stores to become depleted; this happens when ride is 2 hours or longer; drink sports drinks		Not eating premeals or snacks
Avoid Dehydration	Loss of body fluids results in fatigue; carry sports drink, 1 bottle		Not drinking water or sports drinks
	Carry water, 1 or more bottles depending on distance		
50–100 Miles; Over 4 Hours	Eat lots of carbohydrate-rich foods in days preceding the event		Failing on long rides due to poor eating habits
Premeal	Eat a big meal a couple of hours before the big ride		Not eating a premeal
Snack during Ride	Bananas, sandwiches with jam, honey, apple butter, and so on		
	Nibble through ride		Eating too much at once
Water during Ride	Four water bottles		Three or fewer water bottles

10

Field Hockey

INTRODUCTION

Field hockey is one of the oldest organized team sports played in the United States. Field hockey is a team game played on artificial turf or grass in which players use a curved stick and try to drive a hard-core ball into the opposing team's goal. The tactics are similar to soccer, a more commonly played game in the United States.

Modern field hockey evolved in England in the early 19th century. Originally the game was played exclusively by men. Today the game is played by both men and women on six continents. More than 70 countries are members of the International Hockey Federation. In the United States and Canada, field hockey is primarily considered a women's sport.

Field hockey was introduced in the United States in 1901 by Constance Applebee, an English field hockey player. Field hockey became an Olympic event for men in 1928, and an Olympic event for women in 1980.

SKILLS LISTED WITH CUES

We provide cues for the following skills: grip, dribbling—moving with the ball, push pass, receiving—hitting, aerials (flick throw, low lift), shooting, dodging, and defense skills—marking, covering, tackling, and goaltending.

TIPS

1. Players should first learn the skills of running with the ball.
2. Passing and receiving skills should be taught second.

EQUIPMENT TIPS

1. Shin guards and mouth guards are mandatory at the high school level.

2. Recently made hockey sticks have smaller toes that make stick control easier.

3. Cleats (plastic) should be used on grass; turf shoes should be used on artificial surfaces.

TEACHING IDEAS

1. Running with the ball (dribbling) is the first skill that should be taught. It is best taught with competitive relays using obstacles and with small games where everyone has a ball and is moving the ball constantly.

2. Passing and receiving should be taught second and together. You cannot pass to a teammate unless the teammate receives.

3. The hit should be taught only after the preceding skills have been mastered to some degree. In early games the hit should not be allowed.

4. Field hockey can be played in physical education class and should be played in small groups (four, five, six, or seven on each side). STX markets a field hockey training stick that is very useful in physical education classes.

5. A full game consists of two 30-minutes halves with 11 players on each side, including a goalie, and various combinations of players depending on their skills. The most traditional lineup on a field hockey field would be five attackers, three halfbacks, two fullbacks, and one goalkeeper. Many other player lineups are used (4, 3, 2, 1, 1; 3, 3, 3, 1, 1; etc.). At the introductory level of play, smaller games should be incorporated into the teaching session. Small games open up the space, provide more opportunity to play the ball, and make tactics easier to master and see.

6. Training sessions should follow this format:
   • Light jog
   • Stretching
   • Running skills for better movement
   • Ball-control skills
   • Technical skills (passing combos, two-against-one concepts, etc.)
   • Games, cooldown, stretching

FYI

For further information and special help, consult the following organization and resource.

ORGANIZATION

United States Field Hockey Association (USFHA)
One Olympic Plaza
Colorado Springs, CO 80909
Phone: (856) 231-1199

1. The USFHA offers learning packs (sticks and balls).

2. Its youth development committee aids in the development of field hockey in the United States.

WEBSITE

www.usfieldhockey.com

GRIP

SKILL	CUE	WHY	COMMON ERROR
Position	Lay the stick parallel to feet	Ball control	Hands together
	Point to the right		Pointing to left
	Pick up with left hand		Picking up with right hand
	Right hand halfway down stick		Left hand halfway down stick
	Hold stick firmly but comfortably		Holding stick too loosely
Left Hand	Left hand is the holding hand/turns stick		
Right Hand	Right hand is the pulling and pushing hand		

DRIBBLING

SKILL	CUE	WHY	COMMON ERROR
Moving with the Ball (Figure 10.1)	Ball "glued" to stick	Able to control ball	Ball too far in front of stick
	Use small taps for grass play		Hitting not tapping
	Keep ball outside and ahead of right foot for grass play		Right foot behind ball
	Keep ball on the right side at 3:00 position for turf play	Must have full field vision	Wasting dribbles
Strategy	To run with ball		

SKILL	CUE	WHY	COMMON ERROR
Push Pass (Figure 10.2)	Push ball with stick		Wide backswing
	Stick on ball; NO contact noise		Stick off ball, tapping or hitting ball
	Firm right hand	Ball control	Relaxed right hand
	Left wrist pulls stick back		Stiff left wrist
	Short accurate passing		
Strategy	No time to hit ball or shoot		
Receiving	Angle stick slightly forward to deflect ball down	To trap ball	
	Stop ball on stick		Bouncing off stick

FIGURE 10.1 The Dribble

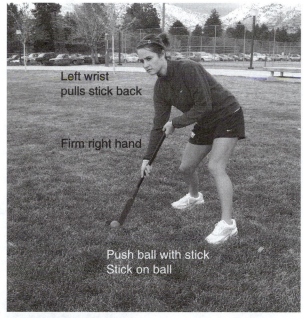

FIGURE 10.2 The Push Pass

SKILL	CUE	WHY	COMMON ERROR
Hitting (Figure 10.3)			
Grip	Slide right hand up stick	Better ball speed	Forgetting to slide hand up
	Bring hands together on top		Hands too far apart
	Contact ball opposite left foot		Contacting ball off same foot
Driving Action	Hip-to-hip swing like a pendulum		Bending wrists
	Toe of stick up on backswing and up on follow-through	Affects direction and control	Toe facing grass
	Right hand guides stick in direction of pass		Hand not guiding stick
	Left arm pulls		
	Bend elbow slightly for a relaxed swing	More consistency and control of ball	Bent left arm
Strategy	Used for passing and shooting		
Shooting	Variations	To beat defender	
	Follow shot	To get rebound	
	Must be in circle	Rule	
	Shots must be on ground or not dangerous	To control danger	

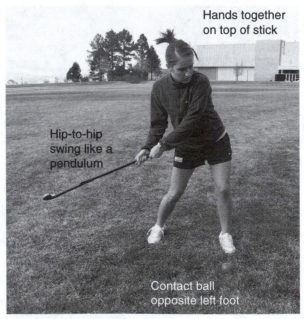

FIGURE 10.3 Hitting

SKILL	CUE	WHY	COMMON ERROR
Flick Throw	Throwing action	Shot variations are important to throw off opponent's reaction time and ability to steal ball	
	Face ball—head, body low		
	Ball between feet (positioning varies) and away from body		
	Toe of stick is extension of hand		
Low Lift	Shovel ball into air, low and gentle		
	Lift the ball up, throwing action		
	Face ball		
	Raise ball slightly—or high depending on what you are trying to do		
Strategy	Used for shooting at close range, penalty, strokes, lifting ball to cover a big distance		
	Used for lifting ball over a defender's stick		

SKILL	CUE	WHY	COMMON ERROR
Footwork	Balance	To be able to change directions quickly	
	Drop		
	Approach attacker with control and balance		
	Break down steps		
	Stay in front space		
	Stick defense at 10:00-2:00 position		
Dodges	Get out of the way!		Backing into the defender
	Execute dodge outside of defense playing distance		Anticipating too late or too early
	Execute dodge right off dribble	Must be able to beat defender with the ball	Stalling
	Accelerate by defender, cut in behind defender		Constant speed and direction
			Crash! Head-on collision
Techniques	1. Pull to the right, accelerate		Backing into the defender
	2. Pull to the left, accelerate		Backing into the defender
	3. Spin and accelerate, must move away from defender		Backing into the defender
Pressuring Defender *Marking*	Stay between your goal and offensive player	To keep attacker from scoring	Not anticipating soon enough or focusing on defenders
	"Face to face" with your opponent at all times		Tumbling with backside to opponent, losing concentration
Covering *Supporting Defender*	Either mark dangerous space or take next dangerous attacker	Take away attacker's options	
Covering Defender	Make decisions on dangerous space, decide to make attacks or cover space		

continued

SKILL	CUE	WHY	COMMON ERROR
Tackling	Body low, frontal body position	To maintain balance	
	Hands and arms away from the body, body in low position, slide stick in, tackle at 5:00 position		
	Block ball hand quick, move away with ball		
Goaltending	Stop ball by making a V with ankles—keep knees together	Easier transition to attack	Feet and knees apart
			Standing straight
	Move by sliding feet across goal mouth		Picking up feet
	Always clear ball to sides		Clearing ball in front of cage
	Stop ball before clearing for better control of direction		Hitting ball before clearing
	Can use either side or tip of boot when clearing		Not focusing on ball

11

Football

When teaching flag football, keep the rules as close to those of the regular game as possible. The students can relate to our national pastime more easily. Football is a huge part of our society. The students will be able to enjoy the game with their family or friends because they will know the skills, rules, and some common plays.

SKILLS LISTED WITH CUES

The cues in this chapter cover the following skills: throwing, catching, punting, catching a punt, snapping the ball, quarterback steps, lateral pass, handoffs (right and left side), tuck away after catch, running down the sideline, blocking, and in, out, and post running routes.

EQUIPMENT TIPS

1. New Tech Tac footballs have an easy web grip. Two sizes are available: 6-inch and mini-footballs. Nerf multicolor footballs and Zwirl footballs are easy to grip and throw, or you may use smaller leather footballs. Avoid using large, regulation-size leather balls, as they are difficult to throw and catch. See the FYI section on page 130 for information on ordering these fun balls.

2. Order a variety of colored vests: red, yellow, green, orange, purple, and blue.

3. Flags with Velcro belts: This avoids the question of whether the player was down.

4. Flip scorecards: If players can see a scorecard, it will add motivation to the game.

5. For those who play recreation and league football, use a helmet, pads, and rubber cleats.

TEACHING IDEAS

Divide students into pairs: a highly skilled student with one with fewer skills. Have them practice the skills together. The highly skilled student can give tips to the other one.

TEACHING PROGRESSIONS

1. Practice throwing a football with the right and left hands.
2. Practice kicking a football with the right foot and the left foot. Play Philadelphia Football.
3. Practice catching a punted ball with a partner. Challenge the pair to catch 10, 15, or 20 balls.
4. Practice plays with three players. One is the center, one is the quarterback, and one is the receiver. Rotate positions after three thrown balls. Teach the quarterback steps and centering skills. Add a defender and teach the defensive skill of back pedaling and mirroring the offensive player.
5. Play 4 on 4 (passing plays only).
6. Practice handoffs and a lateral pass. Play 3 on 3 mini-games with running plays only.
7. Practice a combination of passing and running plays.
8. Let the teams make up their own play patterns and play 4 on 4 games.

MINI-GAMES

1. Philadelphia Football.
2. Mini-games of 2 on 2 and 3 on 3: These games can be played to practice in, out, and post plays, with a defender on each player.

MODIFIED FLAG FOOTBALL RULES

1. Six to eight players on a team.
2. Football field, using 40 to 50 yards for each mini-game.
3. Kick off from the 20-yard line.
4. Each team has four plays to make a touchdown. Why? Players don't have to worry about keeping track of the line of scrimmage.
5. Score the game just like a regulation football game.

   6 points for a touchdown

   1 point for a run-in after the touchdown

   2 points for a pass-in after the touchdown

   2 points for a safety. A safety occurs when the defensive team pulls the flag off an offensive player who is in their offensive end zone (safety zone is 3 yards).
6. Any offensive player on the line can catch the pass.
7. There is a 3-yard neutral zone. The students take three steps back from the line of scrimmage. The line of scrimmage is where the football lays.
8. A lateral pass is the same as in regulation football. The pass must be thrown behind the quarterback or to the side. There are no forward lateral passes.

9. The quarterback must be behind the line of scrimmage in order to throw a forward pass.

10. In this game, no one is standing around. Everyone is moving and having fun practicing all the skills. If you have a class of 32 students, you could organize four mini-games, with four players on each team.

FYI

For further information and special help, consult the following organizations and resources.

ORGANIZATIONS

National Football League
410 Park Avenue
New York, NY 10022

Innovative footballs: Tech Tac web footballs and others
Sportime
One Sport Way
Atlanta, GA 30340
Phone orders: (800) 283-5700
Fax orders: (800) 845-1535
Website: www.sportime.com

WEBSITES

www.goflagfootball.com
A rule book is available at this site, which includes passes, the field, equipment, clock, kicks, handling, deflagging, scoring a tie game, substitutions, interference, unfair and unsportsmanlike conduct, fouls and penalties, and a glossary of terms.

www.afafootball.com

SKILL	CUE	WHY	COMMON ERROR
Grip	Grab top of ball like holding a soda can or a fish's head	More surface area on ball, better control	Grabbing middle of ball
	Put 3–4 fingers on the the laces, depending on the size of your hand	Better grip	
	Finger pads hold laces		Palm holding ball
Throwing Action (Figure 11.1)	Stretch arm way back; make an L shape	For better control and to throw the ball farther	
Stance and Leg Action	Short to medium step	To get rid of the football fast	Overstriding, high stepping, or taking no steps
Release Point	Release at 2:00 with right hand; left hand, 10:00	Ball will go at correct angle	
	Football points upward		
Follow-Through Action	Turn palm out on follow-through; ball comes off index finger	Ball will fly through the air in a spiral motion	

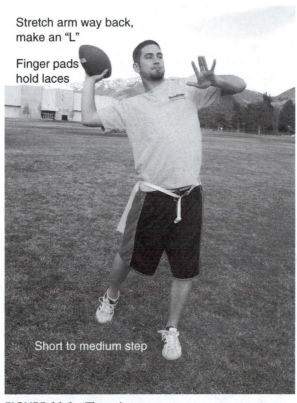

Stretch arm way back, make an "L"

Finger pads hold laces

Short to medium step

FIGURE 11.1 Throwing

CATCHING

SKILL	CUE	WHY	COMMON ERROR
Hand Action (Figure 11.2)	Big hands; reach out; shape hands like a diamond	Won't bounce off chest	
	Catch ball in diamond	Ball fits best	
Eyes	Pull ball into chest; watch ball into chest	Helps to avoid dropping ball	

Shape hands like a diamond

Big hands, reach out

FIGURE 11.2 Catching

KICKING A PUNT

SKILL	CUE	WHY	COMMON ERROR
Punting (Figure 11.3)	Hold ball with two hands away from body	Ball is more stable	
	Drop the ball	Less chance for error	
	Support foot plants at the same time as dropping the ball		
	Pull kicking leg back	More power to send the ball far	
	Swing leg under body	More effective technique	
	Ball makes contact with shoelaces and below knee	More surface area on which to contact ball	
	Toes pointed down		
Follow-Through (Figure 11.4)	Kick high, like a scissors kick	Gives more distance to ball	

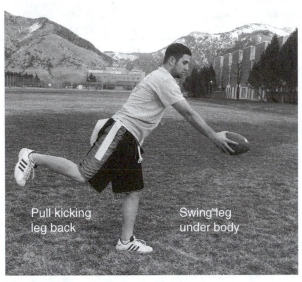

Pull kicking
leg back

Swing leg
under body

FIGURE 11.3 Punting

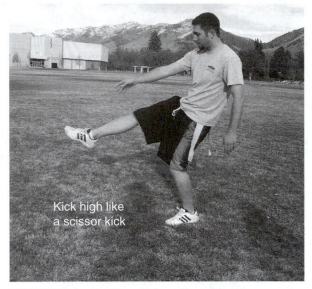

Kick high like
a scissor kick

FIGURE 11.4 Punting: Follow-Through

CATCHING A PUNT

SKILL	CUE	WHY	COMMON ERROR
Elbows (Figure 11.5)	5-point (hand-hand-elbow-elbow-bottom of sternum)	Big area for ball to land	Open arms
	Make a cage with arms	More surface area to catch ball	Arm and hands parallel to ground
	Fingers pointing to sky	Does not hurt the fingers	
	Palms toward face	Place for ball to go	
	Elbows to stomach		Elbows out, ball slides through
Action of Catching	Pull ball toward chest	Ball won't drop to ground	Ball hits to high off chest

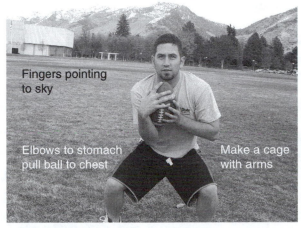

Fingers pointing
to sky

Elbows to stomach
pull ball to chest

Make a cage
with arms

FIGURE 11.5 Catching a Punting Ball

SNAPPING BALL FROM THE SIDE

SKILL	CUE	WHY	COMMON ERROR
Foot Position to the Ball	Feet behind ball	*Rule:* Feet behind the ball on line of scrimmage	
Hand Position on the Ball	Hold top of ball with an eagle claw	More surface area on the ball, more control of ball	
Hiking Action with the Arm	Straight arm to the quarterback	More accuracy with this method	
	Put the ball into the quarterback's hands; focus on hands	Gives you a focus on the target	
		More concentration and better accuracy	

QUARTERBACK DROP BACK

SKILL	CUE	WHY	COMMON ERROR
Foot Action	After receiving the snap, turn to side, and sidestep	These steps help the quarterback have a fast reaction time	Staying forward and throwing
	Grapevine		
	Slide-slide		
	Plant your back foot and throw	The player has better control of the ball at the time of the throw	

LATERAL PASS (A PITCH)

SKILL	CUE	WHY	COMMON ERROR
Hand Position	Hold ball with both hands	Better ball control	
	Wide fingers on ball	More surface area on the ball, better control	
Throwing Action (Figure 11.6)	Underhand throw		
	Arms straight		
	Aim for the number on the jersey		
Rule	Lateral pass has to go behind or to the side	A forward pass is illegal	Ball going forward is a forward pass

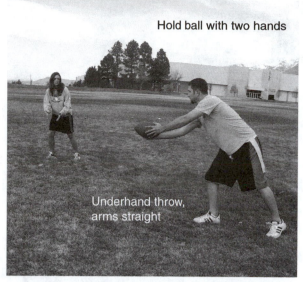

Hold ball with two hands

Underhand throw, arms straight

FIGURE 11.6 Lateral Pass

HAND-OFFS			
SKILL	**CUE**	**WHY**	**COMMON ERROR**
To Right Side of Quarterback			
Receiver Arm Position	Inside elbow up	Better target area for ball to go in	
	Outside elbow down		
	Arms are parallel to each other		
Quarterback Action	Put the ball between the receiver's arms	Target place	
Receiver Action	Squeeze the ball	Ball won't fall out	
To Left Side of Quarterback (Figure 11.7)			
Receiver Arm Position	Inside elbow up	The ball fits in the pocket better	
	Outside elbow down		
	Arms are parallel to each other	Elbow is not in the way	
Quarterback Action	Put the ball between the receiver's arms	Target place	
Receiver Action	Squeeze the ball	Ball won't fall out	

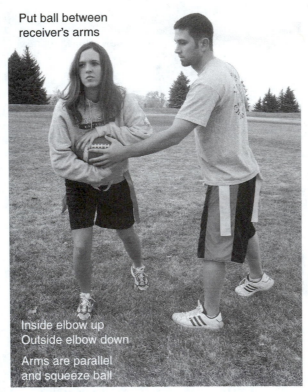

Put ball between receiver's arms

Inside elbow up
Outside elbow down

Arms are parallel
and squeeze ball

FIGURE 11.7 Handoff

BALL-CARRYING TECHNIQUES			
SKILL	**CUE**	**WHY**	**COMMON ERROR**
Tuck Away After Catch	Tuck ball into 4 REEF pressure points:	Ball won't get loose	Ball not on 1 of 4 pressure points
Arm Action	1. Rib Cage (stuff ball into rib cage)	Ball protected	Carrying like a loaf of bread
	2. Elbow (tuck elbow in)	Holds the ball in place	
	3. Eagle claw (spread fingers over point of ball)	Large surface area means more control of the ball	
	4. Forearm (covers ball)	Holds ball against the body, so the ball won't bounce out	
Running Down Sideline	SOAPS (Switch Outside Arm Position)		
Ball Position	Running to the right sideline, carry ball in right hand	If ball gets knocked out, it will roll out of bounds	
	Running to the left sideline, carry ball in left hand	If ball gets knocked out, it will roll out of bounds	

BLOCKING

SKILL	CUE	WHY	COMMON ERROR
Stance	Get into a comfortable squat position, as if you are sitting on a chair		Weight is forward
Arm Action	Arms crossed in front of body, ready to contact the defender	Quicker reaction time	Too much weight on hands
			Stopping feet and lunging
	Feet shoulder-width apart		
Strategy	Keep the opponent away from the ball carrier	Keeps you on the opponent	Not keeping with opponent
Body Force	Push with your upper body, using your legs for strength and balance	Legal position on the block	Using any other parts for blocking

BASIC RECEIVER ROUTES

SKILL	CUE	WHY	COMMON ERROR
In Route (Figure 11.8)	Run straight pivot to outside	To fake opponent	
	Cut to middle: run a straight line to middle; find an open area between defenders	Get to ball faster and run away from opponent	
	Big hands for target for the quarterback	More target area for the quarterback to see and the receiver to catch the ball	
Out Route (Figure 11.9)	Run straight, pivot to inside, and cut to the outside; run toward the sidelines; find an open area between defenders	To fake opponent	
	Run a straight line	Get to ball faster	
	Big hands, for the quarterback to have a target	More target area for the quarterback to see, and the receiver has more surface area in which to catch the ball	

continued

SKILL	CUE	WHY	COMMON ERROR
Post Route	Run straight for 10–12 yards, then cut to one of the goalposts	Fakes defender	
Stop Route	Run straight	The defender will not know in what direction you will be going	
	Stop as if you had come to a stop sign	The defender will be slow to react to your sudden movement	
	Turn around, with your arms and hands ready to receive the ball	Provides a good target to receive the ball	
Fly Route	Run straight until you pass the defender	The defender will not know where you are going	
	Don't stop	Run away from the defender	

FIGURE 11.8   In Route

FIGURE 11.9   Out Route

12

Floor Hockey

Floor hockey is a fast sport because of its transitions, the fact that players are constantly moving from offense to defense, and the speed of the puck or ball. You can substitute players during play without waiting for a whistle. Students have more playing time. Floor hockey develops cardiovascular endurance, core strength, reaction time, hand-eye coordination, foot speed, and agility. Floor hockey also works on skills that transfer to other sports, such as soccer and lacrosse.

Floor hockey is a sport that can be played successfully by all students. There is a role for every student, regardless of physical stature. Each student's personality plays a major role in the cohesion of the team.

SKILL LISTED WITH CUES

This chapter focuses on cues for the following skills: stance, grip, stick position, forehand passing, backhand passing, forehand receiving, backhand receiving, shooting, and goaltending.

EQUIPMENT TIPS

1. Sticks that have a plastic or wood shaft should be used.
2. A plastic puck is recommended for safety reasons because it is easy to control and harder to lift. A plastic ball also works well.
3. PVC nets are recommended for safety and durability instead of metal nets, if you have an option.
4. Safety equipment for all players includes helmet with face mask, gloves, shin guards that cover from the ankles to the top of the knee, and a mouth guard.
5. The goalie needs a helmet with face mask, catcher and blocker gloves, and shin guards.
6. Colored vests should be worn to identify the teams.

TEACHING IDEAS

1. Teach the players to keep the sticks on the floor at all times. This prevents high sticks, which can cause injury. If a player breaks the sticks on the floor rule during a game, that player sits out for 2 minutes, just like in ice hockey. The team plays one player short for the duration of the penalty.

2. Teach the players to watch out for each other. They should avoid hitting another player's ankles, tangling up sticks, or causing a player to fall.

3. Make sure players are in a good hockey stance, stick on floor, knees slightly bent, like making a triangle with stick and feet. Emphasize good posture while in the sitting position: head over shoulders, shoulders over hips, hips over heels.

4. When teaching passing and shooting, make sure to teach the transfer of weight from the back leg to the forward leg. This increases the power of the shot and helps with the accuracy of the follow-through.

5. When teaching passing and shooting, emphasize the wrist rollover during the follow-through. When executed properly, the blade of the stick faces down toward the floor. The stick should point to the target and be a foot or so off the floor.

TEACHING PROGRESSIONS

1. When practicing accuracy, have the students stand 10 to 15 feet from a wall. Each student will pick a spot on the wall or have a target at which to aim, for example, a cone. Having a target helps the student focus on rolling the wrist over and pointing toward the target with the stick.

2. Have students stand 20 feet apart with a partner. Work on passing and receiving skills. When students can do this with control, move the partners closer together and have them speed up the passes. The goal of this drill is to improve passing accuracy, receiving speed, and the releasing of a pass.

3. Hang a vest in the upper corners of the goal and/or place cones on the floor in the lower corners. Have three to four students stand in a semicircle. Have each student shoot for the vests. This improves shot accuracy, speed, and power (Figure 12.1)

FIGURE 12.1 Shooting Drill

MINI-GAMES

Play games of 3 on 3, 4 on 4, or 5 on 5. Set up several mini-games using the width of a basketball court. If a team scores 3 points, it stays on the court, and the opponents step off the court. The next team of three comes onto the court and plays a new game. These games keep the players moving. You can also play these games with goalies at each end.

FLOOR HOCKEY RULES AND GAME

- Due to the physical nature of the game, it is important to abide by a set of rules. Enforcing these rules keeps the sport safe and the game in control.
- If a player breaks a rule, send him to the 2-minute penalty box.
- Slashing (using a stick to strike another player) is a violation.
- Tripping (using a stick, knee, foot, arm, hand, or elbow to cause an opponent to trip or fall) is a violation.
- High-sticking is carrying the stick above the shoulders.
- Interference with the progress of an opponent who is not in possession of the puck or ball is a violation.
- Unsportsmanlike conduct, such as an overly violent behavior, swearing, teasing, fighting, and so forth, is a violation.
- Cross-checking—when a player has both hands on her stick (off the ground) and uses the stick to shove another player—is a violation.

FYI

For further information and special help, consult the following organization and resources.

ORGANIZATION

Olympic training ground for the Amateur Hockey Association of the United States.

USA Hockey
4965 East Fountain Boulevard
Colorado Springs, CO 80910
Fax: (719) 599-5994

PUBLICATION

Ice hockey books have more drills, rules, and information.

SKILL	CUE	WHY	COMMON ERROR
Feet (Figure 12.2)	Slightly wider than shoulder width, flat and firm on floor	Stability, balance, ready to move forward, backward, or laterally	
Knees	Slightly bent, but not over toes	Stability, balance, ready to move forward, backward, or laterally	
Hips	Slightly back	Core stability and balance	
		Helps knees from going over toes	
Stomach/Back	Keep stomach muscles tight and back straight	For core stability	
Head	Head up; looking forward over entire floor	Allows you to see entire floor and what is happening	
Holding Stick	Arms in front, holding stick straight out, forming a triangle with feet and stick	Stability, balance, ready for pass	
	Stick blade flat on ground 2–3 feet in front of feet	More surface area on ground to hit puck	

Emphasize These Cues

1. Feet firm on floor
2. Hips slightly back
3. Back straight, head up
4. Stick flat on floor; form a triangle with feet

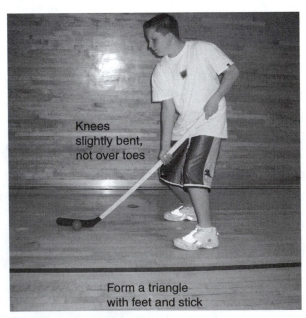

Knees slightly bent, not over toes

Form a triangle with feet and stick

FIGURE 12.2 Hockey Stance

SKILL	CUE	WHY	COMMON ERROR
Right-Hand Shot	Left hand on top; right hand halfway down shaft	Left hand is power hand; right hand is control hand	Hands too close together and grip too tight
Left-Hand Shot	Right hand on top; left hand halfway down shaft	Right hand is power hand; left hand is control hand	
Top Hand	Form a V with thumb and index finger; place at the top of shaft		
Bottom Hand	Form a V with thumb and index finger; place about halfway down shaft	Good control of stick; able to utilize more power	
Knuckles of Each Hand	Knuckles of each hand will face opposite direction of each other	Good control; hand halfway down the shaft utilizes flex in stick for harder and faster shot	

STICK HANDLING

SKILL	CUE	WHY	COMMON ERROR
Stick Position	Hold stick in front of body, forming a triangle with feet and blade	Balance, stability, ready for puck pass	
	Blade should be flat on floor 2–3 feet in front of feet		
Stick-Handling Stance			
Stance	Good hockey stance		
Head	Head up; see puck in peripheral vision	Can see the rest of floor and action going on	
Stick Motion	Blade travels parallel to foot line	Control of puck	
	Blade rotates toward puck at about 45° angle		
	Blade "cups" puck and pulls it forward and backward	Control of puck	
Wrists	Wrists roll toward puck when you catch it	Control of puck	

Emphasize These Cues

1. Keep puck between feet (stick on outside of puck); thus you have to pick up blade and place on other side of puck. Do this while rolling wrists to get 45-degree angle.

2. Use soft hands; there should be noise from the puck hitting the stick.

FOREHAND PASSING

SKILL	CUE	WHY	COMMON ERROR
Stance	Good hockey stance		
Puck Position (Figure 12.3)	Puck starts at heel of blade and behind back foot	Gives proper spin on puck; control	
	Travels forward to toe of blade and then off blade		
	Puck travels parallel to foot line	Accuracy, power, and speed of pass	
Stick	Puck stays on floor	Accuracy, ease of receiving pass	
	Sweep puck parallel to foot line		
	Puck is released from blade slightly in front of front foot		
	Hands on top of stick and halfway down shaft		
	Blade "cups" puck throughout motion		
	Blade should end up 1–2 feet above floor, with blade pointing toward floor		
Head and Eyes	Look at puck position on blade, look at target, look at puck position, pass		
Wrists	Follow puck path to its receiver	Improves follow-through, keeps pass down	
	As you sweep puck forward, roll wrist forward toward target	Puts proper spin on puck, keeps puck down	

Puck starts at heel of blade

Left hand on top, right hand half-way down shaft

FIGURE 12.3 Passing and Shooting Position

Emphasize These Cues

1. Weight on back foot (see Figure 12.4a)
2. Puck starts at heel of blade
3. Blade sweeps puck forward, with a cupping motion
4. See target, then puck, and pass
5. Roll wrist toward target

BACKHAND PASSING			
SKILL	**CUE**	**WHY**	**COMMON ERROR**
Backhand Passing	This motion is the same as the forehand pass, reverse the motion		
	Puck starts on back foot		
	Weight on back foot		
	Transfer weight to front foot		

SKILL	CUE	WHY	COMMON ERROR
Stance (Figure 12.4b)	Good hockey stance		
Head and Eyes	Watch puck come all the way into blade until you have control of puck	Ensures you receive puck and maintain control	
Stick Position	Stick path parallel to foot line	Control	
	Blade flat on floor, slightly in front of foot	Greater area on floor to receive pass, more time to catch pass	
	When puck reaches blade, pull blade backward to absorb pass		
	Blade travels all the way back to back foot	Control	
	Blade cups puck as it moves backward	Control	
Puck Position	Initial catch is on toe of blade (front third of blade)	Control and allows for immediate pass or shot because puck is in proper position	
	As you absorb puck, it should travel forward with heel of blade		
Wrist Position	Wrists roll forward for in-coming pass, as stick and hands absorb the pass	Control; soft hands to to help absorb pass; wrists in position to immediately pass or shoot	

Blade sweeps puck forward with a cupping motion

Roll wrist toward target

FIGURE 12.4a Passing to a Partner

Watch puck come all way into blade

Pull blade backward to absorb pass

Blade flat on floor

FIGURE 12.4b Receiving a Pass

Emphasize These Cues

1. Hockey stance
2. Watch puck into stick blade
3. Absorb puck with blade in a reverse sweeping motion
4. Roll wrist forward when puck meets blade

	BACKHAND RECEIVING		
SKILL	**CUE**	**WHY**	**COMMON ERROR**
Backhand Receiving	This motion is the same for a forehand or backhand pass reception; reverse motion		
	As puck approaches, weight should be on front foot; as you absorb puck with stick and hands, transfer weight to back foot	This makes you ready to immediately pass again or shoot	

SKILL	CUE	WHY	COMMON ERROR
Forehand Wrist Shot (Figure 12.5)	Bottom hand on stick should slide 2–3 inches further down		
	Weight transfer is very important; drive off back leg	Use of legs and hips aids speed and power of shot	
	Sweeping motion of stick should be faster than a pass		
	Bend knees a little more	To add in weight transfer while keeping good hockey stance	
	Roll wrists over and point blade at target		
	Height of follow-through affects height of shot		
Backhand Wrist Shot	Same cues as for forehand wrist shot, reverse motion		
	Momentum from weight transfer should "pull" shooter onto the front foot only		

Emphasize These Cues

1. Good stance
2. Lower hand slides 2 to 3 inches down shaft
3. Transfer weight from back foot to front foot
4. Roll wrists over and point blade at target

FIGURE 12.5 Shooting

SKILL	CUE	WHY	COMMON ERROR
Stance (Figure 12.6)	Head over shoulders, shoulders over hips, hips over ankles, feet shoulder-width apart, bend knees at 45° angle	Having good posture allows quick reaction time to stop the ball or puck	
Hand Position	Hold open catching hand off to the side, waist level	Having the open hand off to the side takes up more space, protecting the net even more	
		It also keeps the hand ready to respond quicker	
	The opposite hand holds the stick so the blade is on the ground in front and makes triangle with feet	Having the stick on the ground in front of the feet provides a barrier between the feet so that the puck does not get past	
	Blade flat on the ground	It also protects more surface area of the net	

Emphasize These Cues

1. Hockey stance
2. Catching hand open, up waist-high, and off to side
3. Stick blade flat on floor, making a triangle with feet

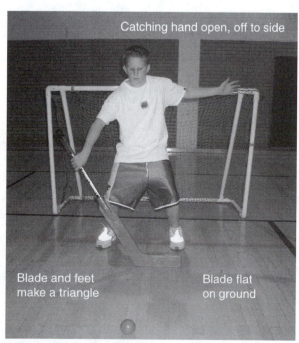

FIGURE 12.6 Goalie Stance

Note

1. The goaltender is the last line of defense. The goaltender has one major goal: to stop the puck. The most effective way of goaltending is to take up as much area of the goal plane as possible. The goaltender's body and the stick help to take up this area.

2. To avoid muscle pulls and strains, always make sure that the goaltenders and players are properly stretched before any activity begins. Goaltenders need to be flexible, because the position requires a quick reflex time, which could cause injury if the player is not warmed up properly.

3. Before beginning the game, let the goaltender's team take practice shots, from a distance, at the goaltender. This drill serves the important role of getting the goaltender's reflex time prepared for scrimmage, as well as warming up the rest of the team.

13

Golf

INTRODUCTION

The game of golf is the fastest-growing sport in the world, and, for a student who has played a satisfying round, it is easy to see why it has become so popular. Golf may be the hardest skill game played today, and it definitely cannot be learned quickly. Three things need to happen with each shot. The golfer must (1) hit the target, (2) shoot the correct yardage, and (3) hit the sweet spot on the club face or hit the ball square on the club face. It takes most recreational golfers years to learn, even naturally gifted athletes. Keeping this fact in mind, teachers should remember to be patient with students, while instructing and encouraging those with a real interest in golf to play as much as possible.

Three to five demonstrations of a golf stroke, associated with one cue phrase, will simplify the learning process and make the skill and stroke more beginner-friendly. Stay with one or two cues until the students are comfortable moving on. Tiger Woods' book, *How I Play Golf,* is a great resource for cues. As one golf pro said, "It's not what you say but it's what the student hears."

SKILLS LISTED WITH CUES

This chapter presents teaching cues for the following golf skills: three different grips, approach to the ball, and the basic swing for iron shots. Once the students have mastered these skills, additional cues provide information for golf shots, which include specifics for wood shots, putting, and chipping. Also provided are cues on how to handle sand shots, windy shots, and different golf lies, including downhill, uphill, and low balls. These particular cues are designed for beginning, right-handed golfers, but they can be adapted for left-handed golfers. Through the use of these cues, you and your students can be successful golfers!

TIPS

1. Type the cues on 3" × 5" note cards, laminate and hole-punch the cards, and place them in your bag for quick reference on different shots.

2. It is essential to grasp and ingrain the fundamentals of golf: grip, stance, backswing, through swing, and finish.

3. Good equipment and good fundamentals of golf equal good golf.

4. Core exercises and stretching are critical to a good golf swing; Tiger Woods' book *How I Play Golf,* covers this well.

EQUIPMENT TIPS

1. Ball differences (colored numbers):
   - *80 compression* (all red numbered balls) suggested for a lady or senior citizen who does not hit the ball very far or has no club-head speed.
   - *90 compression* (red and black numbered balls) suggested for medium to average players, stronger women, and in cold weather for men who hit 100 compression.
   - *100 compression* (all black numbered balls) suggested for stronger men, hot days, fast club-head speed.

2. Standard set of clubs: 1, 3, and 5 woods; 3, 4, 5, 6, 7, 8, and 9 irons; pitching wedge, sand wedge, and putter; and utility clubs: 1 and 2 iron; 4 and 7 wood; and lob wedge.

3. Go to a professional to be fitted for proper club length, proper flex of shaft, and proper lie.

4. Golf shoes with spikes help the golfer stay on the ground and prevent slipping. Golf sandals are popular, but bee stings are common; you might want to wear socks.

5. Artificial-turf doormats can be used to hit the ball indoors. These mats protect the floor.

TEACHING PROGRESSION

Putt first, move to the chip shot, pitch, sand shot, swing fair woods, driver, and then how to handle problem shots. Once the fundamentals are finished, work on mastering the mind.

TEACHING IDEAS

1. Choose clubs beginners can have success with. Clubs that are fairly easy to hit with include 5, 6, and 7 irons. These clubs can be used to help ingrain the swing. When a player begins to feel comfortable with the irons, progress to the woods.

2. The driving range is a place for beginners to practice the skills of golf. Beginners can become easily frustrated on a golf course. When the beginner can get the ball up in the air with consistency, it's time to play a round of golf.

3. Putting and chipping are the least difficult skills to learn; however, to keep the feel for the ball one must practice many hours to maintain these skills.

Use perforated plastic balls

Use cones, hula hoops, and soccer corner flags

Use blue tarps for water

SCORE

SCORE

FIGURE 13.1   Ideas for Modified Golf Equipment and Nine-Hole Golf Course

4. Golf is easy to make complex! The simpler we can make it, the better. Stay away from high-tech words. Progress happens when staying with the fundamental skills and basic swing.

5. Setting up a nine-hole golf course on a football field or large grass field is an excellent way to teach scoring and provide a gamelike experience (Figure 13.1). Equipment and procedures include the following:

    • Scorecard designed by teacher or picked up at a local golf course.

    • Pencils.

    • Jump rope and cones to mark tee box.

    • For holes use soccer corner flags, or attach flags to dowel sticks and stand the sticks in orange cones with holes in top. Place the flag in the center of a hula hoop. Object of game is to hit ball in hula hoop.

    • Regulation clubs, white Wiffle balls, and tees.

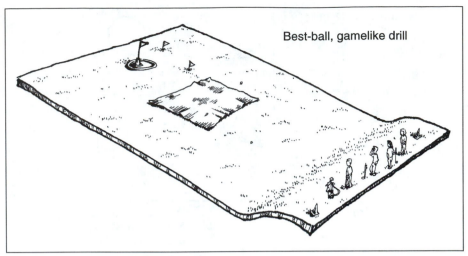

FIGURE 13.2 Early Bird Special Golf Activity

- Set up nine holes that match the pars on the score card.
- Use a shotgun tournament start. Have three or four students on each hole. Give each group one wood, a 5 iron, a 7 iron, a 9 iron, a scorecard, and a pencil. On the whistle everybody starts to play.
- One can play best-ball tournaments and other types. Have fun golfing!

6. Have a contest to see who can hit the ball closest to the hole. Tee shots are made from the top of a hill (if hills are not available, tee off level ground) (Figure 13.2).
   - Set up a tee box area and a par-three hole at the bottom of a small hill.
   - Place a hula hoop about 50 yards out from the tee box with a soccer goal marker or flagstick inside the hoop.
   - Place a blue plastic tarp in front of the hole for a water hazard.
   - Provide 7, 8, and 9 irons for the students to use.
   - A teacher, teacher's aide, or student can place a small flagstick where the closest ball to the large flagstick lands.
   - Each student tries to get her or his shot close to the flagstick. If a student does, the ball is marked with a small flagstick.
   - Closest ball to the hole wins the early bird special.
7. If you don't keep practicing golf, it's very easy to lose your skills. Stay with it.
8. A golfer should spend one-third of their time putting and chipping, one-third of their time hitting range balls, and one-third of their time on the course playing.
9. Try to organize a field trip to the golf course and work on each area listed above. Have the golf pro talk about course etiquette and rules.

For further information and special help, consult the following organization and resources.

ORGANIZATION

Hook a Kid on Golf
2611 Old Okeechobee Road
West Palm Beach, FL 33409

GOLF PROS

Contact the PGA professionals at local golf courses.

Dan Roskelly
PGA Head Professional
Logan Golf and Country Club
Logan UT 84322

PUBLICATIONS

Fronske, H., Wilson, R., & Strand, B. (1996, November/December). Teaching golf creatively. *Strategies,* 10(2), 32–37.

George, J. D. (2004). *Let's golf.* San Francisco: Benjamin Cummings.

Hogan, B. (1985). *Five lessons: The modern fundamentals of golf.* New York: Simon & Schuster.

Mack, G. & Casstevons, P. (2001). *Mind gym.* Chicago, IL McGraw Hill Contemporary Books.

Woods, T. (2001). *Tiger Woods: How I play golf.* New York: Warner Brothers.

WEBSITES

www.golf101.com
www.golfmaestro.net
www.nationalgolfer.com/productions/golf_instruction/butch-harman. ultimate_golf.htm
www.nationalgolfer.com/products/golf_instruction/demo_flicks_on_golf.htm

		GRIPS		
SKILL	**CUE**	**WHY**	**COMMON ERROR**	
Overlap (Strongest)	Little finger of right hand rests on index and middle finger		Gripping too tightly with right thumb	
	Last 3 fingers on left hand and middle 2 fingers of right hand are the grippers	Control of club	Gripping top of club—instinct is to grip with thumb and index finger	
	Fingers are welded together like Siamese twins			
Hand Position	The V of thumb and index finger of each hand points to right shoulder			
	Vs point to right shoulder			
Interlocking	Little finger interlocks with index finger		Little fingers not interlocking	
Baseball	No unity between hands, right hand is strong hand of grip	Control of club	Hands too far apart	
	Hold club like a baseball bat			

		APPROACH		
SKILL	**CUE**	**WHY**	**COMMON ERROR**	
Stance	Stand tall, wide shoulders		Standing straight up; legs stiff or straight	
Arms	Arms hang comfortably		Elbows locked	
	Knees flexed ever so slightly	Can turn back and through the ball		
	Bent over at hips comfortably but not too far			
Focus of Eyes	Look through the lower part of eyes		Eyes and head tilting down	
	Keep chin up through swing	Left shoulders turn under chin	Chin hitting front shoulder during swing	
Head	Head needs to be still			

SKILL	CUE	WHY	COMMON ERROR
Backswing Position	Right elbow points down and away from side	Helps keep club face square and club on line	Elbow up or too close to body
	Left elbow wide and straight	By pushing your left arm away from head as far as you can there is more time to accelerate speed and power on downswing	Left elbow bent
	Wide at the top; the longer and wider you make your backswing the better the swing		Both elbows bent
	Club shaft is parallel to target at top of swing	Helps for a perfect path and plane line through the face of club	
Head Position on Completion of the Swing	Head stays still until trailing shoulder forces it up	More speed and power through the swing	Keeping head down all the way through swing; don't get as much power

SKILL	CUE	WHY	COMMON ERROR
Swing Key 1 **Low and Wide**	Arms wide on the take away	Foundation of a wide swing arc	Downswing too steep or choppy
	Low wide straight		
	Back takeaway		
	Get the feeling of swinging your left forearm more across your chest rather than up		
Swing Key 2	Keep your left knee as quiet as possible while you turn your shoulders		
	A controlled turn is a tight turn		
	Keep left knee in same position as address		
	Push left hip 2 inches to left		Weight gathered on right foot
	80% of weight on right leg; 20% of weight on left leg	More power from weight transfer; ball will go longer	80% on left leg, 20% on right leg
			Not transferring weight to back leg
	Coil		
Swing Key 3	Rip it		Open club face at impact
	Right forearm rotates over the left		90% of balls slice or go to right
	Let the right forearm rotate over the left as aggressively as you can until the ball stops going right; rip it		
	"You finish more around your body than up."		

SLICE

SKILL	CUE	WHY	COMMON ERROR
Slice	80–90% of balls slice	Club face open at impact	
		Forearms rotate too much on takeaway	
		Left wrist is cupped at top of backswing	
		Swing path too much from inside	
How to Correct Slice	You want a flat wrist and square club face at top of backswing		
	Have quicker hands and restrict forearm rotation on backswing		
	Have partner or use mirror to check angle		

HOOK

SKILL	CUE	WHY	COMMON ERROR
Hook		Club face closed at impact	
		Lack of body rotation on through swing	
		Chin buried in the chest	
		Wrist bowed at top of swing	
How to Correct Hook	Flat wrist		
	Maintain triangle		
	Stay connected		

SKILL	CUE	WHY	COMMON ERROR
Stance (Figure 13.3a)	Front foot lines up with ball		Ball lined up with back foot or middle of stance
Tee Ball	Top half of ball should be above club face		Ball teed up too high or low
(Figure 13.3b)	Inside of feet line up with outside points of shoulders	You get more motion in your upper body	
Swing	Tickle grass on backswing		Wood face comes up too soon
	Emphasize low and wide backswing		Hurrying the takeaway swing
	Turn left shoulder under chin		
	Drive tack through ball		
	Sweep the ball off tee		Hitting at down angle
	Keep club head traveling fairly low to ground after impact	Will promote solid contact	
Follow-Through	Belt buckle faces hole		
	Right knee points to target		Left hip faces hole
Focus of Eyes	Head stays still until trailing shoulder forces it up		Raising head too soon or too late

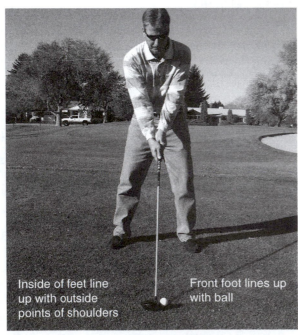

Inside of feet line up with outside points of shoulders

Front foot lines up with ball

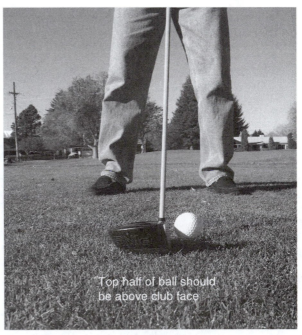

Top half of ball should be above club face

FIGURE 13.3 (a) Stance for Wood Shot

(b) Ball Placement for Wood Shot

SKILL	CUE	WHY	COMMON ERROR
Grip	Hold the putter lightly	Able to feel weight the of putter head at other end	Hold too tightly
	1–10 pressure hold it 5 or less		
Stance	Stand fairly tall	Easy to see path of ball	Hunched over
		Allows for better shoulder swing	
Eyes	Position eyes directly over ball	Keeps you in line with hole	Eyes too far forward or back
	Eyes parallel to line of putt		
	Use bill of cap as a reference point parallel		
Putting Action (Figure 13.4)	Same length back and through	More control of ball	Short too much acceleration at contact
	Shoulders and arm do most of work	Control of ball	
	Left arm and putter act as one	Avoids angles of putter head	
	Keep a steady head and sternum	Keeps putting path stable and true	Head moves right to left
	No peeking	Solid contact	Peeking

continued

PUTTING DRILLS

1. Putt with your eyes closed.
2. Always have a routine. Tiger Woods has an example in his book.
3. Putting is largely about touch to get a feel for speed. The stroke should be easy, smooth, and natural.
4. Start close when putting (the same philosophy as warm-up shooting a basketball). Work yourself back from the hole. Start close to hole and move back gradually from the hole putting close shots to longer shots.

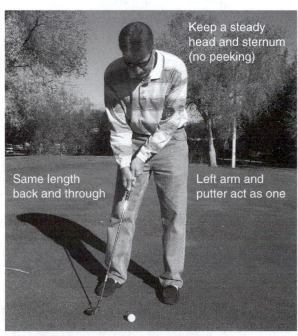

Keep a steady head and sternum (no peeking)

Same length back and through

Left arm and putter act as one

FIGURE 13.4 Arm Swing for Putting

Golf **161**

PUTTING, continued			
SKILL	**CUE**	**WHY**	**COMMON ERROR**
Have a Routine	Always have the same routine when you putt	Puts you in a great form physically and mentally	Routine or process too quick
	Perform it exactly the same way every time		

CHIPPING			
SKILL	**CUE**	**WHY**	**COMMON ERROR**
Grip	Choke down on club	Extra control	
Club	Use 8 or 7 iron	More control—ball does not go as high; more accurate	
Posture	Open stance	See the hole path better	Hunched down on ball
	Chin high		
	Back straight		
Hand position	Set hands slightly ahead of the ball		
Tilt	Lean a little toward target	Promotes a downward blow	
Ball Position	Position ball slightly back of center	Promotes a downward blow	
Read the Shot	See the shot before you hit it		
	Choose a spot you want the ball to land		
	Form a mental picture of the ball traveling there		
Swing Action	Hit down on back of ball	Loft of club will give it height	Stabbing at ball
	Accelerate smoothly		
	Keep eyes focused on back of ball through contact; see grass where ball was		
	Return arm to position at address		

PITCH SHOT

SKILL	CUE	WHY	COMMON ERROR
Address and Club Use	Choose a lofted club sand wedge		
	Open your stance aligning your feet left of target lane		Closed stance
	Open club face to increase loft		Closed club face
	Play the ball forward off your left toe		Play ball back off your right toe
Action Cues	Mini version of the full swing		
	Hips turn slightly back and through	To accommodate the motion of your shoulders, arms, and hands	
	Let the club do the work		
	Slide club head under the ball		
	Accelerate through the swing		Allow club head to stop
End of Swing	Club face should be aiming at the sky	Proves that the loft of the club face has been maintained	

30-YARD PUNCH

SKILL	CUE	WHY	COMMON ERROR
Short Punch from About 30 Yards	Position ball back of center	Helps golfer hit down on the ball	
	Narrow stance; feet between the width of the shoulders		
Backswing	Start the backswing low and wide		
	Left arm fully extended		
	Turn shoulders and hips		
	Simply unturn your hips and let them guide the shoulders, arms, and hands through the downswing		
	A low abbreviated finish	Prove big muscles have directed the motion	Arm and hands directed the motion

SKILL	CUE	WHY	COMMON ERROR
Stance	Be careful not to ground club	Stroke penalty	Placing club face in sand
Feet (Figure 13.5a)	Dig feet into the sand; open face at address	Solid stance	Failing to dig feet into sand, closed face
Stance and Club Alignment	Open stance and club face, weaken left hand	Don't want club face to rotate to closed position	Closed club face, tight grip easer
	Align feet, hips, and shoulders left of target	Preprogramming and out-to-in swing	
	Aim club face to right	Increase loft of the swing club face in order to hit high and soft the back	
	Play ball off left heel	Promotes a higher trajectory	
		Slides club through sand easier	
Swing	Easy does it about technique		Too much strength
	Swing hands back to about shoulder height, easy rhythms		
	Cock wrist firmly	Very hardy shot with little movement in hips or legs	Too much hip with leg movement
(Figure 13.5b)	Slide through the ball		Chopping at ball
	Accelerate through the ball		Fastest speed of club 6 inches beyond contact
Want the Ball to Run After It Hits Green	Hit 3 inches behind ball	Ball comes out without any backspin	Stopping in sand
			Taking no sand
Hit Ball High, Stop Quickly	Hit 1 inch or less behind ball	Ball stops with more backspin	Hitting no sand
			Ball gets away from you
Buried Ball in Sand	Make a divot for a little animal to be buried in line up to left	This little time ball up in the air	
	Forget if there's a lot of effort into shot		
	Swing down firmly, punch		
	Not much follow-through		

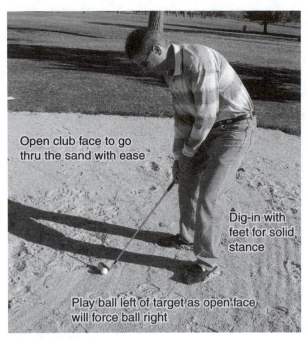

Open club face to go thru the sand with ease

Dig-in with feet for solid stance

Play ball left of target as open face will force ball right

(a) Feet Position

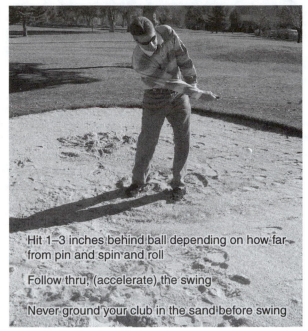

Hit 1–3 inches behind ball depending on how far from pin and spin and roll

Follow thru, (accelerate) the swing

Never ground your club in the sand before swing

(b) Swing Technique

FIGURE 13.5 Sand Shot

WIND SHOT			
SKILL	**CUE**	**WHY**	**COMMON ERROR**
Wind Shot	Wider stance; flex knees more		
	Play ball off back of foot for a low shot just right of center		Playing ball off front foot or middle of stance
	Decrease club number; for example, change from a 5 iron to a 3 iron	More control of ball will go farther in the wind	Using a club number that is too high
	Shorten wide swing, keep hands low; easier swing		Hard, heavy swing
	Take a very thin divot		
	Finish low to hit ball low		

SKILL	CUE	WHY	COMMON ERROR
Golf Ball Lies Downhill (Figure 13.6a)	Play ball off front foot	Where the club face hits ball first for accurate contact of ball	
	Use 1 less club (5 to 6 iron)	Ball goes longer; ball travels farther	Playing ball in a straddle stance or off front foot
	Keep shoulders parallel to the grass like airplane wings		Leaning forward
Beginner	Aim at target line		Aiming straight
Intermediate	Wrists break earlier to close club face		
Golf Ball Lies Uphill (Figure 13.6b)	Play ball off low foot	Where club face hits ground first for accurate contact of ball	
	Play ball off back foot		Playing ball in a straddle stance or off back foot
	Keep shoulders parallel to the grass like airplane wings	Leaning forward	
Beginner	Use 1 more club	Ball will go higher	Aiming straight
Intermediate	Wrists break later to keep club face open longer		

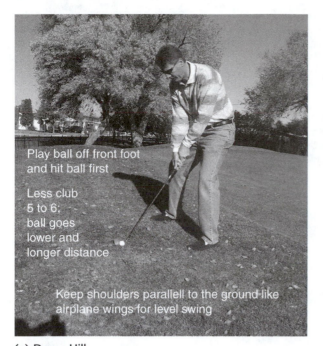

Play ball off front foot and hit ball first

Less club 5 to 6; ball goes lower and longer distance

Keep shoulders parallel to the ground like airplane wings for level swing

Play ball off back foot to make contact with ball first

Play one club more (5 to a 4) as ball will go higher and less distance

(a) Down Hill

(b) Uphill

FIGURE 13.6   Hill Shot

LOW BALLS			
SKILL	**CUE**	**WHY**	**COMMON ERROR**
Feet	Play ball off back foot	More control of ball	Playing ball in a straddle stance or off front foot
	Widen stance		
	Flex knee more		
	Choose more club		
Club Face	Square the club face		Open or very closed club face
Swing	Short wide swing	Ball will stay low	No follow-through
	Keep hands low		

14

In-Line Skating

In-line skating is an enjoyable new sport that can be introduced to people of all ages. Students from elementary, middle, and high schools can enjoy and learn about in-line skating. Many students already participate in in-line skating, and this activity can easily be added to any physical education class.

In-line skating can be incorporated into a physical education program under National Association for Sport and Physical Education (NASPE) Standards. Skate in School is a program developed by NASPE and Roller Blade, Inc., that comes with ready-to-use lesson plans and affordable equipment (skates, helmets, and protective gear).

SKILLS LISTED WITH CUES

Cues are presented for the following basic skills: standing up, ready position, falling, V-walk, using the ABT brake, striding, turning, use of edges, stopping, and swizzling.

EQUIPMENT TIPS

1. Each student *must* wear a helmet and knee, wrist, and elbow pads. You wouldn't play football without a helmet and padding—ouch! Wearing protective equipment helps prevent injury.

2. Organization of the equipment is very important.
   - Mark all of the equipment with permanent markers.
   - Mark skates with the size on the back of each skate. Skates should be stored as pairs on some type of shelving.
   - Mark all protective gear and helmets with S, M, L, or XL.
   - Keep equipment by type or by size. You can use large buckets, one each for knee pads, elbow pads, and wrist pads, or you can use mesh bags that hold one of each type of equipment, all the same size. Choose the method that works for you. You may want to experiment to find out which is better.

3. After each day's use, the equipment should be cleaned with a spray disinfectant and stored in a well-ventilated area to allow drying.

4. The first day of class should be used to go over rules and talk about the physical benefits of skating, the importance of protective gear, and the proper technique of getting and putting away the equipment.

5. Depending on the type of skates and brake pads, you can skate in the gym (with indoor skates) or on a flat, smooth surface outside. For indoor use, you need a nonmarking brake pad, like the ones Roller Blade, Inc., uses in its program.

6. All equipment should be maintained on a regular basis.

7. Skating in water or sand can damage bearings and hurt skate performance. Stick to dry surface.

TEACHING IDEAS

1. Always discuss the importance of protective gear. Don't scare students, but remind them that a broken wrist or concussion is worse than a messed-up hairdo.

2. Talk to students about the physical benefits of in-line skating.

3. Discuss with students the importance of control. If control is maintained, falling should not occur very often. Each student's level of control may be different.

4. Students should be reminded to keep their body weight low and slightly forward, with knees bent, most of the time.

5. Discuss the skating area and use boundary markers and cones when possible. Also, establish traffic patterns for safety.

6. Start nervous beginners on floor mats to ease falls and build confidence.

7. Have students assist each other verbally, but not physically.

8. Avoid hills and declines when starting out. Start on a flat surface—parking lot, tennis court, basketball court.

TEACHING PROGRESSION

1. Rules and procedures
2. Protective gear and skates
3. Standing up
4. Ready position
5. Falling
6. Stopping
7. Rolling and stopping
8. V-walk/stroking
9. V-walk, roll, and basic stop
10. Stride
11. ABT brake
12. Turns
13. Edges
14. Slalom
15. Forward swizzle
16. Backward swizzle

MINI-GAMES

1. *Practice—practice—practice:* Balance on one skate at a time. This helps one to stop better. Skate width of gym and stop. Repeat until skill is mastered. The goal of this activity is for students to practice stopping techniques.

2. *Musical Braking:* Students skate to popular music on a circular course. Periodically, the music is turned off for 3 to 5 seconds. The goal of the activity is that every student should come to a complete, controlled stop before the music is turned on again.

3. *Skating Pins:* Students skate in lanes up and down a flat area. A "wall" of bowling pins is placed at each end, and a line is placed approximately 2 to 3 feet in front of the pins. The goal of the activity is that students perform the basic stop between the line and pins without knocking over any pins.

4. *Slalom Races:* Divide the class into teams of four. Set up a slalom course. In relay fashion, have the teams race through the slalom course, turn around the last cone, and race back to tag the next person in line. Every cone that is knocked down adds 1 second to the overall team score.

5. *Student Routines:* Put the students in groups of four to six. Have the students develop a skating routine to music of their choice. (Be sure the music is appropriate beforehand.) The students need to include at least four different skating skills in the routine. Have students present their routines to the class.

FYI

For further information, consult the following organization and resources.

ORGANIZATION

National Association for Sport and Physical Education (NASPE)
1900 Association Drive
Reston, VA 20191
Phone: (800) 213-7193, ext. 410

WEBSITES

These sites have ideas on how to order skates and how to care for and maintain them, as well as more teaching instruction and competition.

www.aggressive.com
www.rollerblade.com

SKILL	CUE	WHY	COMMON ERROR
Standing Up	Start on both knees	Beginning skaters need to understand the most efficient way to get up, conserve energy, and not get frustrated	
	Lift nonbrake knee and place wheels on ground		
	Place both hands on knees		
	Push up slowly		
	Position skates in a V (heels together)		
Ready Position Figure 14.1	Position skates in a V (heels together)	This position is needed to begin all movements	
	Ankles, knees, and hips flexed		
	Weight forward and low		
	Arms forward and in front of knees		
	Put hands on knees to regain balance if falling backward		

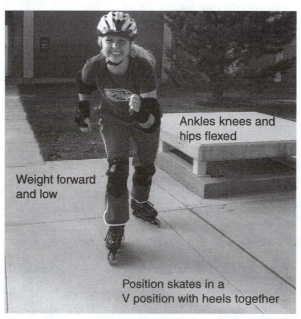

Ankles knees and hips flexed

Weight forward and low

Position skates in a V position with heels together

FIGURE 14.1 Ready Position

SKILL	CUE	WHY	COMMON ERROR
Falling (Figure 14.2)	Drop to all fours (knees, then hands, using plastic part of wrist guard)	Students need to understand that falling forward is the safest way to fall	
V-Walk	Ready position	Basic step for movement	
	Shift weight from one foot to the other	Students are in control of their speed	
	While shifting weight, point toes out like a V		
Stopping #A Open ABT Brake	Weight on nonbrake leg		Failing to lift toe in ABT
	Put brake leg forward		Keeping all wheels on the ground
	Slightly lift toe	Great for beginners	
	Press calf against back of skate		
	Shoulder and arms should be forward		
ABT Brake	Put weight on nonbrake leg	An effective means of stopping; easy for students to have success	
	Slide brake foot forward		
	Press calf against cuff of boot and depress brake		
	Keep shoulders forward		
Standard Brake (Figure 14.3)	Scissor brake foot forward		
	Lift toe and press heel into the pad		
T-Stop Brake (Figure 14.4)	Glide and coast on both skates	Not all students have brakes	
	Lift back braking foot and place behind front coasting foot in T position	Effective for more experienced skaters	
	Apply pressure and ease skate to stop		

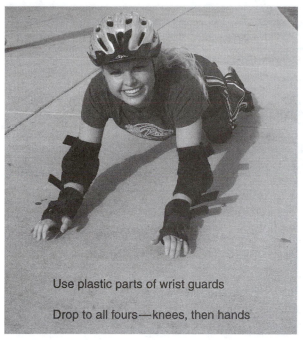

Use plastic parts of wrist guards

Drop to all fours—knees, then hands

FIGURE 14.2 Falling

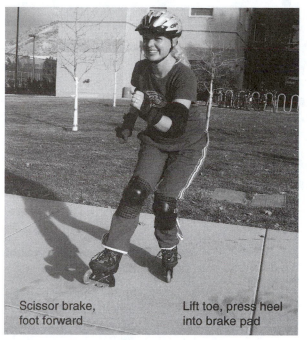

Scissor brake, foot forward

Lift toe, press heel into brake pad

FIGURE 14.3 Stopping Standard Brake

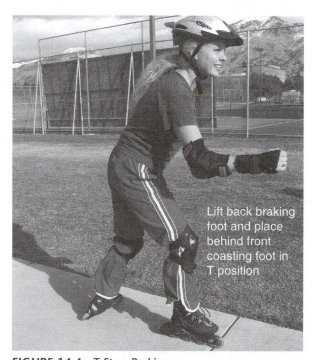

Lift back braking foot and place behind front coasting foot in T position

FIGURE 14.4 T-Stop Braking

SKILL	CUE	WHY	COMMON ERROR
Stride	Ready Position	Short strokes increase power	
	V-walk	Don't twist body while gliding	Twisting body while gliding
	Right foot stroke, push forward; lift left foot off the ground, coast		
	Left foot stroke, push forward; lift right foot off the ground, coast	Keep nose, knees, and toes in forward position	
	Repeat shifting weight back and forth	Take wide strides	
	Note: There is minimal time that both skates are on the ground	Students experience smooth timing	
Turns (for right turns; opposite for left turns)	Look to the right	Don't lean hips out; rather, have upper body lean and leave hips aligned over skates	
	Rotate upper body to right		
	Turn hips and knees to right		
	Skates about 6 inches apart		
	Lean to each side		
Use of Edges	One skate on outside edge	Allows smooth turning	
	One skate on inside edge		
	Roll forward by pressing on edges		

SKILL	CUE	WHY	COMMON ERROR
Parallel Turn	Stride/coast, keeping feet under shoulders and parallel	Use with more experienced skaters	
	Point shoulder to left; skates will follow, using one outside and one inside. Make the right leg lead with the outside edge	Students who feel comfortable on skates will experience success with these skills	
	Lean into the outside edge		
Forward Swizzle	V position	These skills allow the students to move in multiple directions and combine a number of skills	
	Bend knees, lean forward		
	Turn toes inward		
	Push heels out		
	Feet are about shoulder-width apart		
	Then bring feet together		
	Repeat		
Backward Swizzle	Same movement backward		
	Start with toes together (backward V)		
	Put pressure on the inside edge of both feet		
	Turn toes inward toward edge		
	Push heels out		
	Grab heels, pulling them back in (like gripping)		
	Bring feet together		
	Turn toes inward and lean		

SKILL	CUE	WHY	COMMON ERROR
ABT Brake	Put weight on nonbrake leg		
	Slide brake foot forward		
	Press calf against cuff of boot and depress brake		
	Keep shoulders forward		
Standard Brake	Scissor brake foot forward		
	Lift toe and press heel into the pad		
	Heel into the pad		
T-Stop Brake	Glide and coast on both skates		
	Lift braking foot and place in back of coasting foot in T position		
	Apply pressure and ease skate to stop		

15

Lacrosse

INTRODUCTION

"Field Lacrosse is sometimes perceived to be a violent and dangerous game (often called 'brutal' by first-time observers); however, injury statistics prove otherwise. While serious injuries can occur in lacrosse, the game has evolved with an emphasis on safety, and the rate of injury is comparatively low. Played by boys and girls who range in age from six to sixty, lacrosse is one of the fastest growing team sports in the United States. In recent years, lacrosse has experienced unprecedented growth throughout the world.

"A unique combination of speed, skill, agility, grace, endurance, finesse and historical significance, lacrosse may just be, according to basketball inventor James Naismith, 'the best of all possible field games'" (Lacrosse Foundation, 1994, p. 7).

Four major skill areas include catching, passing, picking up ground balls, and cradling. When these four skills are mastered, the rest of the game falls into place. The game has similarities to basketball, ice hockey, and soccer, with the physical contact of football. Lacrosse is a fast-transition game often referred to "as the fastest game on two feet." The cues in this chapter are designed for both men and women. The difference between the men's and women's games is that physical contact is allowed in the men's game but not in the women's game.

Lacrosse is a game played for the love of the sport. There are countless amateur men's club leagues around the nation, and in recent years a new professional men's outdoor lacrosse league has brought the game to national attention. Variations of lacrosse can be added to a curriculum with minimal expense and with such benefits as improved eye-hand coordination, aerobic and anaerobic fitness, muscular coordination, mental toughness, and competitiveness.

SKILLS LISTED WITH CUES

The cues in this chapter are designed to teach the skills of throwing, catching, cradling, shielding the stick, picking up ground balls, individual offensive play, team defensive strategy, and goaltending.

TIPS

1. A good drill for catching is to find a straight wall. Using the stick and a ball, practice throwing the ball against a wall. This is called "wall ball." Catch the ball in the pocket without using the hands. Follow the throwing, catching, and cradling cues. Spending hours throwing the ball against the wall will lead to mastery with these skills. Pick a spot on the wall to aim for, because this method will improve the shooting passing and catching. The goal or cage is 6 feet × 6 feet. This drill can be done in a gym.

2. Cradling is a critical skill that prevents the loss of the ball when moving. Have students run downfield with just a ball and stick, not cradling; then have them cradle and run down the field. This exercise will demonstrate the need for cradling.

3. Body position for passing and catching the ball is important for balance, fluidity of motion, and quick transition to other areas of the game. The ready position consists of knees slightly bent, body relaxed, stick held in the stance position. (See cue for ready position.)

4. Ground ball position: bend at the waist and knees as if attempting to kneel down. Keep head up using peripheral vision to locate and scoop the ball. This allows the player to have visual contact with his own team and opposing players.

5. Develop ambidextrous skills.

6. Throwing tip: When developing stick-handling skills, it is important to emphasize wrist and hand flexibility and strength. One means of doing so after instructing the fundamentals of grip and throwing motion is to have players practice throwing and catching while in a kneeling position. This exercise isolates the upper body and helps focus on the importance of hand and wrist flexibility.

EQUIPMENT TIPS

1. Indoor soccer goals or plastic garbage cans can be used for physical education classes. Soccer balls and volleyballs can be used to teach the tactical skills of the game.

2. Men's equipment differs from women's equipment.

   Men's equipment: Helmet with face mask, shoulder pads, arm guards, gloves, lacrosse stick, lacrosse ball, mouth guard, two goals 6 feet × 6 feet, field 110 yards × 60 yards

   Women's equipment: Stick, ball, mouth guard, gloves optional, two goals 6 feet × 6 feet, field 100 yards × 50 yards

TEACHING IDEAS

1. "Hands high and away" (grip drill): Make players keep their hands higher than their shoulders and away from their bodies throughout the throwing motion like a pull/push or pendulum motion—pulling with bottom hand and pushing with top hand. This drill forces them to use their hands and wrists and deemphasizes the arm motion.

2. Lacrosse can be played in physical education classes in teams of five players each using a smaller goal such as an indoor soccer goal or a plastic garbage can. Lay the can down, and throw the ball into the can. This exercise sharpens shooting skills. The field can be reduced to size available, providing opportunity for multiple games involving the greatest number of players.

3. Scrimmage once a week for at least two regulation periods of 15 minutes each, with full equipment and a regulation field. Regulation play requires 10 players (one goalie, three defenders, three midfielders, three attackers).

4. Physical education teachers could teach the tactical skill of lacrosse with a soccer ball or volleyball carried in the hands of a player instead of a stick. In this scenario one does not need to purchase equipment but can teach the game and rules of lacrosse and present an alternative enjoyable experience.

FYI

For further information and special help, consult the following.

ORGANIZATION

National Lacrosse Foundation
113 W. University Parkway
Baltimore, MD 21210
Phone: (410) 235-6882
FAX: (410) 366-6735
E-mail: info@lacrosse.org
Website: www.lacrosse.org

Materials available:

1. Coaching clinics

2. Teaching videotapes

3. Rule books

4. Lacrosse skills and strategies books

5. Books on history

SKILL	CUE	WHY	COMMON ERROR
Stance (Figure 15.1)	Point and step		
	Stand comfortably, weight evenly distributed on both feet		Stepping toward target with "stick side" foot
	Foot opposite head of stick should point to target		
	As throw is made, make a small stepping motion toward target	This is the direction you want the ball to travel; not stepping or stepping off target can cause the ball to veer off target	Not stepping at all
Grip	Opposing grip		
	With arms hanging by side, hold stick horizontal, in front, with pocket facing up		
	Bottom hand palm down, top hand palm up		
Bottom Hand	Palm the butt end		Leaving 1–2 inches of stick exposed
Top Hand	Shoulder-width apart		
	Approximately 18 inches from bottom hand	Hands too close together give very little control to a 42-inch stick. True for both offense and defense sticks	Sliding top hand down too close to bottom hand when throwing; some reduction of the 18 inches is normal, but do not let hands come closer than 6–8 inches
	Caress it with your fingertips		
	Keep handle off palm of hand and in fingers		Death grip, no gap between palm and shaft of stick
Release (Figure 15.2)	1. *Hands high* Promote hand and wrist flexion by keeping hands at least shoulder high while throwing and catching	The following 3 cues are important for a beginner to remember; they will prevent bad habits from forming that are hard to break	

continued

SKILL	CUE	WHY	COMMON ERROR
Release, *continued*	2. *"One, two . . . crack the whip "* A pull-push motion		Dropping below the shoulders or throwing side arm
	3. *Hit the box* Throw to target every time		
	Put ball in imaginary box that rests on receiver's shoulder		

Note

The top-hand wrist action needed to quickly snap the ball out of the pocket resembles the motion of a whip. In order for a whip to crack, it must first momentarily draw back before it is snapped forward. To help create this momentary "cocking" motion of the top hand, teach the throwing motion as a boxing coach teaches a "one, two combination." The "one" is the initial movement of the bottom hand toward the target (causing the top hand to cock back). "Two" signifies the whipping forward of the top hand. When done quickly in sequence, these two motions will "crack the whip," propelling the ball toward the target.

Keep hands shoulder high while throwing and catching   Hands high

FIGURE 15.1   Throwing

One, two... crack the whip
Quckly snap ball out of pocket

FIGURE 15.2   Throw Release

SKILL	CUE	WHY	COMMON ERROR
Catching	Vertical stick		Turning stick horizontal to keep ball in pocket
	Keep stick oriented vertically throughout catch		
	As long as pocket stays vertical, ball will be guided into belly of netting when it enters		Not having stick in vertical position before pass is thrown
	Give a target, here's your help	A vertical stick provides a target for the thrower both in practice and in games	Letting the stick hang by the waist
	Tilt stick toward passer and let passer know you are there	It lets the thrower know where you want the ball	
	Soft hands, catch the egg: Be gentle with ball and give way as it enters the pocket		
	Catch 'n' cradle: Immediately start a slight cradle motion after catch to "feel" ball in pocket		
Cradling Two-Handed	Opposing grip; bottom hand palm down, top hand palm up; hold stick with ball in pocket facing up		
	Dumb bell curl	Keep ball in the pocket by centrifugal force	
	Curl the top hand to shoulder		
	Nice and smooth	The 2-handed cradle is used by every player in the game; it is the easiest way to control the ball while running	Jerky wrist movements cause the ball to be lost
	Make sure curl motion is nice and smooth		

continued

SKILL	CUE	WHY	COMMON ERROR
One-Handed Cradling *Stick Orientation*	Carry the flag	Used primarily when close to or engaging the opponent	Letting the stick fall horizontal or to the waist
	Hold stick and ball with top hand only		It uses the body to protect the stick
	Hold on side slightly in front, keeping shaft vertical at all times		
	Open, open, open, close, close, close		
	Keeping forearm parallel to ground, coordinate movement of 3 joints into one smooth maneuver: • Open gap between forearm and body by moving stick away • Open wrist by cocking it back • Open hand by loosening grip • Close forearm gap • Close wrist by curling it in • Close hand by tightening grip		
Shielding the Stick	Shield at 45		
	Project free hand between yourself and opponent at a 45° angle to ground		Bending elbow more than 90°
	Show your number, hide your stick		
	Rotate shoulders to expose your back to opponent, completely hides your stick from view		
	Throw and elbow		Hand holding stick moving away from body instead of closer to it
	Elbow on side holding stick should thrust back, thus pulling stick in close to chest		

continued

SKILL	CUE	WHY	COMMON ERROR
One-Handed Cradling, *continued*			
Driving Through a Stick Check (men's game only)	Put up your shield before contact is made with opponent's stick		Reaching out and pushing off on opponent's stick
	Challenging the stick		(Penalty, "warding off," results in loss of ball)
	Drive through the stick, leading with stationary free forearm		Yielding to the check, stopping to see if ball is still in stick
Picking up Ground Balls (Figure 15.3)	Talk, talk, talk; there are 3 things to communicate each time a ball hits the ground:	Communication on ground balls is essential; if a player continues to block once the ball has been picked up, the player can be flagged for any number of penalties	Not making the ball or release calls
	1. *Ball down:* Lets everyone know a loose ball situation exists		
	2. *Ball:* Communicates your intention to pick up ball, thus teammates can direct efforts to blocking opponents who are within 5 yards of ball		

continued

Chest low, parallel to ground

Don't slow down until you are clear of the puck

Sprint through the scoop

FIGURE 15.3 Picking Up Ground Balls

SKILL	CUE	WHY	COMMON ERROR
One-Handed Cradling, *continued*	3. *Release:* Announces you have ball, thus telling teammates to quit blocking opponents; once ball is in your possession, they cannot continue to block for you unless they are in a stationary screen		
	Chest low; bend over at waist and get your chest parallel to ground; this helps shield stick from opponent's check	Using the proper scoop will allow you to scoop up the ball in any field conditions	Exposing arms and stick to opponents when reaching for ball
	Follow with the foot		
	More of a team strategy than a skill		
	Dragging foot after scoop often allows you to kick the ball in front of you for a second shot at it, should the first attempt be missed		
	Sprint through the scoop		
	Accelerate through pickup		
	Don't slow down until you are clear of the pack		
	Pick it up, give it up		
	Helps a team take advantage of an unsettled situation by having players look to move the ball quickly to other players with hopes of catching the opponent out of position		

SKILL	CUE	WHY	COMMON ERROR
Without the Ball	Occupy your man, control his eyes	Off-the-ball movement is essential; quick and even slow organized moves will create holes in the defense and opportunities for the offense	
	Keep opponent from watching the ball and contributing to team defensive scheme		Watching the ball like a spectator; not being aware if opponent is watching you or not
	Know where his eyes are, and if he takes them off you, cut behind him for a pass from the ball carrier		
	First cut away, then cut to: A player always wants to force the opponent to turn his back on the ball		
	When making a cut, first move should be away from ball carrier, thus forcing opponent to lose sight of ball	Moving toward the ball and bringing your defender into the area of the ball	
	Catch or clear, else you clog. When a teammate approaches you with ball, one of three things can happen: 1. Catch: You can offer to take ball 2. Clear: If teammate doesn't want to give it to you, cut through middle of field between goal and ball carrier; this takes your defender out of the way and makes room if the ball carrier wants to dodge 3. Clog: If you don't do step 1 or step 2, you will impede the offensive effort		

continued

SKILL	CUE	WHY	COMMON ERROR
With the Ball			
Driving and Dodging	North–south: Draw an imaginary line between ball and goal you are attacking	Movement laterally across direct route toward goal allows defender to recover and cut off dodger before he or she can get a shot off	
	Always try to move aggressively along this line when dodging		
	Speed in = speed out: Carry as much momentum into the dodge as possible	Keep your options open; if you can't get to the goal with the ball, maybe a teammate can, or already has	Slow starts, gradual acceleration
	Head up, find the open man: The defense will often double-team a dodger; keep eyes on teammate and find player left open because of the double-teaming		Dodger watches feet, opponent, or own stick instead of field of play while dodging
Bull Dodge	Power north–south: Drive through stick check with a solid 1-handed-shield cradle technique; stay close to the north–south line		
Face Dodge	Shake and bake: Quick fake to one side of of defender	Know which move you are going to make before you get to the opponent.	
Roll Dodge	Sin with the chin: Fake a drive to one side, then roll with back to defender, change hands, and drive down other side		Getting way off of north–south line, changing hands too soon, and dragging stick after the change in direction

SKILL	CUE	WHY	COMMON ERROR
Man-to-Man Defense	Maintain the individual defensive postures	Always maintain a position between your man and the goal.	
	Move your defense with your opponent		Lunging after the opponent
	Where he goes you go, stick to him like glue		Failing to maintain your individual strategy—they blow by you
Figure 15.4	One stick-length away		Someone else has to leave his man to pick your man, leaving an open man for outlet pass
Zone Defense	Cover everything in your zone		If you don't keep an eye on your zone, opponents flood it with people
	Split your peripheral view between the 2 offensive players		
	Talk lots		No communication is death
	Conversation between the defenders lets them know where everyone is	As in any defense, communication is key; it lets the other defenders know what's going on around them without having to take their eyes off their man	If you don't talk on defense, they're going to score a goal
Tips	For defense, talk talk talk: always communicate		Getting absorbed in game, forgetting to talk
	Be extremely aggressive on defense, lots of body-to-body and stick-to-stick contact		Out of position
	A good defender has to be very intimidating regardless of size: you know you're going to hurt when you go in his area		

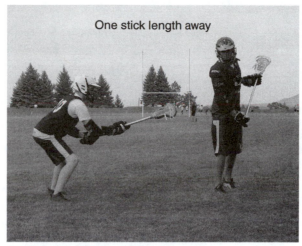

One stick length away

FIGURE 15.4 Team Defense Strategy

	GOALTENDING		
SKILL	**CUE**	**WHY**	**COMMON ERROR**
Quarterbacking the Team Defense	Goalie controls defense like a soccer goalie: *talk*	Goalies must communicate where the ball is at all times as well as instruct defenders when and where to move	Lack of communication
	Calls all the passes and movement of the ball; wherever the ball goes, goalie calls the movement		Concentration and focus elsewhere
	Goalie needs to have good self-opinion, has to maintain motivation of the team		Getting down on a teammate
	Goalie needs to be always up		
Playing the Ball	Goalie needs to move to ball		Not stepping out to meet the ball when possible
	Position body between the opponent with the ball and the goal		

16

Pickle-Ball

INTRODUCTION

Pickle-ball is a combination of tennis, badminton, and Ping-Pong that is played on a doubles badminton court (20 feet × 44 feet) with a perforated plastic ball and wooden paddles. The doubles badminton court on the gymnasium floor can be converted to a pickle-bill court simply by attaching the nets to the volleyball/badminton net standards at a height of 3 feet. Pickle-ball can also be played on the inside singles lines on the tennis court. Pickle-ball is an ideal lead-up game for teaching tennis and racket skills.

The strategies of the game include lobbing, overhead slamming, passing drive shots from the baseline, and fast volley exchanges at the net. The game is played by four people; a fifth person can be designated to be the scorekeeper, which helps accommodate large PE classes and provides the opportunity for that student to learn the official rules of the game. Many teachers have emphasized how pickle-ball has been effective in developing the students' reflexes and eye-hand coordination skills along with quickness and agility. Pickle-ball is a success-oriented game because after the player strikes the ball, the perforations slow the ball down in midflight, thereby promoting longer rallies and providing an equalizing factor for differences in strength, skill, and athletic ability. Many teachers are adding pickle-ball to their curricula because students can become successful with the game the first time they try it.

Pickle-ball is played mainly during the fall and winter months and is a good unit to present before tennis because many of the teaching cues are similar. For example, two cues used for the forehand stroke for tennis and pickle-bill are "Hold your arm in a cast" and "Finish on edge." The only major adjustment would be the longer racket. We have found that students who become successful with the game of pickle-bill are not as intimidated when learning the game of tennis. Another way to introduce pickle-bill is to start with a tennis unit, then add pickle-bill, and finish with a tennis unit.

FIGURE 16.1   Rainy Day

SKILLS LISTED WITH CUES

The cues for pickle-bill skills include the ready position, forehand and backhand swing (grip, stance, and stroke), lob and drive serves, volley and drop shots, top-spin, backspin, and the overhead smash. Also provided are cues for singles and doubles boundaries and scoring, along with singles and doubles strategies.

TIP

A pickle-bill unit can be presented before or after a tennis unit, or on rainy days during a tennis unit. One need not cancel a tennis class at any level because of inclement weather if one has a gym (Figure 16.1).

EQUIPMENT TIPS

1. Tennis courts, badminton courts, volleyball courts, playgrounds, walls with white lines.

2. Wiffle balls of all sizes, softball-size Wiffle balls for beginners.

3. Solid wood paddles. The ball contacting the wood paddle has a tendency to stay on the paddle longer, giving the player the advantage with direct shots on the court. Plastic on plastic tends to spray all over the place and will not stay on the surface of the racket as long. Players have a harder time controlling the shots, and fewer rallies occur. Longer rallies are the result of good equipment.

4. The length of the paddle makes a difference in performance because it is light in weight and short. Players can feel more control with the racket, especially with backhand shots.

TEACHING IDEAS

1. For large beginning classes, have players hit the ball against the wall 10 times. This exercise gives them practice hitting forehands, backhands, and the like by themselves. They progress to the net when they can hit 10 in a row.

2. Use the modified two-bounce-limit rule for beginning classes or less fit players.

3. Have players feed the ball to each other using half-court. This method encourages practicing technique and provides numerous practice trials.
   - Forehand and backhand baseline shot drill provides forehand and backhand stroke practice. This drill is practiced at the baseline.
   - Dink volley game: players stand behind nonvolley zone and hit drives back and forth like volley drills in tennis.
   - Hit offensive and defensive lob shots with a partner.
   - Overhead smash drill with a partner.

4. Volley the ball in the air with a partner. Your goal is to see how many times you can hit the ball back and forth keeping the ball in the air. This drill is good for eye-hand coordination.

5. Score on every serve. The side-out rule can be modified so that a point is scored on every serve. One player serves for a total of 5 serves, then the opponent serves for 5 serves until one player scores 10 points. If time permits, one player serves 10 serves, then the opponent serves 10 serves until one player scores 11 points. Different numbers of serves can be substituted.

6. Provide challenge drills, modified games, games, or tournaments set up before class. These "early bird specials" encourage the students to come early (Strand, Reeder, Scantling, & Johnson, 1997).

FYI

For further information and special help, consult the following organization and resource.

ORGANIZATION

Provides a free catalog on request. A rule book, 9-minute videotape for the game of pickle-bill, textbook, and equipment (paddles, balls, nets, standards, and sets) are also available at this address.

Douglas Smith, President
Pickle-Ball, Inc.
4700 9th Ave Northwest
Seattle, WA 98107
Phone: (206) 632-0119 or (800) 377-9915
Fax: (206) 632-0126
E-mail: info@pickleball.com
Website: www.pickleball.com

PUBLICATION

Curtis, J. (1985). *Pickleball for player and teacher.* Englewood, CO: Morton.

READY POSITION

SKILL	CUE	WHY	COMMON ERROR
Stance	Knees bent		Knees locked
	Weight on balls of feet to ball	Ready to react faster	Weight on heels
	Square to net		Not square with net
Move to Swing	Pivot and step for both forehand and backhand strokes	More control to hit ball in sweet spot of racket	
	Get racket back early		

TOPSPIN-FOREHAND STROKE

SKILL	CUE	WHY	COMMON ERROR
Grip	Index knuckle on ¾— like tennis grip	Puts racket in best position to make contact with ball	Choking the paddle, holding too tight
			Extending first finger behind paddle head
Stance	Pivot and step	Gets player ready to hit	Legs not moving, body is parallel to net
Stroke	Racket back early		
	Arm in cast; firm wrists		Bending wrists or arm
	Swing low to high	More power on ball; gives ball topspin	Scooping ball
	Wait for ball to drop		
	Hit ball in front of right hip	More control	Finishing with paddle flat
Pickle-Ball Drills: Have partners toss ball to partner: Toss, hit forehand Lots of balls Switch			

BACKHAND STROKE

SKILL	CUE	WHY	COMMON ERROR
Grip	Knuckle on 2—like tennis grip		Failing to turn racket
Stance	Pivot and step; get racket back early	Gets player ready to hit	Not taking racket back soon enough
Stroke	Swing low to high	Gives ball power and topspin on ball	
	Wait for ball to drop		
	Hit ball knee-high	Better accuracy	Face of paddle tilted too far up or down
Drill: Have partner toss balls to backhand; Lots of balls Toss and hit Switch places Have partner toss 1 forehand, 1 backhand; switch			

SERVING

SKILL	CUE	WHY	COMMON ERROR
Lob (Figure 16.2)			
Foot Placement	One foot in front of baseline, other foot in back of baseline		Both feet behind baseline
Toss	Drop the ball, then swing the paddle		Throwing ball up or not dropping the ball
Swing	Like pitching horseshoes		
	Follow-through straight up to hit face with biceps		Follow-through too low
	Finish like Statue of Liberty		

continued

SKILL	CUE	WHY	COMMON ERROR
Drive (Figure 16.3)			
Foot Placement	One foot in front of baseline, other foot in back of baseline		Both feet behind baseline
Toss	Ball held waist high and out in front		Ball held too high or too low
	Paddle is held behind you, waist high		
	Wrist in cocked position		
Swing	Drop the ball, then swing		Contacting the ball late
	Arm stiff, like a board, at contact		
Follow-Through	Paddle finishes on edge, shoulder level		
Drills:			
Partners serve lots of balls—to each other			
Partners serve Play the rally out			

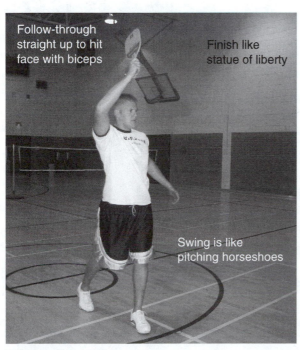

Follow-through straight up to hit face with biceps

Finish like statue of liberty

Swing is like pitching horseshoes

FIGURE 16.2 Lob Serve

Paddle finishes on edge, shoulder level

Arm stiff, like a board, at contact

FIGURE 16.3 Drive Serve

SKILL	CUE	WHY	COMMON ERROR
Ready Position	One foot behind nonvolley zone	Rule	Both feet in front of nonvolley zone (illegal)
	Paddle at eye level	React faster	Paddle held too low
Grip	Knuckle on 2		
Legs and Swing Action	Step and punch		
	Little or no backswing	More control	Too much backswing
	Slight turn of shoulders		Turning shoulders too much
	Meet ball in front of you	Better accuracy to place the ball	Letting ball come to you
	Keep racket in peripheral vision		
Follow-Through	Contact ball in center of racket		Contacting ball on racket edge
	Punch the ball, play patty-cake		Swinging too hard
	Limit follow-through		Too long a follow-through
Strategy	Play just behind nonvolley zone	Rule	
Drill: Feeds toss ball to partner behind nonvolley zone; switch; feeder hit forehand/ backhand volley to partner; switch			

DROP SHOT

SKILL	CUE	WHY	COMMON ERROR
Swing	Graze shorts with racket		Contact to side and front of body
	Slide racket under ball		
	Love tap/soft touch	More control, softer touch to ball	Hitting too hard
Contact	Open-face paddle to give ball underspin		Closing paddle face
	Push, lift, nudge, caress		Fakes opponent because of spin and short
Follow-Through	Look in mirror at finish		Paddle is on edge
Strategy	Swing like a ground stroke when opponent is playing deep		Swinging like a drop shot
Drill: Feeders hit forehand to partner, then hit backhand; switch			

TOP AND BACK SPINS

SKILL	CUE	WHY	COMMON ERROR
Topspin	Swing racket from low to high	Puts topspin on the ball	Swinging racket level
	Like making a candy cane at end of swing		Finishing racket on edge
Backspin	Racket swings high to low	Puts backspin on ball	Swinging racket level
	Shave the ball like shaving your face		Finishing racket on edge
	Cut flat under ball		
Drill: Try backspins against wall; then have partner toss to forehand then to backhand; then have a rally; try to use top- and backspin naturally	Follow through with racquet flat to the net		Stops at contact of ball

SMASH

SKILL	CUE	WHY	COMMON ERROR
Position	Get in back of ball		Too far in front of ball
Contact with Ball	Contact ball in front of body	Better accuracy to get ball down	Contact ball behind head
	Paddle face tilted toward floor		Paddle face tilted toward wall
Follow-Through	Like a volleyball smash		No follow-through
	Recover quickly to ready position		Off balance; can't recover to hit opponent's passing shot
Drill: Have 3 people hitting balls, 1-2-3, hit ball in air, partner returns ball in smash			

SINGLES

SKILL	CUE	WHY	COMMON ERROR
Boundaries			
Court	20 feet × 44 feet		
Nonvolley Zone	7 feet on each side of net		
Scoring	Can only score a point when serving (as in volleyball)		
Drills: After all skills have been taught, use this drill with 3 feeders and 1 hitter: Feeder 1 hit ball to forehand; feeder 2 hit ball backhand; feeder 3 short shot. Then feeders mix up shots. Hitters are to move all over court; rotate hitters every few minutes			

continued

SINGLES, continued			
SKILL	**CUE**	**WHY**	**COMMON ERROR**
Scoring, *continued*	When score is zero or even, serve in right court		
	When score is odd, serve in left court		
	Ball must bounce once in receiver's court as well as once in the server's court on the return: "bounce, bounce"		Volleying the ball before it has bounced once on each side of the net
	Play to 11, win by 2 points		
Strategies	Hit ball deep into opponent's court		Hitting ball in middle of court
	Hit most balls to opponent's weak side (usually backhand)		Hitting ball to player's forehand
	Hit ball to side to cause opponent to move		Hitting ball in middle of court
Server	Vary the serves—deep corners at opponents, hard, soft, etc.		
Receiver	Return ball to opponent's deep court		
Playing	Deep shots to sides		
	Weak sides when possible		
	Wait for errors, then attack net		
	Short volleys followed by deep lob to keep opponent off balance		
	Right at receiver		
	Mix up shots		Using same shot

SKILL	CUE	WHY	COMMON ERROR
Boundaries of Court			
Court	20 feet × 44 feet		
Nonvolley Zone	7 feet on each side of net		
Service Court	6 feet × 6 feet		
Scoring	Server must have 1 foot behind baseline without touching the line		
	Serve across the net diagonally		
	Must clear nonvolley zone		
	Ball must bounce once in receiver's court as well as once in the server's court: "bounce, bounce"		
	First service: team A, 1 player serves		
	Second service: both players on team B serve, then both team A players serve		
	Server switches courts with teammate if point is scored by server		
	Service always starts in the right-hand court		
Strategies	To mix up drive and lob serves		Using same serve
	Accuracy is key over power		Trying to kill shots
Front/Back	Shadow your partner; attack the net		Not following your partner
Side to Side	Don't cross the property line; each one is responsible for ball in own side of court		Playing teammate's ball
	When ball goes close to middle line, call it		Not calling balls
	Communicate		

17

Racquetball

INTRODUCTION

Racquetball is a game of geometric angles that requires agility, speed, and accuracy. One of the great things about racquetball is never having to chase the ball. Racquetball allows one to practice shots and court movements by oneself.

Players should work on their forehand and backhand strokes first. Other strokes, such as the ceiling shot, can be developed from the successful use of these strokes.

When learning the forehand and backhand strokes, many players want to hit the ball hard and fast, but hitting too hard causes the player to lose control. Practicing technique and accuracy will help the player progress to the ultimate goal of hitting the ball harder and faster with better control.

Learning to track the ball is another skill players need to develop. A player must watch the angle of the ball coming off the wall to anticipate the next shot. Experience is the best teacher.

SKILLS LISTED WITH CUES

Included in this chapter are cues for the ready position and grips, forehand and backhand strokes, drive and lob serves, corner and ceiling shots, strategy of service return, singles-game scoring and strategy, and cutthroat rules.

TIPS

1. Always wear proper eye protection approved by the American Amateur Racquetball Association (AARA), no matter what your level of skill is. The ball can travel 80 to 100 miles an hour.

2. Adequately warm up and stretch before and after games.

3. If out of position or unsure, play defensively.

4. Concentrate on proper footwork (i.e., body parallel to sidewall for proper forehand).

EQUIPMENT TIPS

1. Use of proper racket weight and string tension will prevent shoulder and arm pain.
2. Proper eye protection (AARA approved) is required.
3. Proper shoes that provide ankle support and gripping.
4. Be sure racket grip fits hand.

TEACHING IDEAS

1. Use the modified no-bounce-limit rule when starting with younger students and beginners. The player may allow the ball to bounce as many times as desired before hitting it.
2. Use the modified two-bounce-limit rule for older students, junior racquetball leagues, beginning classes, or players who are not physically fit.
3. Stop and hit. Step, drop, and hit. Set up off front wall, step and hit. Continual rally, step and hit.
4. Play with scoring on each rally. Both server and receiver can score points.
5. One player tosses ball to rebound off wall; the other player hits the ball. This drill can be done with forehand and backhand strokes.

FYI

For further information and special help, consult the following organization and resources.

ORGANIZATION

Jim Hiser
American Amateur Racquetball Association (AARA)
1685 West Uintah
Colorado Springs, CO 80904-2921
Phone: (719) 635-5396
Fax: (719) 635-0685
E-mail: racquetball@usra.org
Website: www.usra.org

Materials available:

1. Videos
2. Training materials
3. Racquetball magazine
4. Clothing

It's not always necessary to join a health club to play racquetball. Facilities are available for use at a nominal fee.

PUBLICATIONS

Edwards, L. (1988). *Racquetball*. Scottsdale, AZ: Gorsuch Scarisbrick.
Norton, C., & Bryant, J. E. (1986). *Beginning racquetball*. Englewood, CO: Morton.

READY POSITION AND GRIPS

SKILL	CUE	WHY	COMMON ERROR
Ready Position	Knees bent	Ready to move	Standing upright
	Weight on inside of soles of feet in order to push in either direction		Weight on heels
	Forearms on table	Able to move easily to forehand or backhand position	Arms (racket) to side of body
Forehand Grip	V shape, top of bevel		Gripping too tightly
			Choking up on grip
	Index finger positioned to pull trigger; squeeze trigger finger at impact		Incorrect placement of index finger
	Butt end of racket in palm of hand (for more wrist action)	Creates power	
Backhand Grip	Rotate V one bevel toward thumb	Allows for a more natural arm motion, reducing injuries and creating power	Failing to rotate grip from forehand to backhand
	Turn clockwise		

FOREHAND STROKE

SKILL	CUE	WHY	COMMON ERROR
Hit Prep (Figure 17.1a)	Shoulders parallel to side wall		Hitting with body facing front wall
	Set racket first, then step, and then pivot		
	Elbow above shoulder	More power; less arm strain	Rushed and incomplete backswing
Execution (Figure 17.1a)	Like skipping a rock	Low straight shot	No wrist snap
	Shoulders dictate aim of ball; shoulders parallel, hit parallel	Accuracy	Dropping front shoulder; lifting back shoulder
	Okay to contact ball at knee height; ankle is best	The more parallel to the floor and the lower the contact point, the less bounce	Hitting ball at peak of bounce or ascent
	Wait for it to descend		

continued

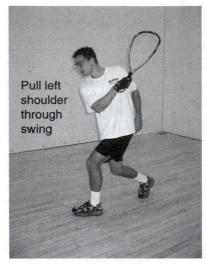

(a) Forehand Execution

(b) Forehand Contact

(c) Forehand Follow Through

FIGURE 17.1

FOREHAND STROKE, continued			
SKILL	**CUE**	**WHY**	**COMMON ERROR**
Execution, *continued*	Step into hit		Ball too high on front wall; racket face tilted up
	Shift weight from back to front		
	Hit ball off front foot or close to front foot, depending on shot		
	Watch ball hit strings	Accuracy	Watching target, not ball
(Figure 17.1b)	Elbow extension plus snap wrist on contact	Power	Wrist in a cast
	Follow-through	Accuracy/power	No follow-through
		Less arm strain	
Opposite Arm (Figure 17.1c)	Pull left shoulder through swing	Power	Left arm hanging at side
	Hit and move to center of court	Ready to retrieve opponent's next shot	Standing still, not moving after shot

SKILL	CUE	WHY	COMMON ERROR
Hit Prep	Pivot—step—set racquet		
	Shoulders parallel to side wall	Accuracy	Shoulders perpendicular to side wall
(Figure 17.2a)	Elbow pointing to ground		Elbow too close to body
	Hitting elbow about 4 inches away from body		
	Wrist cocked		Wrist not cocked
Opposite Arm	Elbow pulling racquet back	Create power on release	Keeping left hand on racket
Execution	Shift weight back to front	Body movement creates power	No weight transfer
(Figure 17.2b)	Okay to contact ball at knee height; ankle is best	Low level shot = less bounce	Hitting ball too high
(Figure 17.2c)	Push belly button to front wall	Power	No hip rotation
	Wait for ball to descend		
	Snap wrist, like backhanding someone	Power	Arm in a cast
	Drive through with hitting shoulder		
	Watch ball hit strings	Accuracy	Watching target or opponent, not ball

continued

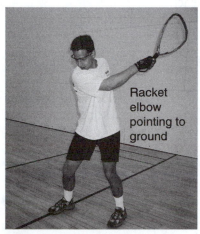

(a) Backhand Execution

FIGURE 17.2

(b) Backhand Preparation

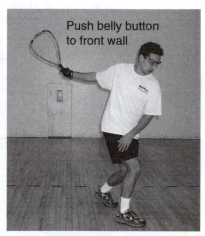

(c) Backhand Follow Through

BACKHAND STROKE, continued			
SKILL	**CUE**	**WHY**	**COMMON ERROR**
Execution, *continued*	Hit ball off front foot	Accuracy	Hitting ball into floor; hitting off back foot
	Shoulder parallel to floor through swing	Accuracy; shoulders dictate direction of ball	Swinging upward or dropping shoulder and skipping ball
	Follow-through at shoulder level		
	Racket in "back-scratch position" (allows for more wrist snap in follow-through)		Open stance
	Hit and move to center of court	Ready for opponent's next shot	Hitting and standing still

SERVING			
SKILL	**CUE**	**WHY**	**COMMON ERROR**
Drive	Visualize bull's-eye on front wall 1–2 feet up	Serve accuracy	Not having a target
Ball Drop	Contact ball between calf and knee		
	Drop ball to allow extension and follow-through or consistent drop		
	Drop—step—drive— move—follow ball		
Bull's–Eye	Should be 1/3 of distance between ball drop and side wall— not more than 1 foot from ground	Aim serve toward the corner—more difficult for opponent to reach	Hitting ball too high
	Hit and move toward center of court	Ready for opponent's return	Inconsistent movement
			Not moving to center after hitting
	Watch ball and know where opponent is		Not knowing where opponent is and not watching the ball

continued

SKILL	CUE	WHY	COMMON ERROR
Lob	Firm wrist	Accuracy	Wrist snap
	Elbow extended	Not too much power	
	Like pitching horseshoes		Hitting ball
	Soft touch		
	Like pushing ball instead of hitting ball		
	Contact ball between waist and shoulder		
	High follow-through	Accuracy	No follow-through
	Pull arm to opposite shoulder		
High	Soft touch	Accuracy	Hitting ball too hard
	Contact on rise 15 to 18 feet: Graze side		
Half	10 to 12 feet: Approach opponent at shoulder height	Difficult for opponent to make offensive shot	No follow-through
	Pull arm to opposite shoulder		
	Hit and move to center of court; gain position	Ready for opponent's next shot	Not moving after serve

CORNER AND CEILING SHOTS

SKILL	CUE	WHY	COMMON ERROR
Corner Shot (Offense Shot)	Pinch in corner	Use when opponent is deep in court—ball stays in front court	Hitting too far from corner and too high
	Low shot		
	Pinch—ball hits side wall and then front wall, or vice versa		
	Near side corner	Hit low on front wall so that it bounces twice before reaching the other side wall (otherwise the ball will pop up off the other side wall)	

continued

CORNER AND CEILING SHOTS, continued

SKILL	CUE	WHY	COMMON ERROR
Corner Shot (Offensive Shot), *continued*	Eyes focus on ball 1–2 feet from front		Eyes wandering
	Hit ball hard	Creates a spin and keeps ball in front court	Can't pinch ball if not hit hard enough
Ceiling Shot (Defensive Shot) *(Use when not in position to make an offensive shot)*	Forehand lob to ceiling		
	Volleyball overhand server motion	Accuracy	
	Aim to hit front lights depending on speed of ball	Should land about 4 feet from back wall and less than 4 feet high on back wall—very difficult for opponent to get an offensive shot	Hitting from wall first

SERVICE RETURN

SKILL	CUE	WHY	COMMON ERROR
Strategy *Beginner*	Keep ball and self in center court		No plan
	Consistency; try to read ball and play		
Intermediate	Control rally with return of serve		On the defense, not offense
	Read serve and place ball to control rally		
Advanced	End rally with return of serve		
	Read serve and place ball to end rally		

SKILL	CUE	WHY	COMMON ERROR
Scoring			
Server	Only the server can score points		The receiver scores points
	Servers permitted 2 serves		1 serve
Receiver	If the receiver wins the rally, the receiver gains the serve and the opportunity to score		
Winning Score	The first player to win 15 points		
	There is no deuce game, overtime, or requirement to win by 2 points		
Match Play	First player to win 2 games		
Each Player Wins One Game	If both players win 1 game, play the next game to 11 points		
	The first player to reach 11 points wins the match		
	Serve in tiebreak goes to player who scored the most points in the previous 2 games		
Strategy	Hit ball away from the opponent		
	If opponent is up close, hit far/passing shot		
	If opponent is back in court, use a dink shot/ pinch shot		
	Mix up shots		
	Mix up serves		
	Mix up sides of court you stand to serve		

RACQUETBALL SERVICE RULES

Single Fault Serves

1. Short serve: A serve that, after hitting the front wall, does not cross the short serve line before bouncing on the floor.
2. Long serve: A serve that, after hitting the front wall, hits the back wall before bouncing on the floor.
3. Three-wall serve: A serve that, after the front wall, hits both side walls before bouncing on the floor.
4. Ceiling Serve: A serve that, after hitting the front wall, hits the ceiling before bouncing on the floor.

Double Fault (Side Out) Serves

1. Two consecutive single fault serves.
2. Any serve that does not hit the front wall first. This includes hitting the front wall and another wall simultaneously (e.g., it bounces off a side wall, the floor, or the ceiling before hitting the front wall).
3. A serve that strikes the server or any part of the server's clothing or equipment.
4. Any serve that leaves the area of the court (e.g., through the observation window).

	CUTTHROAT		
SKILL	**CUE**	**WHY**	**COMMON ERROR**
Rules	Cutthroat is played with 3 players; a server plays against 2 receivers		
Server	Server has 2 serves		1 serve
	Serve has to hit behind second red line		First red line
	Must alternate hitting between server and 2 opponents		All 3 players hit
Receivers	When the server loses the rally, another player earns the serve		
	Rotate clockwise: Player 1 trades with Player 2; Player 2 with Player 3; Player 3 with Player 1		Rotate randomly

continued

	CUTTHROAT, continued		
SKILL	**CUE**	**WHY**	**COMMON ERROR**
Rules, *continued*	After each serve, player goes to the opposite corner of previous position		
Scoring	Only server can score points		
	Serve against the 2 opponents		Receivers can score if they win rally
Strategies	Hit ball farthest away from opponent		
	Go to middle of court after you serve or hit to be ready for the next ball		
Serving Rules	The ball may hit only 1 side wall and must strike the front wall first		A serve that hits the front wall and then either the back wall or ceiling is a fault
Receiving Rules	The ball must bounce behind the second red line before the receiver may return the ball		
After the Ball Passes the Short Line	The receiver must return the ball to the front wall before it bounces on the floor twice		
	The return may hit any number of walls first as long as it hits the front wall		

18

Recreational Walking
and Running

INTRODUCTION TO RECREATIONAL WALKING

Walking for recreation and health has become one of the most popular physical activities enjoyed by adults (Select Marketing Groups of America, 2000). Everyone knows how to walk, it doesn't require any special equipment, it can be accomplished anywhere, and it is a social activity that can be done with a friend or a group. Many people prefer walking over running because it is less strenuous, but they can still get health benefits from their activity. Research has shown that adults who participate in moderate intense activity (such as brisk walking) on most days of the week can significantly reduce their risk for heart disease, or breast cancer, and other health maladies (U.S. Department of Health and Human Services, 1996).

Since walking is such a popular activity for adults, it is important that walking for exercise be taught in the schools so that students learn to value walking as a health-enhancing activity. Physical educators should include some instruction on walking for exercise and give their students an opportunity to walk and be social in their classes. This kind of instruction can teach students that walking and talking together can be valuable and that they don't always have to work at high intensity levels to gain health benefits.

Lately, pedometers have become a very popular tool for monitoring physical activity and are especially useful for monitoring walking. Pedometers are small devices (about the size of a pager) that are worn on the waist band of pants or shorts. They measure vertical movement and can keep track of steps, time, distance, and kilocalories (depending on the model purchased). Pedometers are inexpensive, easy to wear, and easy to read and understand.

WALKING SKILLS

Walking cues are given on the following pages as well as instructions for how to use a pedometer. Additionally, a few introductory pedometer activities are described and some references are given explaining where pedometers can be purchased at a reasonable price.

WALKING CUES

Encourage good posture when teaching walking. Arms should be bent, head up with shoulders back. Walking is an even rhythm, and one foot is always in contact with the ground.

1. Head up, eyes forward, pull chin in
2. Swing arms
3. Shoulders back, tummy flat, chest out
4. Heel to toe

PEDOMETERS

One of the major objectives of physical education is to teach students how they can be physically active both in and out of physical education (PE) class. Walking is a highly beneficial physical activity, and pedometers are a simple way to monitor that activity (see Figure 18.1). Recently, a new pedometer has been developed that measures activity time and step count.

How Pedometers Work

Pedometers have a spring-loaded lever that registers a step count whenever there is vertical movement. Each vertical movement is counted as a step. While not all vertical movement is an actual step (standing up, sitting down, etc.), all vertical movement can still be considered activity. You should be careful to teach students that not every step count is an actual step. Help them understand that the number of step counts recorded can give them an estimate of how active they have been for a given time period.

How to Wear a Pedometer

Proper placement of the pedometer is important for the most accurate recording of steps. Pedometers are worn on the waist band of shorts or pants. They should be worn at the waistline, on the front side of the body, and be located directly above the knee (either right or left is fine). Pedometers should not be worn on the side of the body.

How Many Step Counts Are Enough?

It is important to teach students that step counts are personal. Not everyone will have the same number of step counts. The goal is to encourage physical activity. Some students will accumulate many thousands of steps in a day, while others will only accumulate a few thousand steps. The Presidential Active Lifestyle award (President's Council on Physical Fitness and Sports, 2001) recommends young people accumulate 11,000 to 13,000 steps per day. While this standard will give you an idea of how many steps they need to earn an award, it is unrealistic to suggest students who on a normal day might only accumulate 3,000 to 4,000 steps to set a goal of 11,000 to 13,000 steps. Externally imposed goals may seem unattainable for some students. Personal goal setting should be the objective. Allow students to take a few days to get a baseline of how active they currently are. Once they have a baseline, they can then set personal goals for improvement. A realistic goal for personal improvement might be to add the equivalent of a 30-minute walk to their goal (30-minute

FIGURE 18.1   Pedometer

walk = 3,000 to 4,000 steps, depending on pace). Regardless of the number of steps students are taking, making them aware of their activity levels and helping them improve should be the ultimate objective.

Ideas for Introducing the Pedometer to Students

Following are a few simple activities that will introduce pedometers to students. These activities can be done during the PE class and are designed to help students understand how pedometers work and how they measure physical activity.

Sprint 2/Jog 2/Walk 2

Students set the pedometers to zero. Have them sprint two laps around the gym and stop immediately when they get back to check how many steps they took. Let them catch their breath. Have them jog two laps around the gym and check their steps. Let them catch their breath. Then have them walk two laps around the gym and check their steps. Ask the following questions: Which activity gave you the most steps? Why? Is it better to sprint, jog, or walk? Why? Remember that the focus is that all activity is good for health whether you are walking, jogging, or sprinting.

Develop a Personal Fitness Routine

Have students pair up; challenge each pair to accumulate a total of 1,200 steps together. While one person does a strength (e.g., push-ups, sit-ups) or flexibility (stretching) exercise, the other person does an aerobic exercise (e.g., walking, jogging, locomotor movements) for 30 to 60 seconds. After 30 to 60 seconds have them switch roles and continue working. Every 30 to 60 seconds, they switch roles until they have accumulated 1,200 steps between them. The goal is to teach students to work together while learning that fitness is fun and step counts are personal. One partner may get 700 steps while the other gets 500 steps, and that's OK!! *Note:* It might be more motivating to have music that stops every 30 to 60 seconds, with about 5 seconds in between, playing while students are working.

Get in Sync

Have students select a partner. Encourage them to move in sync with their partner so that at the end of the movement they have the same number (or close to it) of steps. The team with the smallest difference between steps wins. The objective of this activity is to get the students to move in a synchronized way with a partner. Direct them to do walking, jogging, skipping A's, running A's, basketball slide, Karioka, or other movements.

Lowest Count Wins

The purpose of this activity is to teach students that exercise can be done that doesn't accumulate steps and to analyze different movements. Pair students up. The partners must come up with movements that accumulate the least number of steps possible. Partners with the lowest counts wins. They must do something in the following three areas:

1. Ten repetitions of an upper-body strength exercise with correct form (offer students choices)

2. Travel across the floor to the other side of the gym

3. Ten repetitions of a lower-body strength exercise with correct form (offer students choices)

Change Placement

The purpose of this activity is to find creative ways to get the pedometer to count movements that it traditionally does not count. Encourage students to try the following activities and to come up with a way to get the pedometer to accurately count the movement for sit-ups, push-ups, arm circles, bicycle legs, any dynamic stretch or core exercise.

How Much Do Pedometers Cost and Where Can I Purchase Them?

The cost of pedometers varies depending on the manufacturer and the features. All pedometers have the ability to monitor step counts. Many models have features such as date and time, stop watch, miles completed, kilocalories expended, and amount of time spent in activity. Prices generally range between $15 to $40. Educators who are buying multiple pedometers for their school may receive better pricing from vendors. For educators participating in the President's Challenge, pedometers can be purchased through their website. Another good resource for affordable pedometers is Walk4Life. See the FYI section on page 219 for website addresses.

Remember that the ultimate goal of recreational walking and using pedometers is to encourage active lifestyles. Walking is a highly beneficial activity that is overlooked in most PE programs. Teachers need not spend a lot of time on this unit, but including some instruction on the value of walking for healthy living is important. The resources in the FYI section at the end of this chapter will help educators develop appropriate activities for walking and using the pedometer.

RECREATIONAL RUNNING

By far the most popular forms of cardiorespiratory training in the United States are jogging and running. More than 17 million Americans jog or run to develop cardiovascular endurance. Why do Americans participate in these activities?

They require no special skills, expensive equipment, or unusual facility, and they can be performed alone (Strand, Reeder, Scantling, & Johnson, 1997).

Another great reason to run is the way it makes you feel when you're done: the brain is clear, the body is physically refreshed, and the feeling stays with you for hours. The key to running injury-free is to wear a good pair of running shoes. Once you have good shoes, it only takes the first step and you're off to a new adventure experiencing fresh air and different surroundings and letting go of the stress. Start today.

One advantage running has over walking is that a runner can cover a greater distance in a shorter period of time and thus can burn more calories. Jogging is defined as slow running at a comfortable pace for 8 to 12 minutes per mile. Running is defined as a faster pace under 8 minutes per mile (Strand et al., 1997).

RECREATIONAL RUNNING SKILLS LISTED WITH CUES

In this chapter cues have been structured for the following: runner's cues, uphill running, downhill running (short steep hills, gradual hills), building striders, striders, race course preparation, prerace routine, start of race, racing strategy, postperformance routines, and senior high school mileage.

TIPS

1. Have your runners hydrate well before, during, and after jogs, runs, and races.

2. It has been suggested that side ache can be related to weak conditioning, weak abdominals, shallow breathing, a large meal before exercise, and dehydration or excessive exercise intensity. Pain may be relieved by holding the right arm over the head and stretching the side. This condition is not serious, just uncomfortable to the runner (Strand et al., 1997).

3. A very important concept in running is that of pacing. In general, pacing means being able to run at a steady pace for a given length of time. Beginning runners have a tendency to start off too fast when given a certain distance to run. Soon they are walking because they have not been able to maintain the speed and have moved into anaerobic training. Teachers need to teach pacing in a jogging class and let students experience what it feels like to run at a steady state for various intensity levels for various lengths of time (Strand et al., 1997).

4. Have runners wear pedometers.

EQUIPMENT TIPS

1. Get a good pair of running shoes. Spend $50 or more and buy a brand-name running shoe. Make sure the shoe is comfortable.

2. Have water and towels available.

3. Wear clothing that is breathable.

4. Dress in layers for cold weather.

TEACHING IDEAS

1. Teachers sometimes get too caught up in the mechanics of running. If they would block out the upper body and see what the legs are doing, they

would often find that the runner has good mechanics from the waist down. The runner is doing what feels good to her or him. Remember that the runner is propelled along the ground with the legs, not the arms, head, or hands. Arms are for balance. Reasons why runners may not have perfect mechanics might be a leg length discrepancy, spine curvature, or individual structural difference (people are wired differently). You are fooling around with nature when trying to make major changes in the mechanics of runners. The more they run, the more they will develop an efficient and economical running style. Relaxation and running economy are the keys. It also helps to inherit good genes.

2. Prepare an activity in which students are required to walk or run at a certain pace. Have them check their heart rates. Switch the pace during the workout and see if they can hold that pace. Have students talk about what happened during their run. Did they go too fast or slow when they started? What happened when they tried to keep a steady pace? For more running activities read *Fitness Education* (Strand et al., 1997).

3. *Training for the beginning jogger* (Strand et al., 1997):

   a. Jog for 15 to 25 minutes; distance will vary from 1.5 to 3 miles; stretch.

   b. Jog for 20 to 30 minutes; distance will vary from 2 to 3.5 miles; stretch.

   c. Jog for 25 to 35 minutes; distance will vary from 2.5 to 4 miles; stretch.

4. *Training for joggers developing into runners* (Strand et al, 1997):

   a. Warm up with a 10- to 12-minute jog.

      Work out: four 800-meter runs, jog, rest 5 minutes between repetitions, stretch 5 to 15 minutes.

   b. Warm up with a 10- to 12-minute jog.

      Work out: six 400-meter runs, jog, rest 5 minutes between repetitions, stretch 5 minutes.

   c. Warm up with a 10- to 12-minute jog.

      Work out: six 600-meter runs, jog, rest 5 minutes between repetitions, stretch 5 minutes.

5. *Training for fun runs, 5k, 10k, and up:*

   a. *Warm-up ritual/routine:* Jog about 1 mile with flat shoes, stretch out approximately 10 minutes, jog about 1 mile, building striders (2–4). Make the warm-up similar to race preperformance ritual/routine.

   b. *Two workouts per day:* Start with daily early morning runs about 2 to 3 miles during training session at 70 to 80 percent of runner's top speed.

   c. *M–W–F afternoon workouts:* A hard workout might include Monday: long hard run; Wednesday: gradual uphill distance run; and Friday: fartlek training on a grass "hilly" park.

      T–Th–S: Easy workouts to finish running mileage for week's total.

   d. *Hard and easy weeks:* 10 to 15 miles one week, 20 to 25 miles the next week. Gradually build up mileage. Avoid overtraining as it causes injuries.

For further information and special help, consult the following organizations and resources.

PUBLICATIONS FOR WALKING AND PEDOMETERS

Pangrazi, R. P., Beighle, A., & Sidman, C. L. (2003). *Pedometer power: 67 lessons for K–12*. Champaign, IL: Human Kinetics.

Mize, M. & Decker, J. (2002). *Walking games and activities*. Champaign, IL: Human Kinetics.

President's Council on Physical Fitness and Sports. (2001). *The President's challenge physical activity and fitness awards program*. Bloomington, IN: President's Council on Physical Fitness and Sports.

Select Marketing Groups of America. (2000). *The superstudy of sports participation* [print]. American Sports Data. www.sgma.com/research/marketplace/superstudy_sports_participation.html

U.S. Department of Health and Human Services. (1996). *Physical activity and health: A report of the Surgeon General*. Atlanta, GA: Centers for Disease Control and Prevention.

WEBSITES FOR PEDOMETERS

President's Challenge
www.presidentschallenge.org/order_center/index.aspx
Walk4Life
www.walk4life.com

ORGANIZATIONS FOR RUNNING

Road Runners Club of America (RRCA)—National Association of Nonprofit Running Clubs
1150 South Washington Street, Suite 250
Alexandria, VA 22314-4493
Phone: (703) 836-0558
Fax: (703) 836-4430
E-mail: rrcaoffice@aol.com
Website: www.rrca.org

1. Provides information on local clubs.

2. Dedicated to promoting long-distance running as a competitive sport and as a healthful exercise.

3. Mission to represent and promote the common interests of its member clubs.

4. Running clubs join the RRCA for a modest annual fee and receive a range of programs and services in return. Services include nonprofit tax-exempt status, liability insurance, equipment insurance, and others.

5. Provides running books, videos, a curriculum guide for teachers and coaches, and a program guide for parents and children.

American Running Association
4405 East-West Highway, Suite 405
Bethesda, MD 20814
Phone: (800) 776-2732, (301) 913-9517
Fax: (301) 913-9520
E-mail: run@americanrunning.org
Website: www.americanrunning.org

SKILL	CUE	WHY	COMMON ERROR
Relaxation (Figure 18.2)	Work on drills to relax face, jaw, neck, shoulders, arms, and hands	Conserves energy, smoother running technique	Tensing face, neck, jaws, shoulders, arms, hands
	Repeat the word "relax" or other predetermined cues		
Breathing (Figure 18.3)	Belly breathing	Avoids side aches caused by breathing too fast and high in chest	Side aches caused by breathing too fast and high in chest
	Pouch stomach out as you breathe in	Side aches also caused by starting too fast when not trained to do so	

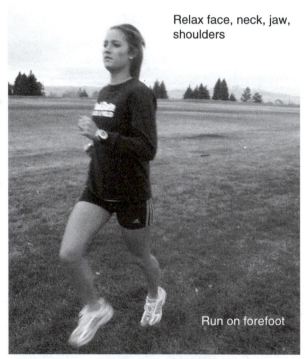

Relax face, neck, jaw, shoulders

Run on forefoot

FIGURE 18.2 Distance Running Relaxation Cues

Belly breathing

Pouch stomach out as you breath

Brush shorts with fingertips

FIGURE 18.3 Distance Running Cues

SKILL	CUE	WHY	COMMON ERROR
Uphill (Figure 18.4)	Short quick steps	Prevents overstriding	Overstriding
	Quickly get feet back to touching ground	Faster	
	Compact stride contained within oneself		
	Run on forefoot		
	May lean forward depending on steepness of hill		
	Maintain the hill and power over the crest of the hill	Prevents slowing down at the top of the hill and losing momentum	Slowing down at the top of the hill
Downhill _Short Steep Hills_	Brake to avoid falling and/or gaining too much speed		Gaining too much speed
	Use a heel-first running stride		
	Shorter braking stride		Overstriding
	Short quick steps		
	Bring arms out further away from body	For balance	Arms too close to body
	Power down the hill with shorter steeper hills	Prevents falling	

continued

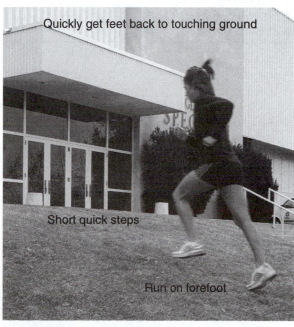

FIGURE 18.4 Running Up Hill

HILL RUNNING, continued

SKILL	CUE	WHY	COMMON ERROR
Gradual Hills	Make body perpendicular to hill		Overstriding
	Keep hips forward		
	Swing out arms away from body	For balance	
	Place foot under center of gravity	More efficient running technique	
	Let gravity work with you		
	Maintain body balance		

STRIDERS

SKILL	CUE	WHY	COMMON ERROR
Building Strider			
1–50 Meters	Start from jog, go into a good pace by 50 meters	Warm up for the race	Sprinting too soon
50–80 Meters	Accelerate to 80% of full speed	Get the muscles ready to race	Accelerating over 80% of full speed
80–100 Meters	Smooth transition to acceleration and then to deceleration		Decelerating too quickly
Strider			
Distance 50–100 Meters	Begin slowly, but by 50 meters athlete is at 80% speed		Athlete is over 80% speed

RACE COURSE PREPARATION

SKILL	CUE	WHY	COMMON ERROR
Knowing the Course	Go over course before race		Not taking time to go over course; arriving too late
	Walk or run course alone	Helps them focus	Running the course with team instead of individually; good for team unity, but all may not focus on course
	Have a tentative plan		
	Know where crucial hills and blind spots are on course		Daydreaming during course

PRERACE ROUTINES/RITUALS

SKILL	CUE	WHY	COMMON ERROR
Prerace	When countdown starts for the athlete, do not interfere	If the coach's job has been done well, there is no need for last minute coaching	Pep talks to teams and individuals just before race
	Athlete knows what is expected early in week		
	40–60 minute warm up before competition. Example: Athlete finds quiet spot; makes restroom stop; jogs about 1 mile; stretches alone; makes restroom stop; puts on spike shoes or racing flats; jogs; 2–6 building striders; walks or jogs 5 minutes		
	A shorter warm-up is needed		
Hot Day Warm-Up	Hydrate well all day		
	Warm up in shade if possible		
	A longer warm-up is needed		
Cold Day Warm-Up	Don't forget to hydrate	Keeps body in top performance; prevents energy loss; gets the muscles ready to go	

SKILL	CUE	WHY	COMMON ERROR
Start	Both arms down		Both arms up
	Dominant leg back	More powerful start	Weakest leg back
	Most weight on back foot		Weight even or too much on front leg
Leg action	Push off back foot first	Faster start; legs will be in correct running stride	Forgetting to push with back leg first
Arm action	Arms come up	To protect yourself at the crowded start	Left arm forward and left leg forward
Strategy			
Beginning of a Race	Begin race significantly fast in order to gain good position	Gives you a jump start	Getting behind at start
	Maintain good early position		Going out too fast for too long
	Be near front		
	Control breathing		High, quick breathing
	Find key people position		
	Fast and relaxed		
	"I feel strong"		
	Draw into oneself, the sport, and opponent		Responding to harassment by spectators
Tactics During Race (Figure 18.5)	Catch someone and pass 'em	Provides a specific goal on which the runner focuses	Not focusing on a runner or group of runners ahead of you to pass
	Catch someone and beat 'em	Keeps the mind alert	
	Don't get into no-man's-land	Other runners motivate and support you for maximum potential; less likely to give up	Not staying with the pack or another runner
	Don't run alone; stay with group		
	Focus on the runner in front of you by imagining that you are connected with a rope and are slowly being pulled in		

continued

SKILL	CUE	WHY	COMMON ERROR
Tactics During a Race, *continued*	Accelerate and pass runners after a turn, over a hill, or through trees	Discourages other runners	Don't attack or charge up hills; it's not energy efficient
	Blind spots are effective for 20–50 yards when runners cannot be seen		
	Use of groups is helpful to break opposing groups (extended acceleration of 100–200 yards)		
Finish Line	Run through the line	A better time	A racer might pass you
Postperformance Ritual	Flexibility exercises, static stretches	Blood is circulating in muscles to get a better stretch	Overtraining runners
	Jogging, easy running (no acceleration, flat terrain, training shoes)	A cool-down helps recovery; gets rid of lactic acid wastes	Could injure legs by overtraining tired muscles

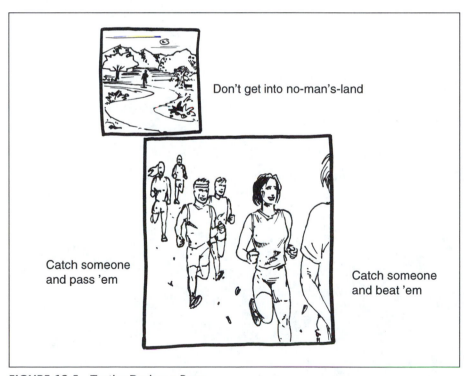

FIGURE 18.5 Tactics During a Race

	MILEAGE		
SKILL	**CUE**	**WHY**	**COMMON ERROR**
High School Distance Races	2–3 miles		Overtraining runners
	Cross-country distance is 3 miles (5 kilometers)		School schedules often require 2 competitions per week. If this is done all season, it may be too much racing
			Injuries from lack of proper adaptation time

19

Soccer

Soccer is a game that everyone can play, a game that keeps you fit and challenges you to the max. Soccer has been around for centuries and is played the world over. It has been termed the Sport of the World, and rightly so, because it is played in every country of the world. In most countries, it is more commonly known as *football,* and here in the United States it is known as *soccer.* What makes it so exciting is the challenge of a whole team trying to score. Soccer is a simple game, one that all students will enjoy.

SKILLS LISTED WITH CUES

The following soccer skills are included in this chapter: ball control and ball control drills; the dribble and dribbling drills; passing and two-player passing; chipping and two- to three-player chipping drills; the long-pass and two-player drills; trapping and trapping drills; kicking-shooting and kicking-shooting drills; heading; throw-in; goalkeeping; goaltending; defense; and offense.

EQUIPMENT TIPS

The first thing you need to consider is proper equipment.

1. A 12-inch ball is appropriate for 12 years and older.

2. One ball for every two to four students is recommended to practice skills. The students can work in small groups, with no standing in line waiting for a turn. This maximizes student involvement.

3. Students should wear comfortable clothes that are appropriate for hot weather.

4. Comfortable shoes (no sandals): Cleats are not needed at this level of play. Decide whether cleated shoes will be allowed in class. Be aware that some toes may get stepped on. However, cleated shoes are recommended for recreational soccer teams.

5. Shin guards are important in preventing injury to the anterior compartment of the shin (very little room for tissue and blood). It is recommended that all students have a pair, especially for games.

6. The field of play can be an actual soccer field or an open, grassy area at the school or a nearby park.

7. Use cones to outline the field. Flags can be substituted for goals. Half cones are great to use in drills. You can make a set of goals 3 feet high × 3 feet wide out of PVC pipe.

8. Use colored vests to divide students into teams.

TEACHING IDEAS

1. A warm-up should be included with every class practice. A proper warm-up includes moderate physical activity, such as jogging or a game of keep-away with the soccer ball. This, along with proper stretching, decreases the likelihood of injury.
   - Warm-up
   - Elevation of heart rate
   - Breaking a sweat is important
   - Ideas for warm-ups: running and dynamic stretching.

2. Safety Concerns
   - Emphasize the importance of playing with control and being aware of others' personal space. Use mini-games to reduce the number of players in a game situation.
   - Be prepared for accidents. Have a first-aid kit available and a first-aid plan.
   - Have plenty of water available during the activity, especially on a hot day.
   - Avoid playing during the heat of the day when possible.
   - Ensure no wearing of jewelry, shirts tucked in, and proper clothing for weather conditions.
   - Have proper warm-up and cool-down periods to prevent possible muscle injuries.

MINI-GAMES

1. Play games of 3 on 3, 4 on 4, and 5 on 5.

2. Scoring options in these games: ball goes over endline, 1 point; ball goes through two cones, 1 point.

For further information and special help, consult the following organizations.

ORGANIZATIONS

American Youth Soccer Organization
12501 S. Isis Avenue
Hawthorne, CA 90250
Phone: (310) 643-6455
Fax: (310) 643-5310
Website: www.soccer.org

U.S. Soccer Federation
1801-1811 South Prairie Avenue
Chicago, IL 60616
Phone: (312) 808-1300
Fax: (312) 808-1301
Website: www.ussoccer.com

Women's United Soccer Association
6205 Peachtree Dunwoody Rd, 15th Floor
Atlanta, GA 30328
Website: www.wusa.com

Major League Soccer
110 E. 42nd Street, 10th Floor
New York, NY 10017
Phone: (212) 450-1200
Fax: (212) 450-1300
Website: www.mls.net

U.S. Youth Soccer USYSA
1717 Firman Drive, Suite 900
Richard, TX 74081
Phone: (800) 476-2237
Website: www.usysa.org

SKILL	CUE	WHY	COMMON ERROR
Ball Control			
Knowing the Ball	Kicking the ball	To get familiar with the ball and how it works	
Kicking Top of Ball	Ball goes down (ball stays low)	Keeps ball low and in control	
Kicking Middle of Ball	Ball goes straight		
Kicking Bottom of Ball (Figure 19.1)	Ball goes up (like a pop-up in softball)	For chipping and defensive clears	
Kicking Left Side of Ball	Ball goes right		
Kicking Right Side of Ball	Ball goes left		
Ball Control Drills			
Juggling the Ball: Try to keep the ball in the air, using only the feet, as long as you can. Goal is 2 balls, then 3, then 4. Players who can do between 5 and 10 have good ball control.		Increases ball touches, familiarity with the ball, thus increasing ball control skills	
Experimenting with Ball (Partner Drill): Players strike the ball on the 5 surfaces listed above		Again, just getting familiar with all the different surfaces	

SKILL	CUE	WHY	COMMON ERROR
Dribble Technique	Caress ball in stride	If you push the ball too far ahead, a defender can easily steal it away	
Dribble Ball with Different Surfaces of Foot (Figure 19.2)	Inside, outside, sole, or laces		
	Close control; keep ball close	Keeps ball close and under control, which makes it much more difficult for the defender to gain possession	
	Push firmly		
	Head up, pull chin back		
	Arms out, with elbows bent for balance		
Action of Dribble	Depending on the situation, change pace and direction		

continued

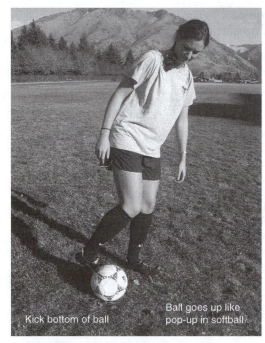

FIGURE 19.1   Ball Control

Kick bottom of ball

Ball goes up like pop-up in softball

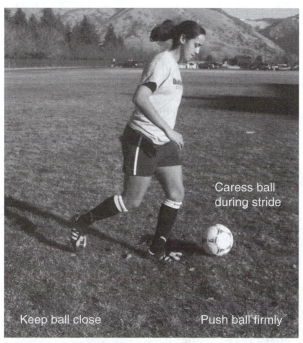

FIGURE 19.2   Dribble

Caress ball during stride

Keep ball close

Push ball firmly

DRIBBLE/DRIBBLE DRILLS, continued

SKILL	CUE	WHY	COMMON ERROR
Dribble Drills Using 6 or 7 cones for each small group, have students dribble through cones in a weaving pattern		Learn how to keep control of the ball while dribbling; cones help players control the ball. The goal is for the player to stay in close proximity to the cones	
Races			

PASSING/PASSING DRILLS

SKILL	CUE	WHY	COMMON ERROR
Passing			
Push Pass	Pendulum swing with the foot (like on a grandfather's clock)	For easy, quick passes to a teammate	
Foot Position	Ankle firm		
Inside	Strike ball with instep of foot		
Outside	Strike ball with outside of foot		
Laces	Strike ball with laces, not the toe	Don't toe ball, because there is no accuracy	
Striking the Ball Action	Knee over ball	To have more control and the ball won't go flying up in the air	
2-Player Passing Drills			
5- to 10-Yard Passes: Pass back and forth to partner, using different surfaces of foot		Gain familiarity with the technique of the push pass	
		Kicking with right and left foot gives you an edge over the average player, who can't pass with both feet	
Passing Accuracy: Player 1 stands with legs shoulder-width apart; player 2 tries to pass the ball through partner's legs; switch positions		Gain accuracy with the push pass	

SKILL	CUE	WHY	COMMON ERROR
Chipping the Ball			
Eyes	Focus on the bottom part of the ball	Clears the ball out of the defense, or for a pass over the opposing team to one of your teammates	
Approach	Approach the ball straight on		
Action	It's a quick, hard stab under the ball (like a shovel)		
	Bring your knee toward your chest		
Chipping Drills			
2-Player Drills: 1. Practice chipping to each other from 10–20 yards apart			
2. Accuracy: Mark off off an area 5–10 feet square using cones (the distance from each box is variable. Two players stand in the coned area and chip to his or her partner			
3-Player Drill: Player 1 passes the ball to player 2, who passes ball to player 3, and player 3 tries to chip the ball over player 2 to player 1. Rotate players so that each player goes to the position spot they passed to (player 1 goes to player 2's spot, player 2 goes to player 3's spot, and player 3 goes to player 1's spot. Repeat			

SKILL	CUE	WHY	COMMON ERROR
Long Pass		Used for crosses and shooting	
Ankle	Ankles firm (no floppy feet)		Stronger, more controlled pass
	Take a slightly angled approach		
Nonkicking Foot	Place it next to the ball	Helps create greater velocity in kicking foot	
	Toe is pointing at target, so ball will go to target		
Kicking Foot	Strike the ball with laces and inside of foot	More surface is on the ball, better control	
Used for Corner Kicks and Clears	Follow through with the foot pointed and leg toward the target		
	Strike the ball where the ball touches the grass; keep your ankle locked when striking; your leg kicks up and into the ball with a good follow-through		
2-Player Drills *At Least 20 Yards Apart:* Player 1 passes to player 2; pass back and forth; have players take a step backward each time they do a successful pass at that distance			

SKILL	CUE	WHY	COMMON ERROR
Trapping			To gain quick possession of uncontrolled ball
Trap	Absorb ball and soften the hit by moving your body away slowly	Controls the ball, brings it right to your feet	
Different Surfaces	Cushion the ball; stop the ball as if catching an egg		
Foot	Trap ball with soft feet		
Thigh (Figure 19.3)	Trap ball with upper front of thigh		
Chest (Figure 19.4)	Trap ball with breastbone		
Head	Trap ball with forehead		
Receiving the Pass	Present the trapping surface to the ball; take the pace off the ball by withdrawing the body part as soon as the ball is received		
Trapping Drills			
Each Player Has a Ball: Have the player throw the ball up in the air, and practice using the different surfaces to trap the ball		Helps player practice the skills of trapping	

FIGURE 19.3 Thigh Trap

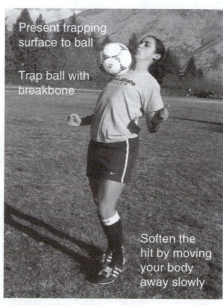

FIGURE 19.4 Chest Trap

Present trapping surface to ball

Trap ball with breakbone

Soften the hit by moving your body away slowly

SKILL	CUE	WHY	COMMON ERROR
The Kick (a striking action executed with the feet—e.g., the long pass kick, corner kick, goal kicks)	Body is stationary and leg is straight, with little flex at the knee; there is minimal movement of the arms and the trunk; concentrate on the ball; hold arms out for balance		
The Shot	Like firing a cannonball		
Leg	Pull back the kicking leg; have it pointing at the target		
Nonkicking Foot	Place the nonkicking foot alongside the ball, toes pointing at the target	Ball goes where the toes point	
Kicking Foot	After shooting, follow through. After the follow-through, land on the kicking foot (not the nonkicking foot).	Puts more power and control in the stroke	
Ankle (of Kicking Foot)	Ankle is firm, toes are pointing down		
Head	Keep head down and chest over the ball to keep the ball low		
Kicking/Shooting Drills Each player has a ball and faces the goal; have each player practice shooting on the goal (no goalie is needed). To prevent injury, don't retrieve balls until all have been shot			

HEADING

SKILL	CUE	WHY	COMMON ERROR
Head	Strike ball with top of forehead (where the hairline meets the forehead)	It doesn't hurt when heading on the hairline; more control	
Eyes	Keep eyes open—watch the ball meet your forehead		
Upper Body	Draw upper body back (pull shoulders back)	It will provide more power in the header	
Chin	Pull chin in		
Follow-Through	You strike the ball—do not let the ball hit you		No power in the header if you let it hit you
Torso	Snap the upper body forward to meet the ball (whip the body through the ball)	Most of the power comes from here	
Offensive Header	Head downward toward goal	Use offensive header for passing and shooting	
Defensive Header	Head upward	Used to clear the danger area	

THROW-INS

SKILL	CUE	WHY	COMMON ERROR
Throw-Ins	When the ball crosses the touchline into out-of-bounds, it is thrown back onto the field (which is the only time a field player may touch the ball with the hands), stand where the ball crossed the line and throw from behind the head (USSF rules)		

continued

SKILL	CUE	WHY	COMMON ERROR
The Throw (Figures 19.5 and 19.6)	Face the field		
	Use both hands		
	Start behind the head, and throw over the head (follow through with both hands)		
	Keep both feet behind the touchline; both feet must stay on the ground		
	Arms throw outward		
Follow-Through (Figure 19.7)	Body snaps through the throw	More power in the throw	
Short and Close Throw	Snap (arms snap down, hands and palms down)		
High and Low Throw	Snap up! Throw up and over		

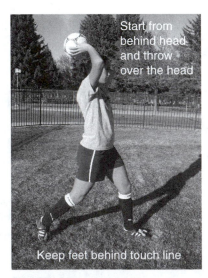

FIGURE 19.5 Soccer Throw-In (Hand/Arm Position, Side View)

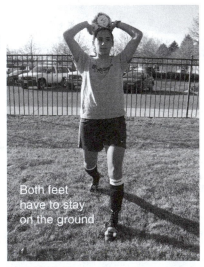

FIGURE 19.6 Soccer Throw-In (Hand/Arm Position, Front View)

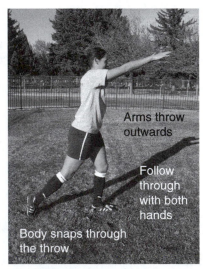

FIGURE 19.7 Soccer Throw-In (Follow-Through)

SKILL	CUE	WHY	COMMON ERROR
Receiving	Goalie calls for the ball		
Low Balls	Scoop into body with hands outstretched, fingers spread; wrap it up		
Hand Positions for Catching in Air	Big hands		
The "M"	Palms up, pinkies together; used to receive low balls		
"Hershey Kiss" or Triangle	Palms out, pointer fingers touching; thumbs create a "Hershey Kiss" or triangle	So ball will not slip through fingers	
Punching	Clear the ball away from the goal, using a flat surface on the hand	Used for high balls hit over the top of the goal; used when diving to hit the ball away from the goal	
Diving (Figures 19.8 and 19.9)	Lunge and cover lots of area with body		
	When diving, land on the outer of the thigh, hip, and side of the upper body; don't land on the knees		
	Reach out with hands		
	Catch the ball and pull it in		
Distributing Ball	Balls can be distributed by punting, rolling, throwing		

Big hands   Lunge and cover lots of area

FIGURE 19.8 Goalie Dive

Reach out with hands, catch ball, and pull in   Land on outer thigh, hip, and side of body

FIGURE 19.9 Goalie Dive Landing

GOALTENDING

SKILL	CUE	WHY	COMMON ERROR
Throwing (10–20+ Yards)	Twisting action will limit bounce for player receiving		No spin on release makes ball bounce and difficult to receive
Rolling (10 Yards or less)	Rolling a bowling ball	To make it easier for player receiving	Holding ball too loose
	Underhand pitch in softball		Too short a follow-through will not allow ball to reach target
	Roll in front of or directly to player's feet		Releasing ball too high causes it to bounce and be hard to control

DEFENSE

SKILL	CUE	WHY	COMMON ERROR
Tactics	Team gets compacts	To give attackers very little room to play in	Team is spread out in front of goal, creating space for attackers to exploit
	Players in front of goal will be close together, closing down goal-scoring options for attackers		Defense posture is loose, allowing goal-scoring opportunities
	*Stagger the defense for depth and support		Players are caught in a straight line across the field, allowing for penetration with a single pass
	*Delay opposition as far away from goal as possible to allow players to recover		Team in possession allowed to freely advance forward
	†Players closest to ball must provide immediate pressure		Closest individual defender does not delay attacker

*Important when the defense brings the ball up; supports the offensive attack

†Important in an attacking situation on defense

continued

SKILL	CUE	WHY	COMMON ERROR
Tactics, *continued*	†Keep playing space narrow for opponents by channeling toward touchline or supporting defenders		Defending with body square to attacker allows for options to the sides or through legs
	†Keep balance of team organized through communication		Confusion and disarray in defense through lack of communication
	If ball cannot be won directly from challenge, clear ball away from danger area either upfield or over touchline	Players in their defensive third of the field attempt to advance ball under extreme pressure and lose possession, possibly creating goal-scoring opportunity for opponent	
	*Once ball has been recovered, offense begins immediately	While defense is on its heats	Slow transition from defending to attacking
	Results can be achieved through man-to-man marking, zonal marking, or a combination		
Objectives	Regain possession		
	Deny penetration		
	Slow down attack		
	Stop shots		
Stance	Bend knees slightly, bend elbows (ready for action), eyes on the ball and the opponent		
Tips	Keep goalside of your opponent		
	Be first to the ball		
	Defend the ball, not the player		

*Important when the defense brings the ball up; supports the offensive attack

†Important in an attacking situation on defense

SKILL	CUE	WHY	COMMON ERROR
Tactics	*Offense begins immediately when ball has been won	To have many options that the defenders must contend with	Delay in transition may result in loss of possession
	*All players are involved in offense from point of recovery		Player fails to move into offense, limiting options
	*Create options by utilizing width of field (spread the field out)		Attacking players squeezing in toward center of field closes down space for players in possession
	†Quickly move ball into defensive half through quick, short, crisp passes to open players, directly to forward target, or thru dribbling	To open up more space for the attackers to play in	Delay in advancing ball allows defense to recover
	†Forward movement of offensive players not in possession creates dribbling or passing opportunities for player with ball		Lack of movement provides few options for player with ball
	Vary focus and method of attack		Team becomes predictable and easy to defend
	Creativity and imagination in final offensive third of field are vital to creating chances for scoring		Lack of imagination and creativity stifles attack
	†Taking risk in front of opponents' goal is encouraged as loss of possession does not create immediate danger	The ultimate objective in soccer is to score goals; therefore, always attempt to end attack with a shot or goal	Without taking risk in front of defensive team's goal, scoring will become difficult

*Important when offense begins an attack

†Important when offense is attacking and trying to score

SKILL	CUE	WHY	COMMON ERROR
Tactics, *continued*			Teams that play not to lose rather than to win develop players who find the game to be dull and boring
Dribbling	Keep head up; look for a pass		Body forward and erect
Off the Ball	Get goalside of the opponent		
	Penetrate the defense		
	Move into empty space, always creating chances		

20

Softball, Fast-Pitch and Slow-Pitch

INTRODUCTION

"Safe!" yells the umpire, as the runner slides into home. The crowd goes wild as the home team wins the tournament.

One of softball's unique features is that it is a hometown game that pulls a community together. Recreation departments accommodate people of different ages and provide opportunities for them to join youth, coed, female, and male leagues. Nearly every town, small or large, has a ball diamond where residents gather to enjoy the cool evenings and chat with neighbors while watching the game.

Opportunities to teach softball skills begin in middle school and continue though high school and college.

SKILLS LISTED WITH CUES

Softball requires a variety of skills: throwing, catching, windmill pitching, hitting, sacrifice bunting, baserunning, runner-on-base techniques, the catcher, sliding (straight-in slide), and slow-pitch skills. The use of these organized cues and progressions can be very beneficial.

TIPS

1. Going over players' positions before the season begins creates harmony and team success. Explain the mental and physical expectations of each player and her or his role on the team. For example, a player's responsibility might be sitting on the bench, warming up ready to hit or run, or perhaps to play second or third base if an infielder is injured or is not having a good game. A team member who plays second base in one game may play shortstop or be a defensive replacement in the next game. This approach develops a team concept, team cohesion, and a sense of personal

responsibility to and for the team. If a player makes an error, have him or her focus on the next play. Direct the energy into a positive focus. Pick up a rock, pretend the rock is the error, and toss it—get rid of it.

2. Make practice fun and competitive! At the beginning of practice have a verbal cue, for example, "blue." When they hear the cue "blue," the players stop and do what the coach explained they would do at beginning of practice. The coach can have a variety of motivational ideas or conditioning exercises to give to the players. For example, perform 5 sprints, 10 sit-ups, 15 push-ups, or some other exercise; give a high five to a player standing next to you; run together and laugh; tell a player something positive; or call a player's name, and have that player tell the team what they are going to do. At completion continue practice where the coach left off. Change off with hitting one day and defense the next day.

3. Vary practice so drills don't become monotonous.

4. Use of batting tees provides instant feedback and helps correct batting errors more quickly. Pitching machines build confidence in batting. Live pitching allows for game-like preparation and competition.

EQUIPMENT TIPS

1. Glove: Outfielder's glove is longer for more range; infielder's glove is shorter for more quickness. Use a batting glove under the glove to help pad it.

2. Batting gloves also can be used to protect the hand when diving back to base or sliding into base or when hitting for bat grip.

3. Boys, girls, women, and men should use a bat light enough to control and swing for quickness. Start with a 22-ounce bat for young girls and boys and go up to a 25- to 28-ounce bat for college-age athletes.

4. Sliding shorts, knee and elbow pads, and sweat bands are especially good for sliding drills to avoid scratches and abrasions.

5. Steel cleats add quickness and agility for defense, running base paths, and preparation for sliding.

6. Make sure equipment is comfortable and functional.

TEACHING IDEAS

1. Warm up arm: First throw short distances (emphasize correct throwing technique); then move to longer distances.

   a. *Progression drill:* Have a partner throw 10 ground balls to the back hand side, 10 on the glove-hand side, and 10 ground balls that need to be charged so that ground-ball technique is emphasized as well as defensive movement.

   b. *Short-hop drill:* Have a partner throw ball at receiver's feet or glove when in a defensive position, so the player can't catch it in the air.

   c. *Short underhand or overhand lob drill:* Correct technique, close and long pop-ups; 10 short hops: always catch with two hands; 10 pop-ups: call pop-ups, move feet, communicate "mine," move with glove tucked.

2. Quick-hands partners drill: Catch the ball with two hands, rotate the glove to see the ball, grip it, and get rid of it as quickly as possible. The goal is to see who can get rid of the ball the fastest while keeping the fundamentals in mind.

3. Soft-toss drill against a fence: Partner stands on bench or chair and drops ball straight down. Hitter works on quick hands, and ball contact.

4. Beach ball drill: Put a beach ball between knees, which forces one to stay closed with hitting. If one opens, ball drops—gives direct feedback.

5. Bingo drill: Place a batting tee and ball at home plate; place another batting tee and ball directly in front of the first tee. The batter's goal is to hit the first ball off the tee into the other ball straight in front of it. Yell "Bingo" if the goal is accomplished. This drill helps timing, batting stride, quick hands, and knowing where the batter should be contacting the ball.

6. Throw ball to fielders, progress to side/side, up and back, hitting ball with bat.

7. Lateral drill: All players line up at third base position; coach hits ball to first player in line. That player fields the ball, then throws home; moves to the shortstop position and fields ball, throws home; moves to second base position, fields ball and throws home; moves to first base position, fields ball, throws home. That player stops at first base and waits until last fielder goes. The fielders in line repeat the same drill. Everyone goes back around. All players in line encourage the fielder who is up.

8. Baserunning and defensive strategy drills are best taught without batting to permit more offensive and defensive plays (repetitions).

9. Give players opportunities to play all positions.

FYI

For further information and special help, consult the following organizations and resources.

ORGANIZATIONS

Fast Pitch World
P.O. Box 1190
St. Charles, IL 60174
Phone: (800) 591-1222

1. Equipment, notebooks, techniques, rules, and umpire information
2. Video: 12 fast-pitch USA videos
3. *Fast Pitch World Magazine*

All junior high, high school, and college coaches are welcome to become members of the National Softball Coaches Association.

National Softball Coaches Association (NSCA)
409 Vandiver Drive Suites
Columbia, MO 65202

PUBLICATION

Kneer, M. E., & McCord, C. L. (1995). *Softball: Slow and fast pitch*. Dubuque, IA: Brown and Benchmark

VIDEOS

Baseball World's *Defensive Drill Video* with Tom Emanski.
A proven training program that improves arm strength, running speed, practice organization, infield/outfield skills, quickness and agility.

Simple Hitting for Youth Coaches, Parents and Players.
Presented by the Rob Andrews Baseball Camps (former MLB player)
Concord, CA

THROWING			
SKILL	**CUE**	**WHY**	**COMMON ERROR**
Grip	Hold ball in pads of 2 fingers	Ball control	Gripping the ball in palm
	Grip ball lightly		
Stance	Stand sideways	Pointing glove helps to know where the ball is being thrown	Standing forward
	Point glove-hand shoulder at target as well as glove		
Throwing Action (Figure 20.1)	Take a long step toward target		Not stepping, stepping too high, stepping across the body
	Keep knees bent		
	Take arm straight down and stretch it way back		Bringing ball behind head
	Make an L with throwing arm		
	Wrist snap	Puts the "zing" on the ball	Keeping weight on back foot
	Follow-through with throwing hand to opposite knee		
Focus of Eyes	Both eyes focus on target	Look where you want the ball to go	Looking anywhere else or path of ball

FIGURE 20.1 Throwing the Ball

FIELDING A GROUND BALL

SKILL	CUE	WHY	COMMON ERROR
Glove (Figure 20.2)	Put fingers of glove in dirt	So balls don't go under the glove	Glove too high
	Keep glove hand palm up, throwing hand with palm down as a shield (aka Venus's Flytrap)	Protects from bad hops hitting one's face	
	Keep glove in front of body	Won't lose track of the ball	Glove off to side of body or behind oneself
Body	Keep body square to ball		Body too high off the ground and stiff
	Keep a good stance		
	Keep buttocks down, like sitting on a stool	Allows for position readjustment if needed	Standing tall
	Stay behind ball		
	Keep knees flexed		
	Head down, chin down		Pulling head
	Eyes on ball		
Action	Call for the ball		
	Give target with both hands	Tells where you want the ball thrown	
	Reach out with hands, pull ball in		Hands too close to body
	Give with ball		Not pulling ball in
	Spread fingers over ball		
	Catch with both hands	Decreases the chance of balls popping out	
Focus of Eyes	Watch ball go into glove or fingers		Taking eyes off ball; not tracking the ball

FIGURE 20.2 Catching and Fielding a Ground Ball

SKILL	CUE	WHY	COMMON ERROR
Glove	Out in front of body		Palm up or glove to side
	Raise glove toward ball		Glove down
Body	Square to ball		Side to ball
	Point fingers upward, thumbs together		Fingers down, hands apart
	Fingers toward sky; thumbs touch		
	Stay behind ball but make one's momentum forward	Forward momentum puts more power behind one's throw	Not getting behind ball
	Block out sun	Don't lose the flight of the ball	
	Get feet in throwing position after catch		
Action	Soft glove		
	Give with catch		Arms stiff
	Cover ball with throwing hand	Balls don't pop out	Catching with one hand
	Catch ball with both hands		
Focus of Eyes	See ball all the way into glove		Looking away too soon in haste to make throw

SKILL	CUE	WHY	COMMON ERROR
Hard Hit	Catch ball as if it were an egg (aka soft hands)		Body stiff and hard hands
	Give with ball; funnel into waist		
	Glove down		
	If you can, get in front of ball	Getting in front of ball gets you in better position to throw afterwards	
Slow Hit	Get behind ball		
	Charge slow balls		Waiting for ball
	Scoop ball as if with a shovel, but keep glove down		
Rolling Ball	Pick and throw on the run	Saves time for your speedier runners	Using the glove to "pick" and then throwing
	Use hand to pick and throw if time is of essence		
Focus of Eyes	See ball all the way into glove	Don't lose path of ball	Looking away or looking at runner
Chin	Keep head down with chin on chest as you go down	Head down, chin down decreases chance of getting hit in throat, face, or chin	Pulling head up too soon
Throwing Hand	Place above glove hand like a Venus's-flytrap for production		Hand prevents bad hops from hitting one's face

SKILL	CUE	WHY	COMMON ERROR
Stance	Square to target	Proper presentation of ball	Perpendicular to target
	Keep front heel and back toe on rubber		No contact with rubber
Grip	3-finger grip (thumb and 3 fingers)	Ball control	Holding ball in palm of hand
	Hold ball in fingers, without palm touching ball		
	Keep ball in glove or hand, waist high		Ball too high or too low
			Ball not in glove
Arm Swing (Figure 20.3)	Raise hand above head		Bringing arm to side
	Momentum should go back to front		
	Back-circle to release point		
Release (Figure 20.4)	Release ball at hip	Pitch's path is level	Releasing in front or behind hip
	Keep weight back		
	Turn belt buckle to target	Hips give the power behind the ball	Letting arm do all the work

continued

Raise hand above head

Back-circle to release point

Release ball at hip

FIGURE 20.3 Arm Swing for Windmill Pitch

Turn belt buckle to target

Snap wrist on release

Push off rubber with back foot

FIGURE 20.4 Release for Windmill Pitch

Softball: Fast-Pitch and Slow-Pitch **251**

WINDMILL PITCH, continued			
SKILL	CUE	WHY	COMMON ERROR
Release, *continued*	Make sure to rotate hips		
	Snap wrist on release	Wrist snaps put the spin on the ball	Keep wrist stiff
	Keeping wrist relaxed		
	Follow-through after wrist snap		Bending elbow as hand finishes up by head
	Point toe at catcher	Push-off puts final momentum on ball	Not striding directly at plate
	Push off rubber with back foot		

HITTING			
SKILL	CUE	WHY	COMMON ERROR
Stance	Stand sideways		Standing forward
	Feet slightly wider apart than shoulder width		Feet too far apart or too close together
	Weight over balls of feet		Weight on heels
	Heels lightly touching the ground		
	More weight on back leg (80%/20%)	Weight back decreases the chances of lunging toward the ball; more power to hit ball	Weight on left leg during the swing
	Front shoulder slightly lower		
Arm Swing	Hitter should think "shoulder to shoulder" (start swing with chin on front shoulder; finish swing with chin on back shoulder), aka "Ike to Mike"		Moving head during the swing
			Head too tense

continued

SKILL	CUE	WHY	COMMON ERROR
Hip Rotation	Snap or rotate back hip at pitcher, drive body through ball, take photograph of pitcher with belly button	Rotating hips provide the power; keeping 80% on back leg gives more power	No rotating hip
	Throw hands through softball: "Slow feet, quick hands"		Using arms instead of wrists
Focus of Eyes		Middle ball contact is solid contact	Not seeing ball hit bat
	Watch ball all the way into catcher's mitt		
	Watch spin and delivery of ball	Pitch detection	
Step	Step 3–6 inches (stride should be more of a glide)		Overstriding causes bat to drop during swing (jarring step)
	"Step to Hit"		Hitter "steps and then hits"
	Step toward catcher with weight on ball of foot	So you don't have upper-body fly open	Stepping "in the bucket"
	Keep front shoulder level		
Follow-Through	Top hand rolls over bottom hand; bat goes all the way around the body		
	Take your right palm to the pitcher; draw a straight line through your chest with left thumb	Leads to quicker hands	
Teaching Progressions	Teach cues in order given (first 3); then add others as needed		Give cues in 3's to avoid information overload
	Remember the 4 basic steps to hitting: 1. Coil weight on back leg 2. Stride 3. Pivot 4. Pop		

SKILL	CUE	WHY	COMMON ERROR
Checkpoints for Coaches	If the batter is not gripping, standing, or holding the bat correctly, coach could correct the player individually	Personal feedback is always more beneficial	Don't use these cues unless a player needs assistance; give 1 at a time
Grip	Hold bat in base of fingers (this technique allows wrist to roll freely and generates bat speed)	Holding bat in palm of hand; squeezing too hard	Loose grip allows for greater wrist rotation/ extension and relaxes forearms
	Align knuckles		
Closed Stance	Place feet shoulder-width apart, then move front foot toward plate (helps untrained hitter step toward pitcher)	Keeps hips in control	Stepping back
			Flying open
Bat Position	Bat held armpit high and far enough away from the body that both of the player's fists could fit	Bat up allows you to stay above the ball	
	Front elbow should resemble an L shape		
	Back elbow held away from body (aka "the box")		Holding bat too close to shoulder
Bat Angle	Straight up in air or up and angled slightly over back shoulder		Cradling bat around head; bat pointing back toward pitcher

SACRIFICE BUNT

SKILL	CUE	WHY	COMMON ERROR
Grip	Grip bat lightly with thumb and 2 fingers		
	Pinch the bat		
Action	Pivot with back foot toward pitcher, square body to pitcher	Presents the bunt	Keeping side toward pitcher
	Bend knees	Allows to go up or down with pitch rather than one's bat	Legs straight
	Slide top hand up to trademark, keep bat at a 45° angle	45° angle helps to push ball to ground and not in the air when contacted	Not keeping bat level at 45°
	Place bat in front of plate at top of strike zone	Increases the likelihood of ball being fair	Keeping bat behind body
	See ball all the way in		
Contact	Play catch with ball	Softens bunt, deadens ball, allows for ball/ bunt placement	Dropping bat to ball
	Give with the ball (aka softhands)		Swinging at a ball
			Going for a pitch out of a strike zone
	Bunt strikes!!!		

Running to First	Push off with back leg	Legs provide one's power	Swinging arms wildly
	Run through base, then breakdown	So momentum doesn't slow	Pointing toes out
	Dig dig dig		Shortening or lengthening stride
	Full acceleration		
	Run with form and run relaxed		Leaping at base, which leads to injury
	Hammer nails		
Extra Base	Make loop midway to base	So you are in position to advance to the next base	Looking at base
			Cutting too early or late
	Hit inside of base	Shortens base path	Hitting outside of base
	Round bag hard and jog back if necessary		Looping too wide
	Always look for the extra bag	Aggressive baserunning is the difference between winning and losing	

SKILL	CUE	WHY	COMMON ERROR
Ready Position	Square body to next base		Keeping body perpendicular
	Take stagger start	Allows for better push-off from base	Keeping feet together
	Keep right foot a stride behind base		
	Push off left foot, stride with right		
Break	Find the pitcher's rhythm	Helps to establish when to lead off	
	Start stride at top of pitcher's windup	Gives you a good jump	Leaving before pitch is released; however, early is better than late

continued

	RUNNER ON BASE, *continued*		
SKILL	**CUE**	**WHY**	**COMMON ERROR**
Break, *continued*	Push off at release or a little prior to		
	Rock'n'go, back-front	Adds to one's momentum	
Approach	Pump arms with stride		
	Hammer in nails		
	Round base and look for coach		

	THE CATCHER		
SKILL	**CUE**	**WHY**	**COMMON ERROR**
Stance	Crouch over balls of feet	Proper stance allows for good reaction time, especially on toes	Body held erect with weight over heels or down on knees
	Align right toe with left heel, toes out (slightly staggered stance)		
	Keep weight over balls of feet		
	Keep knees flexed, butt down		
Glove	Hold glove out as target in front of body	Big glove target gives pitcher an idea where where you want the ball	Holding glove to one side or the other and not out in front of body enough
	Relax hands, give steady big target		Arms and hands stiff
	Runner on: Keep bare hand alongside (slightly behind) glove No runner on: Bare hand behind back	Hand by glove with runner on increases the transition time from receiving to throwing	

continued

SKILL	CUE	WHY	COMMON ERROR
Receiving	Pitch above waist: Fingers up		
	Pitch below waist: Fingers down		
	Frame pitch by catching outside of ball	Framing increases your strikes to ball ratio	
	Block ball in dirt with body with head pulling down		Trying to catch ball in dirt
	Relax hands and draw body in	Relaxed hands give with the ball, which means less bubbled balls	Arms and hands stiff; unable to cushion ball
	Keep weight on the balls of feet		Being caught on one's heels
	Move body over to get in front of and receive inside or outside pitches	Decrease the chances of pass balls	Standing still and trying to reach to one side or other to catch, which leads to pass balls
	Let ball come to you, don't reach		
Throwing	Get up quickly but keep body low, explode forward, drive with legs	Body low keeps ball on direct path to target	Sitting on heels and not getting into throwing position
		Body low is quicker and puts more power behind throw	Standing straight up, which leads to many overthrows
	Push off ball of back foot, step directly toward target with front foot	Less overthrows	Looking at the runner or covering person
	Keep eyes directly on final target		
	Trust your throw!		

SKILL	CUE	WHY	COMMON ERROR
Approach	Inside corner of base on infield side of base (ball is in outfield)	Sliding to the corners of bags positions you to avoid the tag	Sliding straight into plate, which may injure lower extremity
		It is the differ B/W safe and cut	
	Outside corner of base on outfield side of base (ball is in infield)		
Sliding Action (Figure 20.5)			
Leg Action	Lead with top leg straight, bottom leg bent under (looks like a number 4)	Number 4 with legs increases one's momentum toward the base	Not getting bottom leg bent under, resulting in slides upon the knee; not fun
	Slide on outside of calf, thigh, and buttocks		
Torso Action	Sit down		Sitting straight up
	Lean back, relax back	Leaning back keeps one's slide momentum forward	Body tense
Arms	Touchdown signal	Arms above head (prevents injuries)	Dragging arms and hands slows slide, so keep them up

continued

Touchdown signal with arms

Number 4 with legs

Stop scooter with heel, sole up

FIGURE 20.5

SKILL	CUE	WHY	COMMON ERROR
Sliding Action, *continued*			
Head Position	Back with closed fists	Eyes on play lets you know where the ball is, for you may not need to slide	Keeping head up, resulting in a tag in face or head
	Eyes on play		
Base Contact	Lead with heel, like stopping a scooter or slide, sole up	Soles up decreases the likelihood of injury and doesn't slow one toward the base	Soles down and getting cleats stuck in dirt
	Straight leg, but don't hyperextend		Straight leg doesn't give when base is contacted

SLOW-PITCH SOFTBALL DIFFERENCES

1. There are 10 or 11 players rather than 9 players as in fast-pitch.
2. Tenth player extra on defense, called short fielder or rover, plays anywhere on the field.
3. Eleventh player, extra hitter (EH), may not be used on defense. Not allowed in coed slow-pitch.
4. Leading off and stealing bases are not allowed.
5. Bunting is not allowed.
6. Batting requires a lot of patience if you are used to fast-pitch. Basically wait longer for the ball, let the ball come to you, and don't reach for the pitch.
7. Pitched ball must travel through an arc between 6 and 12 feet high.

SLOW-PITCH STRATEGIES

1. Pitch the ball so it is as close to 12 feet high as possible when it is close to the batter.
2. Make the ball drop quickly as it crosses the plate. Placing a forward, backward, or sideward spin on the pitch is also a commonly used legal strategy. One foot must be in contact with the pitching plate when the pitch is released.

SKILL	CUE	WHY	COMMON ERROR
Underhand Slow Pitch			
Grip	Like throwing a ball normally		Gripping the ball too tightly
Setup	Ball in front of chest	Allows for proper presentation of ball	
	Both feet parallel on mound		
	Feet not quite shoulder-width apart		
Arm Action	Pendulum swing	Allows for the pitch's momentum	
Stepping Action	Step with foot opposite to throwing arm	Enhances ball arc, spin, and momentum	
Releasing the Ball	Release ball out in front of you at belt height		
Batting			
Batting Action	The key to slow-pitch batting is waiting for the ball	Let the ball travel to you until it is in your power zone, then explode!	Swinging too soon
	Be patient, be relaxed		Swinging too soon
	Focus eyes on ball spin	To detect the ball's movement and inside or outside pitch recognition	Eyes wandering
			Big eyes
	Swing level	Level contact equals solid, line drive contact	Reaching too high
			Trying to hit it like a golf swing

21

Strength Training

INTRODUCTION

"In the early 1900s Alan Calvert developed adjustable barbells with weighted plates that could be added or removed to change the resistance. In more than 80 years few changes have altered his basic design" (Allsen, Harrison, & Vance, 1983, p. 129).

Free weights have an advantage over machines in that they require the participant to balance the weights when lifting, using more muscles and training all muscle groups. When using free weights, the student progresses more quickly than when using machines. Many bodybuilders prefer free weights.

The use of weights in adolescent strength training is an important part of each person's development. Training adolescents should use dumbbells and training bars to teach correct techniques and form. There is no need to go heavy at this young age, but teaching proper mechanics is important. We start kids playing sports early; why not teach kids strength training under proper supervision? To include weight lifting in the curriculum, teachers need to have the appropriate equipment and be able to offer a weight-lifting program for at least six weeks (the time it takes for the body to adapt to the regimen). By using a different lift for the same muscle group the student can continue to progress.

The purpose of strength training is to achieve your potential. The benefits include increased muscle mass, increased strength and power, increased personal and sport performance, increased self-esteem, and conquering personal challenges.

SKILLS LISTED WITH CUES

We provide cues for the following free-weight lifts: squat, bench press, power snatch, and power clean, as well as safety guidelines. Also provided are guidelines for core exercises: push-ups, sit-ups, and dips.

FIGURE 21.1 Push-Ups, Sit-Ups, and Dips Develop Rapid Strength Gains

TIPS

1. Each muscle group should be exercised two or three days a week.
2. Stretch before and after lifting.
3. Complete the full range of motion during any lift. Don't do partial or half movements.
4. Lifting weights should be a controlled movement. Avoid jerking movements. The positive move (concentric) is usually faster than the negative move (eccentric).
5. Push-ups (modified or regulation), sit-ups, abdominal curls, and dips are great strength exercises that develop the core and that can be done any time, any place (Figure 21.1).
6. Core training is essential to being a well-rounded athlete and should be done during each lift session. It can be done every day.

EQUIPMENT TIPS

1. Use two chairs or benches to perform modified dips.
2. Use mats, carpet squares, or grass to perform sit-ups and abdominal curls.
3. Stability balls should be used in core training.

TEACHING IDEAS

1. Have students chart their progress. Class or individual charts can be used. Students are motivated by seeing their progress.

2. Provide weight-lifting picture charts in weight rooms for students to refer to. These pictures can help teach correct weight-lifting techniques.

3. Always train with a partner, and train with one who has comparable strength. The partner spots the weight for the weight lifter. This method saves time because the partners don't have to keep changing the weight on the bar.

CORE EXERCISES

What is the core? Why is it important to develop the core? The whole body is a pillar—head over shoulders, shoulders over hips, and hips over feet. The center and the most important part of the pillar is the *core* consisting of the area between the bottom of the rib cage and bottom of thigh both front and back. The development of the core is critical because it involves the center of all motion. Developing the core muscles can help improve performance in every sport. There are a variety of exercises to develop the core, including push-ups, abdominal work, and back extensions. While performing each exercise in a lifting session, the athlete should focus on his or her core while completing the lift.

Push-Ups

Start with 10 push-ups per day; work up to 50 to 300 a day.

1. Regulation.
2. Modified with knees.
3. All fours and lift one hand or leg.

Push-up workout: Try three sets of 5 push-ups, working up to three sets of 10–15–20–25.

Sit-Ups

Sit-ups work abdominal muscles. Start with 10 per day; work up to 50 to 1,000 a day done three to five days per week. Variations can be:

1. Arms crossed in front.
2. Arms at side come up and touch toes.
3. Crunches with legs up, bent, twisting side to side.
4. Rowing.
5. Back extensions: Lie face down on ground with arms straight out to side; raise chest off ground.

Sit-up workout: Try three sets of 5 sit-ups, working up to three sets of 10–15–20–25.

Dips

Dips work shoulders, forearms, and back of upper arms. Variations:

1. Place palms on end of bench, feet on ground, and dip.
2. Place palms on end of chair, feet on another chair; dip down.
3. Use dip bars in weight room.

Dip workout: Dips take a little more strength. Start with one set of 5 to 10 and work up to three sets of 15 to 20.

Rapid strength gains take place with lots of push-ups, sit-ups, and dips. You can perform these three strength exercises almost anywhere.

TRAINING

The overload principle involves subjecting the muscle to more stress than it is accustomed to. As a result, the body will adapt to reasonable amounts of stress. Excessive stress will cause the body to break down, leading to injury. The components of overload include load, repetition, frequency, and rest.

1. *Load* refers to intensity and the amount of resistance or weight being used during an exercise.
2. *Repetition* refers to the number of times an exercise is performed during a set.
3. *Rest* refers to the amount of time between sets. The greater the load or the higher the number of repetitions, the greater the amount of rest required between sets.
4. *Frequency* is the number of training sessions per week.

Recommendations for Beginners

1. Load: 50 percent of maximum
2. Repetition: performance lift 8 to 12 times, between two and four sets (usually three sets)
3. Rest: 2 minutes between sets
4. Frequency: two to three times per week
   - Two times a week will maintain strength; three times a week will increase strength
   - Power (speed and strength): 3 to 8 repetions
   - Bulk mass: 1 to 6 repetions
   - Endurance: 10 to 15 repetions
   - Pyramid: ascending in weight, then descending back down
   - Super sets: pairing one lift with another; for example, a back squat with a pull-up
   - Plyometrics: bounding, sprinting, jumping.

Safety

BREATHING

1. Exhale while exerting the greatest force.
2. Inhale while moving the weight into position.
3. Holding your breath causes a decrease in blood volume returning to the heart and impairs the volume and level of oxidated blood returning to the brain. It also affects blood pressure. You may get dizzy or faint. *Never hold your breath!*
4. While not holding your breath, you must hold your core tight. Squeeze your abdominal cavity while performing the required lift. This is an important safety factor during strength training.

CLOTHING

1. Sport shoes provide good support.
2. For serious lifters, weight-lifting belts protect the back when squatting or pulling.
3. Spotters
4. Collars
5. Grips—pronated: bench; supinated: curl; mixed: dead lift

CONCEPTS OF STRENGTH TRAINING

1. Train specially for your sport.
2. Train all year round.
3. Get in shape gradually.
4. Listen to your body.
5. Train first for volume (more reps) and later for intensity (heavier weight).
6. Cycle the volume and intensity of your workouts.
7. Do not overtrain.
8. Train your mind.
9. Become a student of your sport or activity.
10. Always warm up and cool down when lifting.

FYI

For further information and special help, consult the following organization.

ORGANIZATION

National Strength & Conditioning Association
1995 N. Union Boulevard
Colorado Springs, CO 80909
Phone: (800) 815-6826 or (719) 632-6722
Fax: (719) 632-6367
E-mail: nsca@nsca-lift.org
Website: www.nsca-lift.org

BENCH PRESS

SKILL	CUE	WHY	COMMON ERROR
Grip	Grip couple of inches wider than shoulder width	Try and minimize sport movement	Too wide, too narrow
Feet Position	Feet flat on ground	Safety; always have balance	
Back Position	Back flat on bench	Raising buttocks can lead to back strains	Raising buttocks while lifting
Execution	Lightly touch chest when lowering bar	Slow continuous movement	Bouncing bar off chest
		Always control weight; less stress on shoulders	
	Lift should be smooth		If weight wobbles, too much weight
	Chest puffs out		Chest caves in
Incline Bench Press	Same as bench press except bring bar down to lightly touch collarbone		Bringing bar down too low
Decline Bench Press	Same as bench press except execution		
	Bring bar down to lightly touch the lower part of the chest		Bringing bar down too high on chest

SKILL	CUE	WHY	COMMON ERROR
Safety Guidelines (Figure 21.2)	Have spotter		
	Use collars		
	Control bar at all times		
	Inhale during eccentric contraction and exhale during concentric contraction		
	Always keep a tight core, sucking belly button to spine		
Weight Belt	We do not emphasize the use of a weight belt. It takes away from the development of our core strength. Some students will put them on when weight gets too heavy—85% and above. Keep that inn if you want; it is probably a good idea for teachers to have students wear them		

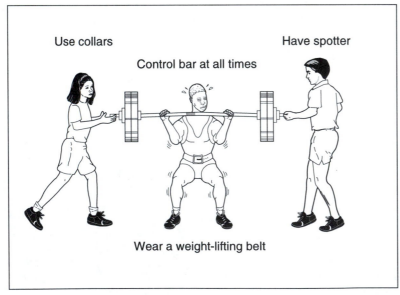

FIGURE 21.2 Safety Guidelines

Use collars

Have spotter

Control bar at all times

Wear a weight-lifting belt

POWER CLEAN

SKILL	CUE	WHY	COMMON ERROR
Stance	Feet shoulder-width apart	Use athletic stance as much as possible	Feet too wide
	Knees slightly bent	Again, athletic position	Knees too straight
	Chest over knees		
	Tight back	Suck belly button to spine	Rounded back
Grip	Just outside of knees		
Execution	Same as power snatch until catch		Elbows not getting high enough
	Rotate elbows under bar		Bar is away from body
	Drop body and catch bar on clavicle and front deltoids		

POWER SNATCH

SKILL	CUE	WHY	COMMON ERROR
Stance	Feet shoulder-width apart	Use athletic stance as much as possible	Feet too wide
	Knees slightly bent	Again, athletic position	Knees too straight
	Chest over knees		
	Tight back	Suck belly button to spine	Rounded back
Grip	Super wide grip (as if carrying a wide table by yourself); form wide V		
Execution	Drive with legs (jumping in the air)		Performing slowly
	Explode hips when bar reaches knees		
	Pull bar high with elbows high and close to body (like putting on your pants)	Everything must go vertical	Bar away from body
	Drop under bar (hold world over head)	Drive heels in ground	No drop
		Catch in athletic stance, same as start	
	Lock elbows and stand	Drop under weight to catch properly	

SQUAT

SKILL	CUE	WHY	COMMON ERROR
Abdominals	Abdominals held in tightly	Important for safety	Being lazy
Stance	Feet shoulder-width apart, slightly pointed out	Always train with an athletic stance	Feet parallel
Execution	Eyes at noon	Keep you from falling over	Looking down or looking up too high (at the ceiling)
	Back straight and shoulders upright and tall		Rounding the back and bending over too much at the waist
	Weight on heels (water-skier taking off or sitting down in chair)	Keep stress on muscles not patella of the knee	Weight on toes with heels off ground
	Knees stay behind toes	Same as above	Knees going beyond toes
	Femur parallel to floor and knees at a 90° angle	Net for depth to full gain all muscles and prevents stress on knees	Going too low

22

Swimming

INTRODUCTION

The swimming and safety cues incorporated in this chapter provide instructors with a variety of creative ideas that students of all ages are able to visualize and implement into their swimming and safety skills. For example, when teaching the prone float, one might instruct the students to pretend they are "Superheroes looking over the city." Other feedback about this cue might be "Look to see if someone is in trouble." Questions could include "How is the person doing down there?" or "Can you see the crooks?" When these cues are used, students' imaginations are stimulated, and critical swimming skills are learned. When teachers use their imaginations with the cues and elaborate on them, the class becomes interesting and fun.

We have designed some very vivid swimming cues to help the swimmer envision the arm stroke, kick, and coordination patterns. For example, making an inverted heart for the breaststroke or an hourglass for the butterfly stroke helps the student learn to perform a difficult arm movement more quickly and efficiently.

Other cues are designed to help refine and polish the strokes—for example, "Thumb brushes side of leg on the finish of the front crawl arm stroke" or "Hand rests on top of leg to finish the arm stroke on the sidestroke." These refinement cues should be used when the swimmer has mastered major arm, kick, and coordination patterns.

Learning correct swimming strokes through the use of cues helps the student feel more comfortable and efficient in the water, which could lead to a lifetime of fitness and recreational activities.

The fundamentals of swimming skills such as floats, etc. are found in *Teaching Cues for Basic Sport Skills for Elementary and Middle School Students* (Fronske, 2002).

SKILLS LISTED WITH CUES

Swimming strokes include the front crawl, back crawl, butterfly, sidestroke, breaststroke, elementary backstroke, trudgen, trudgen crawl, and double trudgen.

Swimming skills include the rotary kick, treading water, front and back open turns, swimming underwater, breaststroke and butterfly turns, speed turns, surface dives, and diving.

TIPS

1. Type the cues on a 3 inch × 5 inch note card, laminate it, and float the card on the water while teaching.

2. Punch holes in the note card, put string through the holes, and tie a knot. Put string around instructor's neck. The note card won't float away from the swim instructor.

3. For laminating the note card, use clear contact paper, heavy Ziploc bags, and clear postal tape.

EQUIPMENT TIPS

1. Goggles help beginning swimmers enjoy the water and open their eyes underwater; they also prevent the eyes from burning when a person swims laps.

2. Kickboards.

TEACHING IDEAS

1. The following is a suggested teaching progression for the five basic swimming strokes: front crawl, back crawl, elementary backstroke, breaststroke, and sidestroke. The sidestroke should be taught after the whip kick has been mastered because of negative transfer with the scissors kick.

2. Front crawl: If students have erratic breathing habits or body twists, have them breathe on the opposite side. This tactic helps them relearn correct breathing patterns.

3. Sidestroke: Have students learn sidestroke on both sides.

4. Breaststroke coordination: When teaching the breaststroke to beginners, have students practice only one stroke. Stop until they master the one stroke; then add two strokes, three strokes, and so on. This method helps develop coordination and gliding for the stroke.

5. Wet base (modified game): A new water game played like baseball in the water. Instructions for the game follow.

   ### EQUIPMENT
   1 kickboard used for the bat
   1 lightweight plastic 8-inch ball
   4 hula hoops used for the bases
   4 10-pound weights to keep hula hoops secure (optional)

RULES

1. Batter stands in shallow end of pool, bats to deep end of pool; pitcher pitches ball underhand, no more than three pitches.

2. Bat like baseball, swim underwater through hoop to first base, then to second base, and so on. Award one point for making it back to home plate.

3. A ball that goes out on deck is a foul ball.

4. Outs are made just as in baseball.

5. Two teams, 4 to 10 players per team.

FYI

For further information and special help, consult the following organizations and resources.

ORGANIZATIONS

Your local American Red Cross

National Headquarters of the American Red Cross
430 17th Street Northwest
Washington, DC 20006
Phone: (202) 737-8300
Website: www.redcross.org/hss

U.S. Swimming, Inc.
One Olympic Plaza
Colorado Springs, CO 80909
Phone: (719) 578-4578
Fax: (719) 578-4669
Website: www.USASwimming.org

PUBLICATIONS

American Red Cross. (1981). *Swimming and aquatics safety.* Washington, DC: American Red Cross.

American Red Cross. (1992a). *Swimming and diving.* St. Louis, Mosby.

American Red Cross. (1992b). *Water safety instructor's manual.* St. Louis, Mosby Life.

American Red Cross. (1993). *CPR for the professional rescuer.* St. Louis, Mosby.

American Red Cross. (2001). *Lifeguard training.* Boston, MA: Staywell.

American Red Cross. (2003). *Lifeguard management.* Boston, MA: Staywell.

Counsilman, J. E. (1977). *Competitive swimming manual for coaches and swimmers.* Bloomington, IN: Author.

Counsilman, J. E., & Counsilman, B. E. (1994). *The new science of swimming.* Englewood Cliffs, NJ: Prentice-Hall.

SKILL	CUE	WHY	COMMON ERROR
Body Position	Be a superhero	More streamline through the water	Hips and shoulders sway
		No wave drag to slow you down	
Head Position	Water level at crown of head	More efficient in the water	Head too far under the water
		Best for streamlined body position	Head too high (creates a drag)
Arm Pull	Use an S pull	Creates power	Straight arm pull
	Thumb to middle of leg		Head-first recovery
Arm Recovery (Figure 22.1)	High elbow recovery	More energy efficient	Dragging elbow in water
		Prevents elbow drag in water, which slows you down	
	Drag thumb lightly along the water		Straight arm recovery
			Hand is higher than elbow during recovery
Hand Entry	Spear a fish that is 2–3 inches below the water and in front of you	Gets the arm in position for greater pull under the water	Palm enters the water first
		More speed	
		More water to pull creates more power in the stroke	
	Try to make a spear with arm; reach with arm		Hand starts to pull too soon
Leg Action	Point toes like a diver	Reduces wave drag, to swim faster; more streamlined	If feet are flexed stiff, swimmer does not move forward, can even go backward in the water
	Kick heels to the surface	Less wave drag	
	Feet relaxed, like throwing a fishing line		
	Kick generated from large muscles of buttocks and thigh give more power		

continued

FRONT CRAWL, continued

SKILL	CUE	WHY	COMMON ERROR
Breathing	Follow the elbow back; look through window	Creates way for air, efficient breath	Head too far under the water (causes exaggerated roll)
		Keeps body streamlined	
	Roll chin to shoulder	Less wave drag	
	Rotate body on skewer	Less drag	
	Hum while face is in water	More efficient air exchange	Water gets in mouth
	Exhale through nose	Avoids getting water in mouth	

High elbow recovery

Boil the water

Only heels break surface

Spear a fish that is 2–3 inches below water

FIGURE 22.1   Front Crawl

SKILL	CUE	WHY	COMMON ERROR
Body Position	Iron rod down back	Less wave drag	Hips and shoulders sway
	Eyes look at toes splashing water		
Head Position	Lie down, as if head is on a pillow, water touching ears	Less wave drag	Head is too far back, eyes looking at the ceiling
Hand Recovery (Figure 22.2)	Thumb leads coming out of the water as if a string is pulling the thumb up	Specific goal for swimmer to heed	Fingers lead coming out of the water
	Thumbs up, making the OK sign	More streamlined; more efficient to cut through the water	
Shoulder Recovery	Lead with shoulder; straight arm	More streamlined	Arms are bent
	Raise hand to ask question	More efficient for best power position	
	Graze your ear with your arm		
	Skim the ear		
Hand Entry	Pinkie finger always leads going into the water	More efficient	Arms enter too far out to the side of the body
	Palms facing away	Less splash	Hand or elbow enters first
Arm Pull	Make a question mark with each arm pull	Creates power to move body forward	Straight arm pull
		Less stress on shoulders	
Leg Action	Point toes like a diver	More streamlined; move through the water faster	Flexed stiff feet; swimmer does not move forward well, knees and heels break the surface of the water
	Kick toes to the surface	More efficient	
	Make water boil	Less drag	
Body Rotation	Hip to sky	Keep body streamlined	
	Rotate body on skewer	More efficient	

FIGURE 22.2 Back Crawl

	BUTTERFLY STROKE		
SKILL	**CUE**	**WHY**	**COMMON ERROR**
Arm Pull	Draw an hourglass with high elbow pull	More power	Straight arm pull
	Push arms; explode out of the back of stroke; touch thigh with thumb		
	Stay low		
Arm Recovery	Elbow is being pulled by string upward	Gets arms ready for power phase	Elbows stay in water on recovery
		More efficient stroke	
	Thumbs drag along the water to keep elbows high		Arms drag along the water
	Pinkies exit first		
Hand Entry	Catch the water with hands		
Leg Action	Legs are together, like a mermaid	Gets legs in position for power phase	Legs too far apart
	2 strong kicks		Whip kick or frog kick
	Make kick like a metronome		
Coordination	Lead with head	Better coordination of stroke	
	As hands enter in front, chest is down, buttocks up		

continued

BUTTERFLY STROKE, continued

SKILL	CUE	WHY	COMMON ERROR
Breathing	Keep chin near the water when breathing	Easier to take the breath	
Body Roll	Body roll through a relatively narrow band of water at the surface	Body is streamlined to move through water	
	No deeper than 1–2 feet	More efficient	

SIDESTROKE

SKILL	CUE	WHY	COMMON ERROR
Body Position	Lay head on arm	Keeps body streamlined to move through water more efficiently	Ear and head too far above the water
	Lower ear is in water		Lying on stomach
Arm Pull	Tie a big knot	Creates best power from the arms	Both hands start above head
	Pick an apple from a tree and put it in your pocket	Keeps upper body above the water	
Arm Recovery	Rest the top hand on the top leg during glide	Keeps body streamlined and aerodynamic to move through the water	Top arm pushes too far past the leg
Leg Action	Draw both heels toward buttocks	Legs in best power position	Whip or frog kick used
	Tuck the knees, flex the top foot, and point the bottom foot		
	Do the splits	Gets body ready for power phase	Legs too close together when trying to make the splits, legs go up and down, not sideways
	Splits done sideways		
	Legs do not pass each other when kick is finished	Keeps swimmer on side and streamlined	Legs pass each other on the kick
	Avoid up-and-down splits, close legs like scissors	More efficient	
Coordination	Stay streamlined	Rest	
	Count to 3 on glide		
	Stay parallel with side	Keeps body aerodynamic in water	Roll or lie on stomach

SKILL	CUE	WHY	COMMON ERROR
Body Position	Arch back to bring shoulders out of water		Body vertical in water
Head Position	Eyes focused on wall	Streamlined to move through the water more efficiently	
	Crown at water level		Hair submerged in water
Arm Pull/Arm Recovery	Make a small upside-down heart; start at the point of the heart, trace it with hand, then split it in half with hands	Creates power in the stroke	Heart shape is too wide or long
Arm Glide	Fully extend arms and count to 3 before starting to pull	Creates aerodynamic	Starting to pull too soon
Leg Action (Whip Kick)	Kick buttocks with heels	More power	Knees too far apart
	Try being knock-kneed		Frog kick
	Knees a fist apart		
	Keep knees closer together than ankles		
	Draw circles with heels		Knees outside ankles
	Push feet/squeeze legs		
Breathing	Lift chin, not head to breathe	Easier to breathe	Head too far out of water
Coordination	Pull, breathe, kick, glide	Saying these words helps with the coordination of the stroke	Gliding when arms are at waist

SKILL	CUE	WHY	COMMON ERROR
Body Position	Ears in the water	Helps streamline body to move through water more efficiently	Head too far out of water
	Arms down at sides		
Arm Recovery	Tickle sides with thumbs all the way to the armpit	Creates more pull for power	Hands do not come to armpits, half stroke
Arm Pull	Palms out	More power	Hands and arms come too far above head
	Make a T		
	Make a snow angel	Creates more pull for power	
Leg Action (Whip Kick)	Drop feet straight down	Requires less energy	Buttocks drop, knees bend to chest
	Make penguin feet	When knees come up, body sinks	
	Try being knock-kneed	Gets legs in position for power phase	Knees are outside of ankles
	Feet outside knees	Action with feet faster	
		More power	
	Upper legs form a table		Knees come out of water
	Draw heels toward buttocks		
	Try drawing circles with your heels	Action phase more powerful	Scissors kick with 1 or both legs
	Push feet, then squeeze legs		
Coordination	Recover the arms first, kick and pull, then glide		Arms and legs start at the same time
	U-out together, glide		

	TRUDGEN STROKES		
SKILL	**CUE**	**WHY**	**COMMON ERROR**
Trudgen	Front crawl		Breathing on both sides
	Roll hips to side	Creates power	Whip kick staying on stomach
	Scissors kick when breathing	Help with timing to breathe	Kicking when head is in water
Trudgen Crawl	Front crawl		
	Roll hip to side		Hips flat
	Scissors kick when breathing, flutter kick when face is in water	Create more power in the stroke	Forgetting to flutter kick
	Breathe on one side		Breathing on both sides
Double Trudgen	Front crawl with no flutter kick		
	Scissors kick—scissors kick	Creates more power	Kicking only one side
	Roll hip to each side when performing a scissors kick on each arm stroke		Not rolling hips
	Breathe on one side only		Breathing on both sides
	Head stays in water on one arm stroke and 1 scissors kick; keep head in water	Helps with the coordination of the stroke	Turning head right and left
	Try to keep arms moving and in sequence with each scissors kick		

SKILL	CUE	WHY	COMMON ERROR
Rotary Kick (Figure 22.3)	Sit on horse, back straight		Standing straight up
	1 foot rotates clockwise, the other foot, counterclockwise		Legs going same direction
	Eggbeater		
	"Wax on! Wax off!" with your feet (as in the *Karate Kid* movie; same motion, but use feet)		
Tread Water	Look over fence		
Arms	Figure 8 with hands, palms up, palms down or like spreading butter with sides of hands		Hands pushing down
Legs	Scissors/breaststroke/rotary		
Body Position	Relaxed		Body too rigid, not relaxed
			Too much energy, too tight
Front Open Turn	Drop 1 shoulder, meet hands above head		Grab wall with both hands
	Knees tuck against wall; submerge in water		Not tucking
	Spring off wall		Not pushing
	Stay submerged	More streamlined	Staying on top of water, not submerging
Back Open Turn	Drop 1 shoulder, meet hands above head		Arms by side
	Spring off wall		Not tucking
	Be a torpedo	Creates power	No power
Sidestroke Arms and Coordination	See sidestroke cues		
Swimming Underwater	Be a submarine	Body is streamlined	Swimming on top of water
	Scrape a big bowl with hands	More power; more efficient pull	Straight arm pull
	Be a frog		

continued

Sit on horse—
legs spread

COUNTERCLOCKWISE

CLOCKWISE

One foot rotates counterclockwise   One foot rotates clockwise

FIGURE 22.3   Rotary Kick

SWIMMING SKILLS, continued			
Butterfly Arm Stroke and Coordination	See butterfly stroke cues, pages 277–278		
Breaststroke Turn	Drop shoulder, hands meet above head; submerge	Gets body underwater for more efficiency	Shoulders level
	Superhero looking over city underwater	More streamlined	
Sidestroke Turn	Touch wall with leading arm		Touching wall with both arms
	Drop one shoulder		
	Spring off wall		
Speed Turn and Pull Out for Breaststroke	Drop 1 shoulder, meet hands above head	Gets body in streamline position	
	Spring off wall		Not tucking
Arms	Draw lightbulb to thighs (feel water move down legs to toes)	More power	Shallow pull
Legs	Whip kick and stretch	More power	Kicking too quickly after pull

continued

SKILL	CUE	WHY	COMMON ERROR
Flip Turn for Front Crawl	Front somersault (1 stroke from edge of pool)	Gets body in ready position to be more efficient during turn	Body stays flat, too far from or too close to wall
	Bend at waist; be a hinge		
	Put buttocks in air		Not tucking
	Throw legs out of water	More power	
	Find wall with feet		Finding wall with buttocks, too close to wall, finding gutter instead
	Put footprints on wall	More power to push off	
Flip Turn for Backstroke	Turn on stomach 1 stroke from edge	Won't run into wall	
	Do a front flip turn		
	Push off on back like a torpedo, arms above head	Creates better control and power in push off	
Pike Surface Dive	Swim with continuous motion into pike; pull water up; drive your head down	Creates momentum to get body down	No power into pike
	Hands touch toes		Body stays flat
	Be a hinge or break like a pencil at hips		Stay in bent position
	Shoot legs up or put pencil back together as you dive down	Creates energy to get down to bottom of pool	
Tuck Surface Dive	Swim front crawl with continuous motion		No power into swim
	Drive your head down; pull water up	Creates momentum to get body down fast	
	Swim and roll into ball or cannonball		Head remains up
	Cannonball explodes, shoot feet up in air	Gets body in a straight position to go down	

continued

SWIMMING SKILLS, continued

SKILL	CUE	WHY	COMMON ERROR
Feet-First Surface Dive			
Arm Action	Start in T position		Starting with hands at side
	Perform jumping-jack action with arms	Gives body momentum	Keeping arms down at side
	Arms and hands push down like a jumping-jack and push back up like a jumping-jack or push arms back up like a referee's signal for touchdown	More power to get down	
		Keeps body streamlined	

DIVING

SKILL	CUE	WHY	COMMON ERROR
Safety Rules	Dive in deep water (9 feet or more)	To prevent serious permanent injury	Diving in less than 9 feet of water can cause spinal or head injuries
Side of Pool Dive			
Kneeling Position	Kneel on 1 knee; grip pool edge with other foot	If head is up, the student will flop in the water	Kneeling on two knees
	Head between arms and fingers pointing to water		Hands and arms moving to front of body
	Focus on target on bottom, 4 feet out or surface 1–2 feet from side		Not focusing on target (causes a belly flop)
Action of Dive	Lean forward, try to touch water		Jumping in water with head lifted
	Push with front foot		Somersaulting in
	Keep hips up and dive over barrel	Keeps diver from falling into water	Hips down
	Straighten legs		Legs bent
	Push downward in water with hands	Breaks water with hands, not head	Pushing upward
		Does not hurt the head	

continued

SKILL	CUE	WHY	COMMON ERROR
Side of Pool Dive, *continued*			
Compact Dive	1 foot forward, 1 foot back		Staying on knee
	Kneel and rise		Staying on knee
	Head between arms, point fingers at water		Head not between arms
	Hips up, stretch, and touch surface of water	Reaching for water gets body into position to go head first	Hips down, hands in air
	Lose balance, push off toward water	Gets students going in head first	
	Ankles together on water entry		Legs apart
Stride Dive	Walking stance		Legs together
	Front toes grab edge		Foot is not at edge
	Head between arms		Head is up
	Bend at the waist like breaking a pencil		Body is straight
	Kick back leg up, hips up	Correct body angle for water entry	Not kicking leg
	Once body is underwater, point fingers to surface of water		Fingers pointed down
Long Shallow Dive	Push and stretch		Falling in or plopping in
	Spear into the water		Pointing fingers to bottom of pool
	Over the barrel and through the hoop		
	Hands enter through donut hole	Helps divers dive out, not deep	
	Go through the tunnel just below surface of water		

continued

SKILL	CUE	WHY	COMMON ERROR
Diving from the Board	Hips up, arms stretched, fall forward, focus on target in water		Hips down
Approach Hurdle	Lift knee like a tabletop or a stork position	Gets diver up in the air	Keeping knee down
	Arms back, like pushing ski poles		
Jump off Board	Arms up to touchdown position		Arms staying down
	Use approach hurdle position		One or 2 steps in approaching hurdle
	Arms back like a back arm circle	Gives diver power to get up—not out	
	Land on both feet and push off board	Balance and control	
Jump, Tuck Position	Use approach hurdle position		
	Jump off board		
	Lift knees to chest in fetal position; straighten back up in spear position		Not getting in a tuck position
Tuck Dive	Use approach hurdle position		
	Jump in tuck position		
	Lift hips		Hips down
	Drive heels into ceiling	Keeps body straight at entry point	
	Push hands into water, above head		Hands down
Pike Dive	Use approach hurdle position		
	Hips up	Power	Hips down
	Break the pencil		Bending at hips
	Fingers to toes		
	Drive heels into ceiling	Keeps body straight at entry point	

23

Team Handball

INTRODUCTION

Although a popular Olympic sport for men and women throughout the world, team handball is an emerging sport in the United States that often suffers from an identity crisis. Most of the world calls the game "handball," but in the United States there is already another sport with that name. When most Americans hear "team handball" mentioned, they mistakenly envision a game like racquetball, played on a court and involving hitting a small black ball with both hands. Without a doubt, team handball is *not off the wall!*

Team handball is a dynamic sport that is fun to play and exciting to watch. Natural athletic skills such as running, jumping, throwing, and catching provide the action for the game. Players and spectators alike enjoy the fast continuous play, body contact, and goalie action. First-time spectators describe team handball as soccer with your hands, but they also notice elements that remind them of basketball, water polo, and ice hockey.

Team handball is played between two teams, each with six court players and a goalie, on a court larger than a basketball court. The object of the game is to throw a cantaloupe-sized ball into the opponent's 2-meter × 3-meter goal and defend one's own goal from attack. A regulation game is played in 30-minute halves with no time-outs. A coin toss determines which team starts the game with a throw-off. From that point, the action is continuous. The clock stops only for injury or at the referee's discretion. A successful scoring attempt results in the award of one point. Goals scored per game typically range from the upper teens to midtwenties.

A semicircular line 6 meters from the goal marks the goal area. Only the goalie occupies this area, and both attackers and defenders must remain outside. Basic defense is designed to protect the goal area by placing all six players around it, forming a wall. Defense techniques are similar to basketball with the exception that more contact is allowed. Body contact with the torso is permitted, but players may not push, hold, or endanger an opponent in any way. Excessive roughness results in two-minute suspensions.

When in attack, players are called back courts, wings, and circle runners. Passing is the primary way to move the ball in attack. A player is allowed three steps with the ball before and after dribbling, but while stationary may hold the ball only three seconds. The attacking player's task is to find a way over, around, or through the defensive "wall." This is done by strategies similar to basketball, incorporating the concepts of the "give-and-go," screen, pick-and-roll, and overload. The offense may run set plays, but a freelance style usually dominates.

SKILLS LISTED WITH CUES

The cues listed for team handball include passing and catching (overhand pass, catching on the run), individual movement in attack (piston movement and sidestepping), shooting (general principles, set shot, jump shot), goalkeeping, defense (basic stance, individual tactics, shot blocking, small-group tactics, team defense: 6–0 zone), offense (attacking the gap, small-group tactics, team offense: fast break, 3–3 formation), and essential team handball rules.

TIPS

1. Write or call the United States Team Handball Federation (see the FYI section) to order the *Introduction to Team Handball* video, a televised game from the Olympics, and basic rules.

2. Set up the VCR and TV in the gym the week before you begin a team handball unit. Show the *Introduction* video and five minutes of the game video the first day of class.

3. Give each student a handout of the simplified rules.

4. Let students experience the game right away with just a few basic team handball rules using skills they already know from other sports like basketball and softball. Add rules as the game develops.

5. After a goal is scored, the goalie puts the ball back into play right away. As a result, the defense must move back quickly. If the court is small, this practice allows more playing area than would be available if the throw-off were made at half-court.

6. Call plenty of 7-meter penalty throws on major fouls, and let the player who was fouled take the throw (a major foul is one that destroys a sure chance to score or any dangerous play, i.e., pushing, tripping, hitting, undercutting a jumping opponent, or grabbing an opponent's arm). This approach helps keep the game safe, and players will learn faster about serious fouls, clear chances to score, and dangerous play.

EQUIPMENT TIPS

1. Regulation indoor court, 20 meters × 40 meters, approximately 65 feet × 131 feet, one-third larger than a basketball court.

2. Indoors with limited space, that is, only a regulation or smaller basketball court:

   a. Try to maintain 18- to 20-meter width by using extra space outside basketball court.

   b. Small basketball court: Have no sideline boundaries, and play balls off the side walls. Reduce players to five plus a goalie.

c. After a goal, goalie puts ball back into play with throw-off from the goal area rather than restarting from center court. Goalie cannot leave area or shoot.

3. Outdoor court: playground, grass field, sand beach. For continuous action put an extra ball and student "chaser" behind each goal. Goalie picks up extra ball when shot goes over end line, and student chases the other ball and returns it behind the goal.

4. Marking the court: The most essential lines are the arced 6-meter goal area line and the 7-meter penalty throw line. Use gym floor tape, basketball court three-point line, cones, rope, "chalk dust," paint, or white flour on grass. The dashed free-throw line is optional.

5. Modified goals, 2-meter × 3-meter opening: Tape on wall, portable standards made with rope or old volleyball nets, large crash mat against wall, field hockey or indoor soccer goals, goals built from PVC pipe.

6. Team handballs (about 23 inches in circumference): For safety reasons, the official men's or women's leather ball is not recommended for beginning players or coed classes. Use Sportime's "Supersafe Elite" handball, a dense foam ball, or a slightly deflated volleyball.

TEACHING IDEAS

1. Teach noncontact basketball-style defense. The official handball rules do allow some body contact, but it is not recommended for beginning players.

2. Use the "teaching rules" during scrimmage to encourage players to develop passing and shooting skills along with increasing goalie safety:

   a. Three passes before the team can shoot.

   b. No dribbling or a limited number of dribbles.

   c. Shoot only bounce shots or play without a goalie in the goal area using targets in the goal corners, that is, towels, cones, hoops, and the like. Only the designated goalie can go into goal area and put ball into play after a shot.

FYI

For further information and special help, consult the following organizations and resources.

ORGANIZATIONS

Available resources for sale: team handball basic rules sheet; team handball rule book; videos: ask for video listing; suggestions: *Introduction to Team Handball,* Olympic games, international games (designate men's or women's).

USA Team Handball
One Olympic Plaza
Colorado Springs, CO 80909
Phone: (719) 575-4036
Fax: (719) 575-4055
E-mail: info@usateamhandball.org
Website: www.usateamhandball.org

U.S. Team Handball Federation
1903 Powers Ferry Road, Suite 230
Atlanta, GA 30339
Phone: (770) 956-7660
Fax: (770) 956-7976

Team handball Special Olympics volunteer coach training school manual can be ordered here.

Special Olympics International
Sports Department
1325 G Street, Northwest, Suite 500
Washington, DC 20005-3104
Phone: (202) 628-3630

SUGGESTED EQUIPMENT COMPANIES

Sportime
Phone: (800) 283-5700
Supersafe Elite Handball (6¾ inch), practice/portable goals, and goal nets

Fold-A-Goal
Phone: (323) 734-2507
Practice, portable goals recommended for school programs

Jayfro
Phone: (860) 447-3001
Folding regulation goals and goal nets

PUBLICATION

Clanton, R. & Dwight, M. P. (1996) *Team Handball: Step to success.* Champaign IL: Human Kinetics.

The authors, physical education teachers/coaches and 1984 Olympians, present an illustrated 12-step progressive program of basic skills and strategies. An excellent teacher resource including drills for increasing and decreasing difficulty of skills, lead-up games, a student rule handout, and more. This book can be ordered from the publisher at (800) 747-4457.

SKILL	CUE	WHY	COMMON ERROR
Overhand Pass	Pass with 1 hand, catch with both		
Preparation	Fingertip grip	Improper grip	Holding ball in palm of hand
	Lift ball up and back with elbow flexed at 90°	Poor throwing grip	Elbow too close to body—ball too close to head
	Weight on back foot		
	Shoulders perpendicular to target		
Throwing Action	Step toward target		
	Rotate and square shoulders to target	Pattern	No shoulder rotation—always facing target
		Physically weak	
	Lead with elbow; whip forearm and snap wrist	Poor mechanics	The ball is pushed from shoulder and hand, and ball leads
		Inexperience	
		Physically weak	
Catching on the Run (Figure 23.1)			
Preparation	Maintain running rhythm	Difficulty following flight path	Stopping to catch the ball
Position	Hands up, form a triangle with thumbs and forefingers almost touching		
	Push off one leg, extend arms toward ball		
Receiving Action	Soft hands—catch while flexing elbows to give with ball	Take eyes off ball	Ball rebounds off hands
		Hands too tense	
		Needs soft hands and flexed elbows	
	Land on other foot		

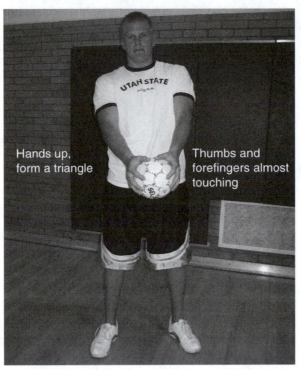

Hands up, form a triangle

Thumbs and forefingers almost touching

FIGURE 23.1 Catching on the Run

INDIVIDUAL MOVEMENT IN ATTACK			
SKILL	**CUE**	**WHY**	**COMMON ERROR**
Piston Movement	Fundamental movement of backcourt players; sum of 3 actions similar to up-and-down motion of a piston in a motor cylinder		
The Three Actions	1. Run to receive; catch ball while running toward goal		Standing in 1 spot to receive pass
	2. Use 3 steps to attack goal; rules: allow 3 steps with ball (i.e., a right-hander should step left-right-left); on third step, shoot or pass, throw off foot that is opposite to throwing arm		Throwing off foot on same side as throwing arm, or passing ball while backing up
			Poor timing

continued

SKILL	CUE	WHY	COMMON ERROR
Piston Movement, *The Three Actions, continued*	3. Back up quickly; prepare to attack again		Forgetting to back up and staying too close to defense
			Watching for action; not moving
Sidestepping	Fundamental movement for circle runners along or near 6-meter line		
Position	Balanced position, knees bent, feet shoulder-width apart, hands open ready to catch		Standing upright with hands down, not ready to catch
			Has not created own space
			Must compete with defense to create space
Leg Action	Step sideways using quick, small steps without crossing feet, maintain balanced position		Bringing feet together or crossing feet
			Off balance; poor footwork

SHOOTING

SKILL	CUE	WHY	COMMON ERROR
General Principles	Shoot on move— piston movement		
	Watch goalie and shoot for open corners of goal; may choose to bounce ball when shooting low		
	Take shots between 6–9 meters; avoid from severe angles	Learn to dive into circle to improve angle	Shooting a set shot from a wing position
	Shoot only when there is an opening (shoot over and between defenders)		Charging into a defender or carelessly shooting a ball that hits a stationary defender
			Poor judgment

continued

SHOOTING, continued			
SKILL	**CUE**	**WHY**	**COMMON ERROR**
Set Shot			
Preparation	Run to receive and attack using 3 steps		Standing still when shooting
	Weight on back foot (same as shooting arm)		Shooting off same foot as shooting arm
	Elbow flexed at 90° or greater		
	Shoulders perpendicular to goal		Facing target, shoulders square to goal
	Head up and eyes on goalie, shoot to open corner; equals "cobwebs"		
Throwing Action	Step forward, transferring weight from rear to front foot		
	Rotate and square shoulders to goal		
	Lead with elbow, whip forearm, and snap wrist		Pushing ball forward from shoulder
Follow-Through	Momentum continues forward and arm motion continues across body		
Jump Shot	Use jump shot to shoot over a defender, or when jumping into the goal area to score		
Preparation	Run to receive and attack using 3 steps		
Jumping Action (Figure 23.2)	To jump: plant foot opposite throwing arm and drive other knee up (changing forward momentum into upward momentum)	Did not read spacing properly	Charging into defender
	Raise shooting arm up and back; make an L		
	Rotate shoulders square to goal while whipping throwing arm forward (elbow, shoulder, forearm, wrist)		

continued

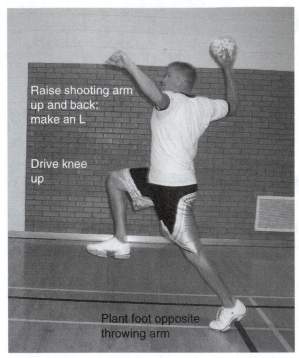

Raise shooting arm
up and back;
make an L

Drive knee
up

Plant foot opposite
throwing arm

FIGURE 23.2 Jump Shot

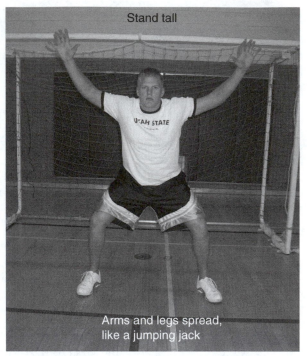

Stand tall

Arms and legs spread,
like a jumping jack

FIGURE 23.3 Basic Position of the Goalie

SHOOTING, continued			
SKILL	**CUE**	**WHY**	**COMMON ERROR**
Throwing Action	Pike slightly at waist and land on takeoff foot		Shot lacks velocity, all power coming from strong upper-body action
			Poor mechanics

GOALKEEPING			
SKILL	**CUE**	**WHY**	**COMMON ERROR**
Rules	Goalie isn't permitted to 1. Leave goal area while in possession of ball (free throw) 2. Receive a pass from a court player while inside the goal area (penalty throw)		
Goal Throw	Stand inside the goal area and throw ball to a teammate		

continued

SKILL	CUE	WHY	COMMON ERROR
Goal Throw, *continued*	Goal throw is awarded when 1. Ball is blocked and recovered in goal area 2. Blocked ball goes over the end line 3. Ball is thrown over end line by attacking team		
Goalie Protection	Train all beginning players in basic goalie technique; make sure each player gets a chance to play the position		
	Play with a dense foam ball at beginning level		
	Wear long sleeves and pants		
	Males wear a protective cup		
Basic Position (Figure 23.3)	Stand tall with knees slightly flexed, weight on balls of feet, hands up, eyes on ball (like a jumping jack)		Bending at waist with hands low, similar to basketball defensive position
			Poor mechanics
			Fatigue
Movement in Goal	Step out about ½ meter from goal line and follow ball by moving with quick shuffle steps, keeping body aligned with the ball		Standing in middle of goal and not moving
			Poor vision
			Inexperience
	Get stable prior to shot, ready to block shot		Feeling off balance when shot is taken
	Protect near post		Poor balance
			Mechanics

continued

SKILL	CUE	WHY	COMMON ERROR
Blocking High Shots			
Footwork	Take small step in direction of ball, push off leg farthest from ball, and leap in direction of shot		Leaning, reaching for ball rather than moving body
			Poor mechanics
			Fatigue
Blocking Action	Extend arm(s) in path of ball and attack the ball; block ball, don't try to catch it		Ball goes through hands when trying to catch it
			Taking eye off ball
			Weak hands
			Fatigue
Blocking Low Shots			
Footwork	Take small step in direction of ball, push off leg farthest from ball		
Blocking Action	Extend opposite leg and arm(s) in path of ball to block	Strength	Shot goes over leg—failing to block with both leg and arm(s)
		Balance	
		Flexibility	
Blocking Wing Shots			
Position	Stand tall close to goalpost, with weight on goalpost-side leg		
	Goalpost-side arm up, elbow bent about 90° with forearm in front of face, other hand out to side bent about 90°		
Footwork	As shooter jumps into the goal area, take one step out from the post and move with quick shuffle steps to keep body aligned with ball		
Blocking Action	Block high shots with arm(s) and low shots with leg and arm(s)		

SKILL	CUE	WHY	COMMON ERROR
Individual Basic Stance	Feet shoulder-width apart, knees slightly bent, weight forward on balls of feet, body upright, arms out, hands up	Fatigue	Upper body bent forward, hands down, like basketball defensive stance
		Poor mechanics	
Individual Defense Tactics *Movement*	Shift along 6-meter line in direction of ball		
	See ball and direct opponent at all times		
	When your opponent attacks, step out from 6-meter line to meet attack—play basketball defense, no contact	Slow to react	Attacker is able to get a shot off from 7 or 8 meters
		Fear of contact	
	Wing defenders should not step out, as a set shot or jump shot is not likely to be successful from such a bad angle	Out of formation	Attacker drives around player and jumps into goal area for a shot
		Good offense	
	Stay between opponent and goal		
	When opponent passes the ball, recover to the 6-meter line	To cover attacker with ball	Leaving space for circle runner to run behind you
		Out of formation	
Shot Blocking *Action*	From basic stance, extend one or both hands into path of ball		
	Attack ball similar to volleyball blocking	Take eye off ball	Ball goes through hands toward goal
		Fatigue	
		Weak hands	

continued

SKILL	CUE	WHY	COMMON ERROR
Small-Group Defense Tactics	Help triangle—when player steps out, 2 adjacent players squeeze in slightly for help on both sides	Defensive miscue	Big open space is left along 6-meter line
	Communicate—each defender should know who is stepping out, who is staying back to help	Defensive miscue	Two players step out to meet 1 attacker, or no one steps out to meet attacker
		Good offensive	
Team Defense *6–0 Zone*	All 6 defenders take positions along 6-meter line, forming movable wall in front of goal		
	Shift as a unit in direction of ball movement		
	Each defender is responsible for attacker in his/her area of zone—each attacker should be accounted for by 1 defender	Defensive miscue	One defender guarding 2 attackers, or an attacker left unguarded
		Good offensive	

SKILL	CUE	WHY	COMMON ERROR
Individual Offense Tactics			
Attack Gap: Space Between 2 Defenders	Use fakes to get in a gap		
	Create a workable space from defense		Attacking too close to defenders; causing free throws, which interrupt flow of attack
	Be a threat to score; look to shoot first, then pass		Not maintaining proper passing
	Break through gap for a shot from 6-meter line		
	Create overload by drawing 2 defenders and passing to an open teammate		
Small-Group Offense Tactics	2 or 3 players work together to create scoring opportunity		
Basketball-Type Tactics	Give-and-go		
	Pick-and-roll		
	Crossing		
	Screens		
Three Phases of Team Offense			
Fast Break	Primary—long pass from goalie to breaking wing		
	Secondary—goalie shoots outlet pass, and team moves ball up floor quickly		
Organize into 3–3 Offense Formation; Move Ball in Support Points	3 players near the 6-meter line: left wing (LW), right wing (RW), circle runner (CR)		

continued

SKILL	CUE	WHY	COMMON ERROR
Three Phases of Team Offense *continued*	3 players outside 9-meter line in back court: left back court (LB), center back court (CB), right back court (RB)		
	Move ball with short, quick passes, wing to wing		
	Run to receive, play in good timing with teammates		
Execute Small-Group Tactics	Play with patience, wait for good scoring opportunity		Trying to score too often one-on-one

SKILL	CUE	WHY	COMMON ERROR
Goal-Area Line or 6-Meter Line	The most important line on court		
	No one is allowed inside area except goalie; players may jump or dive into area prior to releasing ball		
Players	6 court players, 1 goalie per team		
	Throw-off starts the game and is repeated after every score		
	Offensive team lines up on center line—defense at least 3 meters away		
	Offense passes from center of court to teammate, and play begins		
Playing the Ball	Player is allowed to 1. Run 3 steps (violation = free throw) 2. Hold ball 3 seconds (violation = free throw) 3. Dribble with no limit, with 3 steps allowed before and after dribbling (no double dribble)		
	Player is *not* allowed to 1. Throw a ball that endangers opponent 2. Pull, grab, or punch ball out of opponent's hands		
Defending an Opponent	For beginners, noncontact basketball-style defense		

continued

SKILL	CUE	WHY	COMMON ERROR
Throw-In	Awarded when ball goes out of bounds on sideline or when ball is last touched by defensive player (excluding goalie)		
	Place 1 foot on sideline to throw in		
	Defense 3 meters away		
Free Throw (Minor Fouls and Violations)	Awarded to the opponents at exact spot foul or violation occurred		
	Defense must be 3 meters away; if foul or violation occurs within 3 meters of goal area line, put ball into play at 9-meter line (free-throw line)		
	Thrower must keep 1 foot in contact with floor		
7-Meter Penalty Throw (Major Foul)	Awarded at 7-meter line when a foul destroys a clear chance to score		
	One-on-one shot with the goalie		
	All other players behind the 9-meter line (free-throw line)		

24

Tennis

INTRODUCTION

No one can describe the stress, intensity, and exhilaration one goes through when stepping up to the line to serve for the big point in tennis. No other sport can match the beating the body gets after a three-hour match played in 105-degree weather. No other feeling can top the desire to scream a forehand past your opponent after a rally that has made your legs burn. You know it's all up to you. No other game can be as exciting, different, and rewarding for each individual point. No other situation can be as maddening, frustrating, and absolutely glorious as a match of tennis. It gets better every time you step out on the court.

Tennis is not only a sport for a lifetime, but it also helps build character. It teaches you about speed, endurance, agility, anticipation, and quick reaction time. Tennis also tests your mental skills. You learn to control your temper and stay mentally tough to earn those big points that determine who wins the match. To be successful, you must be creative in combining mental and physical skills. Once you are able to do this, you will learn to construct points. It is very gratifying to put the different shots and strokes together to earn a point. The satisfaction comes when you hit a great shot. You keep coming back to the court for more.

The more you play, the more fun it gets. You can always reach for the next level. This is why we believe tennis to be one of the most fun sports to play.

SKILLS LISTED WITH CUES

This chapter present cues for the following tennis skills: grip, ready position, volley, forehand, teaching progressions for forehand stroke backhand, teaching progressions for backhand stroke, lob, drop shot, serve teaching progression for the serve, serve receive, backspin, overhead smash, singles and doubles scoring tiebreaker, and strategies for singles and doubles.

EQUIPMENT TIPS

1. Tennis rackets: Go with the full-size racket unless a player is really young, because they grow out of them so fast.
2. Balls: The teacher needs lots of tennis balls, at least 10 per student.
3. Clothing: Tennis shoes and comfortable clothing are recommended.

TEACHING PROGRESSIONS

1. Teach grip and ready position. Move to forehand and backhand volley, hitting balls with forehand stroke only, then hitting balls with backhand stroke only. The next step is to alternate the forehand and the backhand. Play a game with a forehand stroke to feed the ball and get the game started using volley forehand and backhand skills. Teach the tennis serve last.
2. Try not to hit in the *donut hole* area—the center—of the court. Why? Because your opponent can stand there, hit the ball back and forth, and move you all over the court.
3. When working on positioning, imagine two magnets. One magnet is centered behind the baseline, while the other is at the center of the court, about one to two steps from the net. Have the magnets draw you to one of these two spots on the court. The goal for the receiver is to stay out of donut hole which is in the middle of the court. Players can pass you easily by hitting a shot deep into the court.
4. See teaching progressions after each skill.

MINI-GAMES FOR TENNIS

1. *Quarter-Court Games* (see Figure 24.1)
   a. Play games inside the service area using volleys, where points are quickly scored.
   b. The game is started with a volley and the ball is hit directly to the receiver.
   c. Players begin to volley the ball back and forth.
   d. Whoever has the ball can start the point.
   e. You can play games to seven points and switch sides.
2. *Half-Court Games* Two players play on a half-court. The rules are the same as a ground-stroke game. Play games to seven points.
3. *Ground-Stroke Points*
   a. To put the ball in play, bounce the ball and hit it underhand anywhere in the opposite court.
   b. Singles court lines for singles games and doubles court lines for the doubles.
   c. The ball can only bounce once in your court.
   d. Whoever has the ball can start the point.
   e. Pick a total, such as 11 points, and the first one to reach the score wins. You can play best of three or best of five and rotate with your neighbors.
   f. This drill is great for learning to put points together.
4. *Regulation tennis game, one serve.* Only hit a second serve.
5. *Regulation tennis game, two serves.* You can hit a harder first serve.

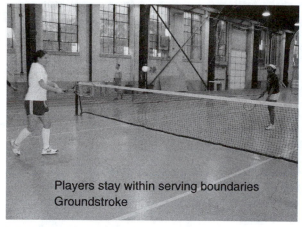

Players stay within serving boundaries
Groundstroke

FIGURE 24.1 Quarter-Court Games

6. *Five Misses:*

   a. Four players on a court at a time with "alternates" at the net post. (There can be just one player at the net post).

   b. Players play out a ground-stroke point together, and whoever misses goes to the net post.

   c. One at a time, the alternates replace the misses.

   d. As soon as a player has five misses, the game is over and you form new teams.

   e. You can also do this game with a feeder in one of the posts. The feeder tosses the ball in the court to start play.

   f. Players rotate after each point with alternates at each net post.

FYI

For further information and special help, consult the following organization.

ORGANIZATION

U.S. Tennis Association (USTA)
70 West Red Oak Lane
White Plains, NY 10604
Phone: (914) 696-7000
Fax: (914) 696-7167
Website: www.usta.com

SKILL	CUE	WHY	COMMON ERROR
Forehand Grip (Right Handed) (Figure 24.2)	Shake hands	Puts racket in proper position	Overgripping
	Hold the end of the racket	Greater speed with a longer implement and greater reach area to contact the ball	
	Index knuckle on third bevel close to fourth bevel	Gives you vertical hitting surface so ball does not go into net or fly long	
Backhand Grip (Figure 24.3)	Turn racket clockwise	The ball flies long if you don't rotate your grip. Remember: "Grip wrong ball long"	
	Index knuckle on second bevel	Gives you vertical hitting surface so ball does not go into net or fly long	
Two-Handed Backhand Grip (Right Handed)	Same cues for regular backhand	Quick reaction time	
	Keep left hand up to anticipate hitting a backhand	More power with both hands	
	Grip left hand above right hand on racket	Proper racket position	
	Left index knuckle on third bevel		
Bevel	Top bevel of the racket is number 1; second bevel is number 2; third bevel is number 3; and fourth bevel, number 4		
Right-Handed Players	Right-handed players rotate bevels in a clockwise direction		
Left-Handed Players	Left-handed players rotate levels in counter-clockwise direction		

FIGURE 24.2   Forehand Grip

FIGURE 24.3   Backhand Grip

	VOLLEYS		
SKILL	**CUE**	**WHY**	**COMMON ERROR**
Forehand Volley	Index knuckle on second bevel for both forehand and backhand	No time to change for quicker reaction time to ball	Thinking that swinging will give you more power
	Pivot, step, and punch	Power	
	Boxing—don't throw a punch from the side; skip forward and throw a quick punch from inside		
(Figure 24.4)	Firm wrist, firm grip	Prevent the racket from coming out of hand, especially if the ball is hit hard into the racket	
	Hand below ball, racket and wrist form L; don't let racket head drop	Firm contact when you hit the ball, better control and accuracy	
	Racket never goes behind front shoulder;	Keeps you aggressive at the net; better shot accuracy	
	Keep racket in peripheral vision	Faster reaction time	

continued

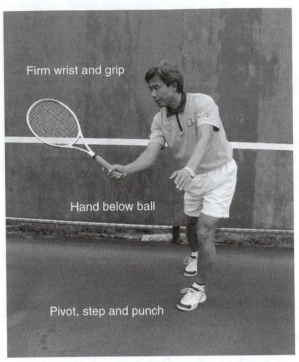

Firm wrist and grip

Hand below ball

Pivot, step and punch

FIGURE 24.4   Forehand Volley

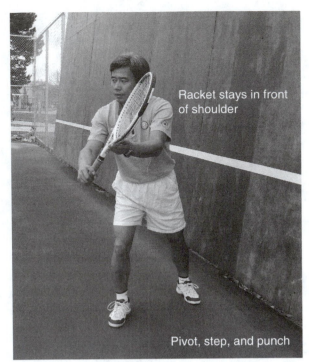

Racket stays in front of shoulder

Pivot, step, and punch

FIGURE 24.5   Backhand Volley

VOLLEYS, continued			
SKILL	**CUE**	**WHY**	**COMMON ERROR**
Forehand Volley, *continued*	Be aggressive; in this shot, go get the ball, don't wait for the ball to come to you	Places the opponent on the defensive	
	Bend at the knees and keep the back vertical		
Backhand Volley (Figure 24.5)	Same as backhand cues, just hitting on backhand side		Pulling racket with right hand; lead with your left
	Bow and arrow position		
	Index knuckle on second bevel		

SKILL	CUE	WHY	COMMON ERROR
Grip	Index knuckle on 3rd bevel close to the 4th bevel	The ball does not go high and you can get under the ball	
Foot Work	Pivot and step	Good position for ball contact	
Stroke Action (Figure 24.6)	Racket back early/ closed face	Good preparation; ball won't fly high and out of bounds	
Contact Point (Figure 24.7)	Contact point, racket is in vertical plane	Accuracy	
	Hit ball even with front hip	Accuracy	
Finish and Follow-Through (Figure 24.8)	Swing low to high and finish on edge		Pulling up too quickly on follow-through
	Point elbow toward the opponent when done	To get good top spin; ball won't go out of bounds	
	Kiss your bicep	The friction created with "over the ball motion" will give more powerful top spin	
	Bend knees and get low	Ball will not go into net if you will get low and bend your knees	Ball goes into net

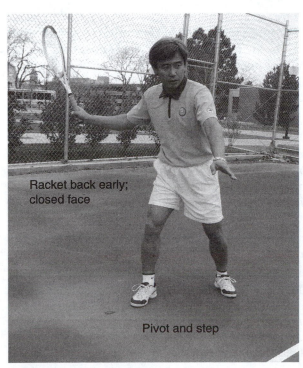

Racket back early; closed face

Pivot and step

FIGURE 24.6 Stroke Action

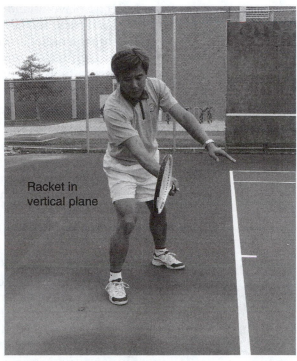

Racket in vertical plane

FIGURE 24.7 Contact Point

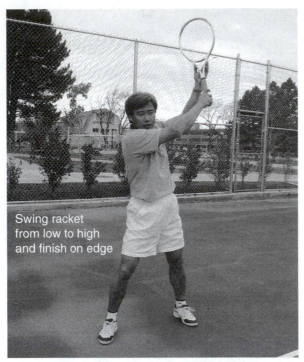

FIGURE 24.8   Forehand Stroke Finish and Follow Through

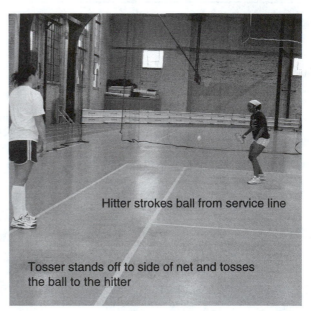

FIGURE 24.9   Partner Forehand Drill

TEACHING PROGRESSION FOR FOREHAND

Check grip first—always, always, always.

To practice the grip, have students bounce the ball with their racket, using the appropriate grip. They can bounce the ball up or down and count how many they get.

1. Have players stand 1 to 2 feet away from the tennis fence. Start with racket head back, and in closed position swing the racket to contact point. Make sure the racket is vertical. On the follow-through, racket goes over the opposite shoulder and elbow points toward the opposite court. Swing from low to high and finish "kissing the bicep." Step 5 feet away from fence, drop the ball, and hit it into the fence.

2. When students' stroke is done with control, move to the court. Drop-hit a ball over the net. Give them a target to aim for—for example, hit down the alley.

3. Next, teach students how to toss to a partner. One student tosses a ball underhand so that it bounces 5 to 8 feet in front of his or her partner. Toss a ball back and forth until they have good accuracy. The ball should bounce at least waist high.

4. When ready, the students toss the ball to their partners. The tosser stands off to the side of the net and tosses balls to his or her partner, who is standing at the service line ready to stroke the ball (see Figure 24.9).

5. The tosser is on one side of the net and tosses balls to his or her partner, who is standing on the baseline ready to stroke the ball. Encourage students by saying it doesn't matter where the ball is landing, but stress the importance of good form on their stroke. When they have some accuracy, allow them to hit forehands back and forth with their partner.

SKILL	CUE	WHY	COMMON ERROR
Grip	Left hand up early, grab racket	Reaction time	
	Right hand index knuckle to second bevel	Accuracy for shot	
	This hand is only there for support		
Foot Work	Pivot and step	To get in good position to hit the ball	
Stroke Action (Figure 24.10)	Bend at knees, back vertical	Better shot accuracy	
	Racket back early, face closed low by your shoelaces	Better power, better accuracy	
Contact Point (Figure 24.11)	Contact point vertical and off the front hip	So ball will land in court	Not leading with the left hand
Finish (Figure 24.12)	Follow through high and finish over opposite shoulder	To achieve top spin	
	"Kiss your biceps"		

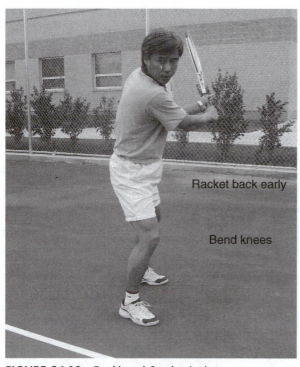

Racket back early

Bend knees

FIGURE 24.10 Backhand Stroke Action

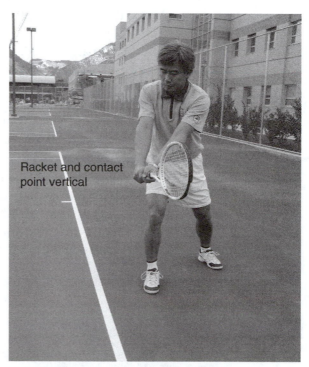

Racket and contact point vertical

FIGURE 24.11 Backhand Contact Point

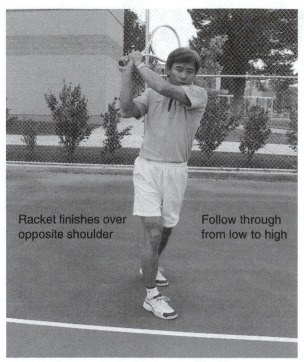

Racket finishes over opposite shoulder

Follow through from low to high

FIGURE 24.12 Backhand Finish and Follow-Through

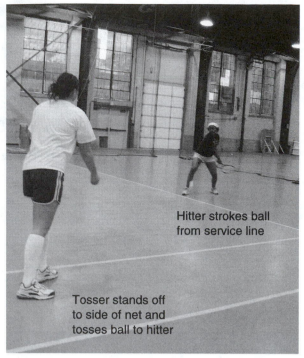

Hitter strokes ball from service line

Tosser stands off to side of net and tosses ball to hitter

FIGURE 24.13 Backhand Partner Toss Drill

TEACHING PROGRESSION FOR BACKHAND

1. Demonstrate the backhand grip. Line students along the fence and have them shadow-swing from low to high following the cues.

2. Partner drop-feeds the ball to partner. Hit into the fence.

3. When they feel comfortable with the stroke, line students on the baseline and partner feed. Give them a target to hit ball in the court, down the line, or cross court.

4. When the students are ready, pair them up. Have one student stand off to the side of the net and toss balls to his or her partner, who is standing at the service line, ready to stroke the ball (see Figure 24.13).

5. Have partner feed ball from the other side of the net.

6. Rally backhand to backhand.

7. Partner tosses the ball to alternating sides. Forehand, backhand, forehand, backhand, etc. This drill gets players to change grips, move feet to the ball, and learn how to hit backhands in a gamelike situation.

8. Teach a ground-stroke game. It incorporates all the skills they have learned and gives them gamelike practice with lots of repetitions.

LOB AND DROP SHOT

SKILL	CUE	WHY	COMMON ERROR
Lob	Rotate racket opposite of backhand		
	Swing low to high	Ball goes up in air	Hitting ball too hard
	Soft touch		
	Pull racket arm to opposite shoulder		No follow-through
Offensive	Lob must be height of fence; lob over fence		Not aiming lob
	Hit to big square	Having a place to aim gives play more control and accuracy	Lob too short; not following through
	Clear fence (good practice height)		
Drop Shot Slice	Act like hitting a backhand or forehand but cut shot in half	More control of ball	Full follow-through
	Soft touch at contact		

SERVE—RIGHT HAND

SKILL	CUE	WHY	COMMON ERROR
Grip	Right-hand index knuckle on second bevel	Accuracy and control	
Foot Placement	Point left foot toward right net post or, if left handed, right foot toward left net post	This allows for good shoulder rotation and power	
	Back foot comfortable position	Stability and balance	
Toss	Hold ball in finger pads	Control of ball	
	Hold the ball down by leg	Control and accuracy of toss	
	Gently toss the ball high	Timing for serve	
	Keep arm straight all the way up	Accuracy of toss	
	Hold arm up until ball contacts racket	You will "feel" the ball better	

continued

SKILL	CUE	WHY	COMMON ERROR
Stroking Action	Hit high and in front of you	Power and good contact point	
	Nike swoosh symbol shows position of how stance should be	Racket head speed the fastest up there	
	Racket motion is just like throwing a ball	Creates a powerful serve	
Follow-Through	Arm action comes across the body	Completes the motion of your serve and power isn't lost	
	The shoulder of the arm that hits the serve replaces where the other shoulder was	The movement naturally provides more power as body weight goes into serve	
Let	Ball hits top of net, goes over net into court; serve is taken over again		Calling it a fault or double fault (on first or second serve)
Ace	Serve is in, and receiver cannot touch it		
Double Fault	Neither of 2 serves goes into court		

TEACHING PROGRESSION

1. Teach the ball toss first. Place the racket on the ground at a 30-degree angle and place foot at the end of the handle. Toss the ball up and try to hit the strings of the racket.

2. Have students throw a ball into the service box. If they can throw it into the box, they can serve it into the box.

3. Teach the entire serve.

4. If the student has difficulty with the serve, have her or him start the serve with racket up behind head (see Figure 24.14).

5. Allow beginners to serve up close and then move back to the baseline when they are ready.

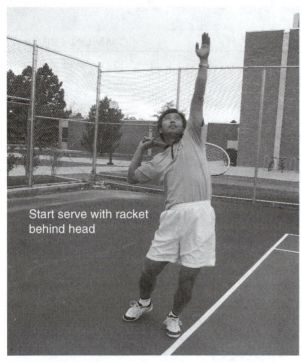

Start serve with racket behind head

FIGURE 24.14 Serve Progression

RECEIVING SERVE			
SKILL	**CUE**	**WHY**	**COMMON ERROR**
Powerful Serve	Short backswing	Better control of ball	Bringing racket too far back
	Watch ball go into racket		
	Block ball		Overhitting
			Big follow-through
	Like a volley		
Less Powerful	Hit ball into court		

SKILL	CUE	WHY	COMMON ERROR
Topspin	Racket swings low too high		Swinging level
	Candy cane swing		
	Racket starts knee-high and finishes nose-high		
Backspin (Slice) (Figure 24.15)	Racket swings high to low		Swinging level
	Cut through ball		
Overhead Smash	Hit like the serve		
	Racket back to neck		
	Left foot in front; power with left foot		Power comes from both feet or back foot
	Point elbow to ball with left hand		Misjudging ball by losing focus of ball

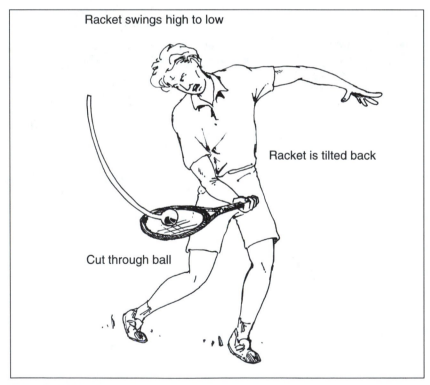

Racket swings high to low

Racket is tilted back

Cut through ball

FIGURE 24.15 Backspin

SINGLES SCORING			
SKILL	**CUE**	**WHY**	**COMMON ERROR**
Rules	First score is the server's score		Saying receiver's score first
	In this game *love* means zero		
	Love (0), 15, 30, 40, game 15–0 = 15–love 0–15 = love–15 30–30 = 30 all 40–40 = deuce		
	Win by 2, deuce and ad		
	Scoring is used for game, set, and match		
	Ad in: server's advantage		
	Ad out: opponent's advantage		
	Or in "no ad": 1–2–3–game		
	No ad after 3–3		
	Next point is game point		
	Receiver chooses side on which to receive serve		
Playing a Set	Change sides on the odd-numbered games: 1, 3, 5, 7		
	Win 6 games; win by 2 games		
	If each player wins 6 games, a tiebreaker is played		
Match Play	Win 2 out of 3 sets, women		
	Win 3 out of 5 sets, men		

SKILL	CUE	WHY	COMMON ERROR
Rules	Partner A1 serves 1 complete game		
	After the set you can serve 2 in a row (at the end of first set and beginning of second set the server can serve 2)		
	Partners always serve from opposite sides of court		
	Opponent B1 serves 1 complete game		
	Partner A2 serves 1 complete game		
	Opponent B2 serves 1 complete game		
Doubles Receiver	*Deuce court* is the right side		Switching during set
	Ad court is the left side		
	Beginning of set, each player chooses which side to receive—deuce or ad court		
	Must stay in that court to receive serve		Receiver's teammate stepping into server's box
	Change sides of court every odd game		

	TIEBREAKER		
SKILL	**CUE**	**WHY**	**COMMON ERROR**
7-Point Tiebreaker	Service begins with the player who received in the 12th game		1-love
	Don't call zero love in a tiebreaker (1–zero)		
	Player A serves first point from deuce (right) court: 1 point		
	Player B serves from ad (left) court first and then from deuce (right) court: 2 and 3 points		
	Player A (C in doubles) serves from ad (left) court first and then from deuce (right) court: 4 and 5 points		
	Player B (D in doubles) serves from ad (left) court first and then from deuce (right) court: 6 and 7 points		
	Change courts after every 6 points		Stop match by having a rest
	Cannot take more than 90 seconds		
	Grab towel and move to court		
	First player to score 7 points wins		
	Win by 2 points		

25

Touch Rugby

INTRODUCTION

Touch rugby is a highly enjoyable running game with the objective of scoring tries. Developed in Sydney, Australia, in 1960, it is a noncontact version of the rugby league game that can be played anywhere by men and women of all ages and abilities. It is a great way to raise your level of fitness and improve your ball-handling skills, and besides all that, it's just a lot of fun. It's always coed, and unlike touch football, there is no specialization in positions. It's continuous; there's no stopping to make plays, so think while you're running. The faster you are able to get in position and move the ball, the greater the advantage you will have.

SKILLS LISTED WITH CUES

The cues in this chapter cover the fundamentals of the sport such as passing and catching. It also covers offense and defense, some basic strategies, and basic rules.

TIPS

Start by teaching players how to catch and pass. Then, run wings unopposed (this is called "all-blacks"). A wing is when players line up on a 45-degree angle approximately 3 to 5 meters apart. Players advance together, holding this formation until the ball is passed to them. Once they receive the ball, they pass it to the next player in the line and retreat behind the player who now has the ball to stay onsides. When players can do this efficiently, it is time to split into teams and play a game.

EQUIPMENT TIPS

1. A rugby ball looks like a big football with rounded tips; they can be purchased on rugby Internet sites.
2. A touch rugby pitch (field) is 70 meters long × 50 meters wide. There is a halfway line with two 10-meter lines on each side of the halfway line.
3. Pullover vests.

TEACHING IDEAS

1. Referee can limit the number of touches before the ball is turned over.
2. Generally played with 7 players on each team, but the game can played with as few as 5 or as many as 10. Modify the field to account for more or less players.
3. If teams are uneven, the scrum-half (player who picks up the ball after the roll ball) on the short team can run with the ball.
4. A rule can be made that any dropped ball (even if it is knocked on by the defensive team) is a turnover.
5. Rules for kicking can be adapted for more advanced teams.

BASIC RULES AND GAME PLAY

1. Officially, the game is divided into two halves of 25 minutes each. There is a 5-minute break at half-time, and teams change direction in the second half.
2. To start the game, the ball is tapped at the halfway mark. This consists of a player releasing the ball. The ball touches his or her foot and returns to the player's hands. The ball is then live. Defensive players must be 10-meters behind the halfway mark but can advance as soon as the ball is tapped. A tap is also used to recommence play after a try is scored and on penalties (Figure 25.1 on page 324.)
3. Offensive team forms wings and uses strategies to gain field advantage attempting to score tries.
4. Each team is allowed six touches before change of possession. A legal touch includes touching the ball, shoes, hair, shirt, etc. When the defense makes contact with the ball carrier they should stop, raise their hand, and verbally call out "touch." The offense must initiate the roll ball from that spot.
5. The defensive team marks players and attempts to cause the offensive team to make errors to receive possession of the ball.
6. Penalties are awarded in cases of shepherding (blocking), offside infringements, forward passes, and player misconduct. The defensive team must be back at least 10 meters on a penalty tap.
7. A roll ball is used to restart play after a player is touched (Figure 25.2 on page 324).
8. During a roll ball the defense is required to be five meters back.

VOCABULARY

1. *Pitch:* In rugby, the field of play is called a pitch.
2. *Touch Line:* This is the out of bounds line.
3. *Forward pass:* The ball is not passed backward or lateral; but it is passed to a teammate who is in front of the passer. This results in a penalty.

FIGURE 25.1 Tapping the Ball

FIGURE 25.2 Roll Ball

4. *Dropped ball:* Anytime the ball is not caught it is considered a dropped ball. The result is a turnover.

5. *Try zone touch down:* This is similar to an end zone in football. To score, the player with the ball must cross into this zone and touch the ball under his or her control to the ground.

6. *Shepherding:* A player who is on offense and prevents a defensive player from tagging his or her teammate who has the ball is shepherding, and it is a turnover. No, this isn't football and you can't block. It results in a penalty and the defense must start back 10 meters.

7. *Roll ball:* Used to restart play after a player is touched or the ball is turned over.

8. *Offsides:* An imaginary horizontal line runs across the field where the ball is situated. Players must stay on his or her side of the line; if the line is crossed, the player is offsides. Interference with play from an offsides position is a penalty.

9. *Scrum-half/acting-half:* The player who picks up the ball after a roll ball is in the scrum-half/acting-half. This player role changes with each play depending on who is closest to the ball (the idea is to get the ball out quickly to catch the defense off guard). The scrum-half has the choice to run with the ball or pass the ball, but if this player gets touched, it is a turnover. Additionally, this player cannot score since at least one pass must be made to score.

For further information and special help, consult the following organization and resource.

ORGANIZATION

Australian Touch Association
P.O. Box 9078
Deakin, ACT 2600
Australia

WEBSITE

www.touchrugby.com

CATCHING

SKILL	CUE	WHY	COMMON ERROR
Call for Ball Support	"With you" or "On your left/right," etc.	More likely to gain field advantage if your teammates know they can pass to you	Not letting your teammates know where you are
Hands Out (Figure 25.3)	Chest level	Give a target	Hands too big, ball slides through and bounces off chest
	Form trianglelike setting in volleyball (but in front of you instead of over your head)		Hands too small, jammed fingers, dropped balls
	Hands should be just a little wider than the ball and collapse easily around the ball as contact is made		

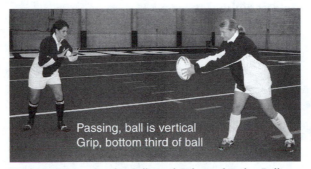

Passing, ball is vertical
Grip, bottom third of ball

FIGURE 25.3 Catch, Call, and Release for the Ball

SKILL	CUE	WHY	COMMON ERROR
Eye Contact	Make eye contact with the person the ball is going to	Make sure of recipient of pass	Passing without looking
Stance	Stand sideways	Use core muscles in rotation for greater power	Facing the target
Grip	Hold with both hands		
	Hold on bottom third of ball	Harder for opponents to knock ball from hands	Grabbing middle of ball
	Thumbs point toward sky, fingers wide and spread around ball	Ball is wobbly in the air and hard to catch	Ball not vertical at time of release
	Ball is vertical		
Leg Action	Short to medium step with leg closest to target	Innacurate	Overstriding
	Rotate at hips	Less power	No rotation
Arm Action	Arms firm	More power and accuracy in pass	Using only 1 hand
	Swing like a pendulum or an elephant's trunk across body	Uses shoulder muscles instead of arm muscles	Arms too loose or too rigid
		Poor flight path	Trying to spin the ball (long passes will have a natural spin)
Release (Figure 25.3)	Underhand, sideways toss	Most accurate and controlled way to pass	Trying to pass like a basketball (forcing from chest rather than letting arms swing)
	Release right at the top of the pendulum swing		
	Ball must go backwards or lateral	If ball goes forward, it is a turnover	Trying to pass like a lateral pass in football
			Releasing too high or too low
			Passing forward

SKILL	CUE	WHY	COMMON ERROR
Roll Ball (Figure 25.3)	The ball is placed on the ground and rolled between the legs with either the hands or foot	To restart play after a touch or a turnover	Too slow, allowing defense to get set
	All defensive players must be back 5 meters		
Scrum-Half Pass (Figure 25.2)	An offensive player picks up the ball after the roll ball and passes to another teammate (the person closest to the ball picks the ball up; this player is the scrum-half for that play)	Puts the ball in play; once the scum-half has both hands on the ball or passes it, the ball is live and the defensive team can attack	The scrum-half cannot score off a roll ball; at least 1 pass must be made to score
	This player can run with the ball, but if touched, possession is lost		
Wings	Players line up on a 45° angle approximately 3–5 meters apart	To receive the ball, you must be behind the passer, lining up like this gives you the chance to catch the ball at full speed, and therefore you will advance further	Players lineup straight
	Players advance together, holding this formation until the ball is passed to them		
	They pass it on before they are tagged and retreat behind the player, who now has the ball to stay onsides		Passing the ball forward
			Catching the ball flat-footed
	Run straight up the field	Running across the field takes away field space from teammates	Running sideways, trying to cut corners

continued

SKILL	CUE	WHY	COMMON ERROR
Basic Strategies			
Loops	First player in wing passes the ball and then loops behind teammates to take a pass on the far side; this causes an overload	If you can get a player open on the end, you can gain field advantage with an overload	Shepherding
			Not communicating
			Getting ahead of the person with the ball; can't make a pass forward
Skips	Passing past the next player in the line to an open player; can skip 1 or more players	Get the ball to a player who can break through a hole	Receiver not ready to catch
Cutting/Switching	Making a sharp cut off the hip of the player with the ball	To hit a gap and break through the defensive line	Too far away from ball carrier
Scoring (Figure 25.4)	1 point is awarded when the ball carrier crosses into the tri-zone and touches the ball to the ground without losing control	Losing control of ball	Results in a turnover; not touching the ball to the ground; no point awarded; roll ball 5 meters from tri-zone; no turnover
			Dropped ball, turnover 5 meters from tri-zone

FIGURE 25.4 Try Zone/Touch Down

FIGURE 25.5 Legal Touch

	DEFENSE		
SKILL	**CUE**	**WHY**	**COMMON ERROR**
Tagging (Figure 25.5)	Touch the player with the ball; a legal touch includes contact with ball, shoes, hair, shirt, etc.	To stop advancement; forces the offensive team to reset; when tagged 6 times, the ball is turned over	Excessive force as called by the ref can result in a penalty
Marking	Pick a player; if that player moves, follow him or her; if he or she has the ball, tag him or her	Easier defense for beginners	Letting your man through a hole
	Watch the waist	Don't get juked/ faked out	Watching the head, ball, or feet
Sliding	Zone defense rather than man	Physically easier; more fun	Not reacting fast enough
	If offensive player loops/cuts/switches, the defensive team slides to mark the new man	As in any sport, communication is very important; always let your team know where you are and who you are guarding	Not communicating effectively
	If you call the end, you always mark the offensive player who is on the end; if you call 2 in, you always mark the player second from the end		Offensive team develops overload or breaks through holes, thinking your team-mate will make a tag that should be yours
Interception	If you catch a pass from the offensive team, the play continues in your possession	If you make a play from an off-sides positions, it is a penalty	You cannot hang out in the passing lane waiting for a pass; you must charge a pass from your line and catch it cleanly to gain possession
Offsides	Defensive players cannot be behind the ball; they must start 5 meters back from roll ball, then must remain even with the ball during play	Results in a penalty	Going too far forward

26

Track and Field Events

INTRODUCTION

How can I go over the hurdle faster? How do I improve my sprint time? What's the best way to exchange the baton? Students and athletes might ask you questions such as these. Are you ready to answer without giving them too much technical information?

An effective way to teach track and field skills is to provide teaching cues that are simple and to the point. Good visual teaching cues help athletes create visual images for better concentration and consequently help to perfect techniques. For example, when teaching the use of starting blocks, have students make a check mark with their hands at the starting line. The check mark cues the student to establish the correct hand position. Another example: When teaching the long jump, feedback from the coach might include "Mark, I really liked how you arched your back like a C in the air; however, make sure you close the jackknife on your landing a little sooner."

Giving students or athletes visual teaching cues can make a significant difference in the outcome of a race or event. A tenth of a second faster time or one inch difference in a throw or jump could mean advancing to regionals and then state competition.

SKILLS LISTED WITH CUES

Teaching cues in this chapter include the following: pillar, sprinting form, skills and drills, relays, low hurdles, steeplechase, distance running and jumping events (long jump, triple jump, high jump), and throwing events (shot put and discus).

Each event is broken down into its component phases, and cues are provided for each phase of the skill. The cues can be used in teaching the beginner or in helping the experienced athlete perfect his or her technique.

FIGURE 26.1 Equipment Ideas for a Track and Field Unit

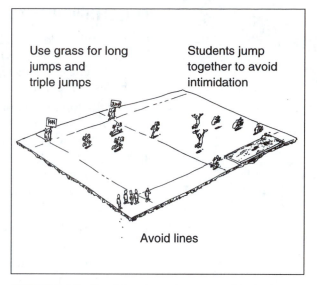

FIGURE 26.2 Teaching Long Jump to a Physical Education Class

TIP

When using a four-station rotation system for a large class, do not include more than one dangerous event. (For example, do not include both shot put and high jump.) The four stations might include starts, shot put (a dangerous station where the teacher should be present), distance runs, and long jump.

EQUIPMENT TIPS FOR RUNNING EVENTS

1. Starts: Blow a whistle to replace gun; use toilet paper for finish line.
2. Use large orange cones, dowel sticks, PVC pipe, or bamboo poles to make hurdles, or use foam rubber practice hurdles. Students are less likely to get hurt because foam hurdles are lightweight (see Figure 26.1).

EQUIPMENT TIPS FOR JUMPING EVENTS

1. High jump: Use elastic surgical tubing as a crossbar (see Figure 26.1).
2. Use grass for long jumps and triple jumps for large classes (see Figure 26.2).

EQUIPMENT TIPS FOR THROWING EVENTS

1. Use lightweight safe substitutes for competitive implements. If you don't have enough equipment, introduce the event as a station activity.
2. Shot put: Use tennis balls filled with lead shot and bound in tape or soft softballs.
3. Discus: Use rubber rings, small hula hoops.
4. Javelin: Use balls.

TEACHING IDEAS

1. Have all students practice long jump and triple jump together, shoulder to shoulder on the grass instead of one at a time in the pit, until they gain some proficiency in the sport. Everyone will get more practice, and students may be less self-conscious than they might be jumping in front of their peers.

2. For the long jump, place a low hurdle or cone in sand. Have student jump over object. Place the hurdle or cone further out or higher up to challenge the student.

3. For the triple jump, place three hula hoops equidistant apart on the runway. Have students run down the runway and place a foot (for each phase) in the hula hoops. Gradually lengthen the distance of the hula hoops to challenge the students.

4. Let student roll the discus on the ground, making sure the disc is coming off the index finger. See how far he or she can roll it before it falls over.

5. Teaching progression: Teach shot put first, and discus second. Use modified equipment for large classes or beginners as described under "Equipment Tips."

Warm-Up

Start the warm-up with a one- to three-minute jog, and then move to dynamic stretches.

Dynamic Stretches

Dynamic stretching is a method of warm-up for explosive, high-speed activity. Dynamic stretches stimulate the body's ability to move faster by promoting more efficient nerve firing and more blood flow to deeper muscle tissues. Dynamic stretching is thought to be superior to static stretching because of the positive effects on the nerves. Static stretches are thought to dampen nerve firing. Dynamic stretches move the limbs through a full range of motion. Basically, the joint is moving continuously through various coordinated and sport-specific motor executions (Winkler & Schexnayder, 1998).

It is important to start gradually, then progress to greater speed and muscle recruitment. Warm up the large muscles first, and then go to smaller, more specific muscles. Most of the following progressive exercises can be performed while jogging, skipping, running backward, or zigzagging (Pfaff et al., 1991, p. 50).

1. Big arm circles: Move the arms forward, backward, swimming backstroke, front crawl, and windmill type of motion alternating one arm forward, the other arm backward. Use your imagination to create ways to move the arms while also moving the legs.

2. Bend over sweeps: Bend over at the waist, swing the arms left and right, and move to a cross swing.

3. Torso twist: In a standing position, straddle the legs and twist the torso back and forth.

4. Leg swings: Stretch by swinging the leg in front, back, and to the side of the body. Hand extends out to balance against a wall or partner's shoulder.

5. Speed skater stretch: Slowly lean in squatting speed skater position and do a stretched lunge to right and left sides.

6. Slow forward leg lunges: Take slow, long lunge steps moving forward.

7. Ankling: Roll from the heel to toe alternating each foot. Place heel next to instep of opposite foot rolling forward with half steps. Swivel the hips while moving forward to toe.

8. Ankle rolls: Draw the alphabet with toes so ankle rotates.

9. Inverted scissors: Lie on back, roll up on your shoulders. Hands and forearms are flat on the ground or floor. Move the legs above your head in a scissors motion, forward and backward, side to side, and crossing the legs.

10. Inverted bicycles: Lie on back, roll up on shoulders. Hands and forearms are flat on the ground or floor. Move your legs like riding a bicycle.

Rule of thumb: Anything goes! Be creative and have fun. As long as you are staying in continuous motion, you are stretching or moving dynamically.

All elite, explosive athletes, including sprinters, warm up in this dynamic manner because of its positive effect on nerve firing. These same high-level athletes avoid static stretching while warming up for high-speed performance because of its negative effects on nerve firing. This does not mean that static stretching is bad, only that it is inappropriate as a warm-up for high-speed performance (Winkler & Schexnayder, 1998).

Core Exercises

Prior to and during the teaching of sprinting technique, emphasis needs to be placed on exercises that develop the core of the body from midtorso to midthigh. Core exercises develop the ability to stabilize the core into a pillar-like configuration. The core can be strengthened with exercises that require the use of core musculature in any or all planes. A general fitness block that includes extensive core development would be appropriate to teach before beginning a skill block that includes sprint technique. See the strength training chapter (Chapter 21) for more details on the core and exercises.

FYI

For further information and special help, consult the following organization and resource.

ORGANIZATIONS

USA Track and Field
RCA Dome, Suite 140
Indianapolis, IN 46225
Phone: (317) 261-0500
Fax: (317) 261-0481
Website: www.usatf.org

Jamie Bennion (heptathlete)
270 N. 530 East
American Fork, UT 84003
Phone: (801) 756-4689

PUBLICATION

Carr, G. (1991). *Fundamentals of track and field*. Champaign, IL: Leisure Press.

PILLAR

SKILL	CUE	WHY	COMMON ERROR
Pillar	Critical for many sport skills	Foundation of correct body posture in most sport skills	
Head Position	Head over shoulders	Creates more efficiency in runners' sprinting technique	
Shoulder Position	Shoulders over hips		
Hip Position	Hips over feet		
	Make a pillar with your torque when performing sprinting drills and sprinting		

SPRINTING SKILLS AND DRILLS

SKILL	CUE	WHY	COMMON ERROR
Toe Action (Figure 26.3)	Toe up	To allow foot contact	
		To be as close under the hips as possible—allows for sprinting to be a pushing action, instead of a pulling action	
		Decreases time spent on the ground and places the foot in an optimal position to come up under the hip and eliminates "dangle time"	
Heel Action	Heel up	To shorten the lever as quickly as possible by bringing the heel directly under the buttocks; avoids "dangle time" (leg extended behind you after it leaves the ground)	
Knee Action	Knee up	Increases stride length	
	Make a backwards L		
	Thigh parallel		

continued

SKILL	CUE	WHY	COMMON ERROR
Arm Action	Hold arms at 90° angle; fingers come to the eye on the front side		
	Don't pass the hip on the back side ("cheek to cheek")		
	Shoulder joint only joint to move		
	Fingers "eye to hip"		
Pillar	Run tall and make a pillar with torso: head over shoulders; shoulders over hips; hips over feet; abs like an accordion	Prevents upper body from leaning back	

FOUR PROGRESSIVE SPRINT DRILLS

Drill 1: Pawing Action

In this drill, students focus on pulling the heel directly under the buttocks and raising the thigh to a position parallel to the ground. The drill is performed by standing sideways, placing one hand on a wall, and raising the opposite leg so the thigh is parallel to the ground. The ready position is, knee parallel to the ground, and standing on the balls of the feet, heel under the buttocks, toes flexed toward the knee. The student then makes a pawing action on the ground, similar to a bull threatening to charge. Throughout the whole sequence, the toe stays flexed, emphasizing contact on the ground directly under the hip.

Drill 2: Walking A's

Walking A's are very similar to the pawing action. Begin by standing in the start position (knee parallel to ground, toe flexed, and heel to buttocks). Perform the pawing action one leg after the other and begin moving forward. Emphasize the cues of toe up, knee up, and heel up, arms "cheek to cheek" and keeping core tight (Figure 26.3, page 336).

Drill 3: Skipping A's

This drill emphasizes the powerful snap of the leg to the ground under the hip. A skip is performed. The student focuses on the cues, thigh parallel, toe up, and heel up, in addition to placing the foot in the optimal position under the hip upon contact with the ground. Arm action again should be "cheek to cheek".

Drill 4: Running A's

Sometimes known as "High Knees." Running A's put all the drills together and emphasize frequency of contacts with the ground, not distance traveled. The student focuses on the same cues as the walking and skipping A's, emphasizing a stable core (abdominals like an accordion).

FIGURE 26.3 Walking A's

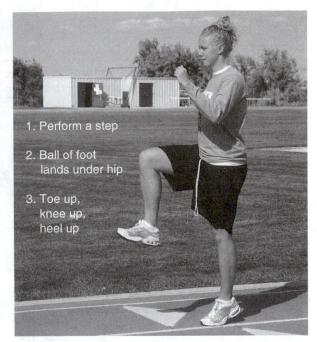

1. Perform a step

2. Ball of foot
   lands under hip

3. Toe up,
   knee up,
   heel up

FIGURE 26.4 Skipping A's

SPRINT ACCELERATIONS

A sprint acceleration is a gradual acceleration from a standing position to full speed over 100 meters. The purpose is to develop and rehearse the conceptual model of acceleration and transitioning to full speed.

SPRINT ACCELERATION AND TRANSITION SKILLS			
SKILL	**CUE**	**WHY**	**COMMON ERROR**
Sprint Accelerations (Initial 15–30 meters)	Push back into the track on balls of feet	More time needed on the ground during the initial acceleration phase to obtain a faster top end speed	
	Angle of body at 45°		
	Low heel recovery (heels don't come above the opposite knee)		
	Toe up		

continued

SKILL	CUE	WHY	COMMON ERROR
Transition (through 50 meters)	Uniformly progress from an emphasis on pushing to a "pawing action"	Allows sprinter to maintain speed that has been generated from the acceleration phase	
	Foot contact gradually becomes upright under hip		
	Toe up, heel up, knee up	When the knees drop, deceleration occurs; the longer a sprinter can keep the knees up, the longer he or she will maintain full speed	
	Body must be a "pillar," like an accordion		
	Transition from low heel recovery to high heel recovery (heel under buttocks)		

SPRINTING			
SKILL	CUE	WHY	COMMON ERROR
Full Speed	Toe up, heel up, knee up!	When knee drops, deceleration occurs; the longer a sprinter can keep the knees up the longer he or she will maintain full speed	
	Maintain knee parallel to ground		
	Hold arms at 90° angle		
	Fingers "cheek to cheek"		
	Make a pillar with your torso (hips up, abs tight)	Prevents students from leaning back when running	
	Run tall		
	Ball of foot lands under hip		

BLOCK STARTS

SKILL	CUE	WHY	COMMON ERROR
Initial Block Setting	Front block 2 foot lengths from start line	Strongest position from which to push	Feet too far apart or too close together or front foot is too close to or far from back foot
	Back foot 3 foot lengths from start line		

STARTING BLOCKS

SKILL	CUE	WHY	COMMON ERROR
"On Your Marks" (Figure 26.5)	Back into blocks		No routine, no order, no sequence
	Toes barely in contact with track		
	Front foot goes in first, back foot second		
	Hands make a bridge with fingers and thumb (behind starting line)	Raises center of gravity	Weight on thumb and knuckles
	Shoulders over hands	Engages forward momentum	Weight back, shoulders behind hands
	Weight forward		
	Eyes looking down	Keeps head neutral	Dropping the head
	Head is level		
	Sit in blocks		
"Set" (Figure 26.6)	Buttocks up in 1 motion	Less stress on supporting arms	Coming up too slow, buttocks lower than head
	Lean until you are just about ready to fall	Get you ready for the 45° angle of your body	
	Shoulders over line		
	Body still like statue		Moving body
	Front leg at 90° angle		
	Back leg at 120° angle		
	Both feet pushing back hard into pedals	Gives sprinter pre-tension in legs	

continued

FIGURE 26.5 "On Your Mark"

FIGURE 26.6 "Set"

FIGURE 26.7 "Gun"

STARTING BLOCKS, continued

SKILL	CUE	WHY	COMMON ERROR
"Gun" (Figure 26.7)	Drive opposites (right arm, left leg or left arm, right leg)	Helps extend body while coming out of blocks	Right arm and right leg come out of blocks first or left arm and left leg
	Drive arm out and up		
	Push both legs equally hard		Stepping with forward leg first
	Explode out of the blocks at 45° angle	Helps sprinter push back into track rather than pulling	Standing straight up
			Pulling motion
	Short, quick steps		
	Feet contact track directly under hip		

SPRINTING—50, 100, 200, 400 METERS

SKILL	CUE	WHY	COMMON ERROR
Racing Form *Hip-Torso Action*	Tall, as if being picked up by the hair	Allows sprinter's knees to come up to 90°	Hips turned down
	Tummy flat (tight like accordion)		
	Make a pillar with the hips and torso		
	Buttocks tucked under	Keeps hips turned up	

continued

SKILL	CUE	WHY	COMMON ERROR
Racing Form, *continued*			
Arm Action	Sharp elbows		Arms crossing midline of body
	Back arm stays at 90°; "cheek to cheek"		
Hand Position	Hold a newspaper		Fists clenched
	Hold a penny		Floppy hands
Leg Action	Heel to buttocks		Not enough knee flexion
	Step over opposite knee		Knee lift too low
	Thigh parallel to ground		
	Point toe to sky		Pointing toe to ground before contact
	Claw ground with foot		
	Snap leg down		Not snapping leg down
	Ground contact with ball of foot directly under hip	Energy efficient	Stopping foot on contact with ground

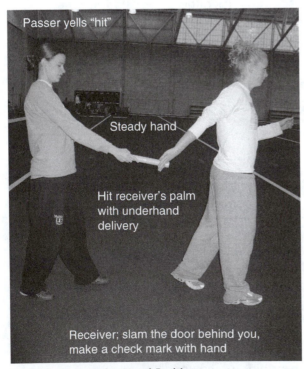

FIGURE 26.8 Relay Hand Position

FIGURE 26.9 Relay Passer's Code Drill

SKILL	CUE	WHY	COMMON ERROR
Receiver's Arm Position (Figure 26.8)	Slam the door directly behind you, keeping arm straight	Gives the passer an accessible target	Arm extended outward
	Thumb in toward backbone; make check mark toward ground		
Receiver's Hand Position	Steady hand and arm		Hand and arm moving
Passer's Arm Position (Figure 26.8)	Hit the palm with underhanded delivery	Prevents passer from missing receiver's hand	Trying to pass before target appears
	Focus eyes on hand; hit target		
Passer's Code	Tape mark for takeoff		Leaving too early or too late
	Leave when incoming runner crosses tape with body		
Exchange (Figure 26.9)	Passer yells, "Hit," a signal for the receiver to lift arm back	Minimizes the time of the exchange	Passer is too fast
	Receiver and passer at full speed when exchange takes place		Receiver is not at full speed

SKILL	CUE	WHY	COMMON ERROR
Receiver	Turn head back over left shoulder toward passer, judge incoming runner's speed	To be able to match passer's speed, minimizing the time of exchange	Taking off too soon or too late
	Take 2 accelerating steps, then turn		
	Point hand at incoming runner with palm up and elbow down		
	Take the baton from the incoming runner like you're taking the money and running	Decreases the chances of dropping the baton	Dropping the money (baton)
Passer	Put baton in receiver's hand, arm fully extended at shoulder level	Decreases the chance of dropping the baton	Watching other competitors
	Full speed until receiver has baton		Slowing before pass

SKILL	CUE	WHY	COMMON ERROR
Receiver's Arm and Hand Position	Arm and hand parallel to ground		Hand bent up at wrist
	Elbow facing up		Arm and hand too low
	Make a check mark with palm facing up	Creates a big target	
Passer's Arm Position	Punch baton into target	Minimizes chance of passer missing the hand	Passing the baton from above shoulders coming down
	Piston-type motion		Passing baton before target appears
	Focus eyes on hand		Eyes wandering
Passer's Code	Tape mark		
	20–30 steps; leave when incoming runner hits tape	Minimizes the time of the exchange	Too soon or too late
Exchange	See target before pass		Passer is too fast, receiver not at full speed
	Passer yells, "Hit," the signal for the receiver to put arm back		

1. Stay tall
2. Keep normal running action
3. Drive elbows back

FIGURE 26.10 Going over Low Hurdle

SKILL	CUE	WHY	COMMON ERROR
Body Position			
Before Hurdles	Short last step		
	Pawing action (like a bull)	Prevents hurdler from going high over hurdles	Sitting, planting drive leg in front of hip
Over Hurdles	Exaggerated sprinting form over the hurdles	Maintains hurdler's speed over hurdle and in between	Jumping over hurdles
Between Hurdles	Sprinting form between hurdles		Last step before hurdle is too long
	Heel to buttocks, toe up		
	Thigh parallel to ground		
	Body erect, tall		
Trail Arm	Drive elbow back	Arms in close to body	Swings back too far
	Cut knee off with thumb		
Lead Leg (Figure 26.10)	Upper leg flexed	Fast lead leg	Straight lead leg
	Heel to buttocks		
	Extend like a switchblade		
	Snap foot downward and backward		Toe contact too far forward of hips
	Ball of foot lands under hip		
	Vigorous pawing action		
	Hips stay level		
Trail Leg	Hips parallel to hurdle		Hips not parallel
	Lead with knee and bring knee back to parallel	Helps maintain speed throughout race	Leading with thigh
	Toes averted		Toes pointed down
	Foot flexed		
	Snap foot down "quick"		
Equal and Opposite Reaction	Stay tall over hurdle, then tall position when foot touches ground	Similar to normal running position, which is more natural	Getting tall too soon or too late
			Leaning over hurdle

STEEPLECHASE

SKILL	CUE	WHY	COMMON ERROR
Water Jump	Stay short		Standing tall
			Arms flapping around
	Lean forward	Limits amount of time over hurdle	Slowing down before the hurdle
	Keep center of gravity close to hurdle		
	Push off the back of the hurdle		Stepping on top of hurdle
Stationary Barriers	Same as 400 hurdle		
	Stay tall		
	Accelerate into the hurdle	Maintains speed going over hurdle	
	Keep up speed		
	Be conscious of trail leg		

DISTANCE RUNNING

SKILL	CUE	WHY	COMMON ERROR
Body Position	Relax the face, neck, shoulders, and arms	More energy efficient	Face, neck, shoulders, and arms are tense/tight (wasted energy)
	Body erect		
Hand Position	Thumb rests on the index finger, as if reading a newspaper (relaxed)	Limits energy lost	Clenched fist or floppy hands
Arm Position	Arms swing forward and back moving shoulder joint only	Energy efficient	Arms cross midline of the body—high arm swing
Leg Position	Use shorter steps than sprinting		Bouncing up and down
			Long stride
	Toes and knees up	Prevents runner from getting sloppy	
Foot Position	Strike heel and roll to toe	Calves wont get tired as quickly	Striking toes first
	Toes straight ahead or slightly out		Feet are pigeon-toed
Head Position	Head and eyes straight ahead	Keeps runner focused on task	Head down or up

continued

DISTANCE RUNNING, continued

SKILL	CUE	WHY	COMMON ERROR
Breathing	Breathe from stomach (avoid side aches)	Receive more air	Breathing from the chest
	As if taking a breath to play a musical instrument		
Thought Process	Think positive thoughts: "I feel great"; "I am strong"; "Body is moving well"	Helps motivation	Thinking negative thoughts

LONG JUMP

SKILL	CUE	WHY	COMMON ERROR
Approach	Start with takeoff foot forward		Changing starting/ jumping foot
	12–18 strides; younger athletes, fewer strides; faster athletes, more strides	Get tired easily	Too many strides
	Accelerate to maximum usable speed		Changing speed of approach
	Same approach every time	Makes runway accurate	
	Knees up and tall in last strides as if being lifted by the hair		
Takeoff	Last 2 steps, like a layup in basketball— long-short	Ensures last step will be under hip	Last step too long
	Jump up and out		
	Drive up knee and opposite arm vigorously	Provides better leverage	Not driving up free knee and opposite arm
	Overemphasize knee lift and arm drive		

continued

SKILL	CUE	WHY	COMMON ERROR
Action in the Air (Figure 26.11)	Body makes a curve, like a half moon	Sets jumper up for a landing	Upper body ahead of hips
	Arch back like a C		
	Knees and feet behind hips		
	Arms above head and behind shoulders		
	Close jackknife	Brings legs up higher in air which allows for greater distance	Little or no leg action
	Extend legs and throw arms past knees		Arms are not thrown past knees
Landing	Collapse buttocks to heels upon landing	Greater distance	Feet apart
	Arms thrust forward		
	Feet together		

FIGURE 26.11   Going over Low Hurdle

TRIPLE JUMP

SKILL	CUE	WHY	COMMON ERROR
Approach	Start with jumping foot forward		Changing starting/jumping foot (takeoff foot)
	12–18 strides—younger athletes, fewer strides; faster athletes, more strides	They tire easily	
	Knees up and tall in last 5 or 6 strides as if being lifted up by the hair		Overstriding or sitting
	Maximum speed		Last step too long
	Same approach every time	Makes runway accurate	
	Last 2 steps like a lay-up in basketball—long-short last 2 steps	Ensures last step will be under hip	
Hop	Take off and land on same foot	The rule	Landing on the opposite foot
	Tall upper body	Knees come up better	Leaning forward at waist
	Head and eyes level		Looking down at ground, head down
	Look ahead		
	Knee up, toe up		Straight leg
	Snappy, pawing action	Gets jumper ready for next phase	No pawing action
	Active landing		Leg does not snap down
Step	Long step, as if stepping over mud puddles		Hopping again
	Take off and land on opposite foot		
	Tall upper body	Knee comes up better	Leaning forward at waist
	Head and eyes level; look ahead		Looking down at the ground, head down
	Split in air		Short steps
	Wide thigh separation during step		

continued

SKILL	CUE	WHY	COMMON ERROR
Step, *continued*	Landing—snappy, pawing action	Gets jumper ready for next phase	No pawing action
	Active landing		
Jump			
Arm Action	Reach for the sky; drive arms upward	Provides better leverage	Not driving arms upward
Head and Eye Position	Head and eyes level; look ahead		Looking down
Body Action	Close jackknife		No hips
	Extend legs from hips		
	Throw arms past knees, as if driving ski poles back at the start of the race	Allows for greater distance	Reaching hands to feet
	Collapse buttocks to heels upon landing		Straight-leg landing on buttocks
Ground Contact	Even cadence throughout jump	Greater distance	Uneven cadence
	Even rhythm		
	Feet make "ta–ta–ta" sound (even–even–even step)		Feet make "taaa–ta–ta" sound (long–short–-short step)

HIGH JUMP

SKILL	CUE	WHY	COMMON ERROR
Approach	Start just on the outside of the standards	Allows for better curve	
Running Stride	Make a J		Running straight at the bar
	10-step total approach		
	Get speed in run first		
	The last 4 steps start the turn for the J		
Body Position	Lean into curve		Standing tall in curve
	Inside shoulder a little lower than outside shoulder		
Running Stride	Last 3 steps medium, long, short	Ensures last step will be under hip	Last 3 steps too long or too short
Takeoff			
Legs	Take off from outside foot		Inside foot used to take off
	Foot placed parallel to bar		
	Takeoff foot down quickly, as if stepping on a bug	More power	Take off with both feet
	Plant power leg, active landing		Failing to plant power leg, no power in run or jump
	Drive the lead knee vigorously up	Provides for greater leverage	Not driving knee up
Arms	Drive both arms up	Provides for greater leverage	Using legs only
Flight			
Body Position	Arch like a banana	Makes better arch	Flat back
	Head back		
Arm Position			Hands not visible
			Dropping fists

SKILL	CUE	WHY	COMMON ERROR
Enter/Exit Position	Enter ring from rear	The rule	Entering and exiting ring from side or front
	Exit from rear	The rule	
Hold Shot	Cradle shot	Allows for better release	Dropping the elbow and having the shot roll into palm
	Hold shot on finger pads		
	Push shot firmly against neck		
	Elbow up		
Release of Shot	Push shot through head		Throwing like a baseball
	Shot leaves from neck, a "put" not a throw		
	Release is fast like a punch and at a 45° angle		Punch is horizontal
Start of Glide	Bend support knee		Hurrying start and keeping weight back
	Kick backward with nonsupport leg		Trying to throw before reaching power position
	Land both feet simultaneously still facing back		
	Hips open up quick like a baseball swing		
	Free arm swings up as if slapping a giant	Creates torque	
Explosion of Glide	Push with both legs	Makes throw more powerful	Legs collapse on thrower
	Keep shot back last		
	Release shot at 45° angle		
End of Throw	Slap and pull with free arm	Shorten lever to speed rotation	

DISCUS

SKILL	CUE	WHY	COMMON ERROR
Enter/Exit	Enter ring from back	The rule	Entering and exiting ring from rear
	Exit ring from back	The rule	
Holding the Discus	Open-handed eagle-claw grip	Allows for correct release and flat disc in air	Letting discus fall from hand
	Carry a textbook		
	Relax fingertips on edge of discus		Not gripping solidly
Release	Discus leaves off index finger as if releasing a bowling ball	Better flight	Holding on to discus too long
The Wind	Twist and shout	Shout makes discus go farther	Only half winding
	Keep body wound up until throw, then shout	The more torque, the farther the disc will go	
	Keep arm back		
Explosion of Throw	Hips lead like a baseball swing	Creates torque	Throwing before reaching power position
	Hips open quick like a baseball swing		
End of Throw	Long pull (smooth like a golf swing)	Creates long lever	Hurrying the throw release (will cause discus to flutter like a dead duck)
	Head and chest up facing sector		Legs collapse

27

Tumbling

INTRODUCTION

Tumbling is the most popular event in gymnastics because not much equipment is required for it. All that is needed is a flat surface area—a lawn, a living room, a football field, a basketball floor, a trampoline. Tumbling can be done anywhere and everywhere.

Tumbling is a sport that combines flexibility, strength, and coordination. It is for all ages. There is something exciting and intriguing about the body in motion. The wonder of the sport is the skills and movements that defy the limits placed on us by gravity.

SKILLS LISTED WITH CUES

Included in this chapter are simple cues to help instructors teach the following skills more efficiently: forward roll, front roll straddle, backward roll, backward roll straddle, handstand, back extension roll, cartwheel, and round off.

TIPS

1. Students should not be forced to do any tumbling skills. Ninety percent of injuries occur when students try to perform skills they are not ready to do on their own, often causing students to "chicken out."

2. The student should be completely confident before performing a skill. If a student is fearful or has had a bad experience, let the student choose which skill he or she would like to perform.

3. The most basic position is the handstand position. If a student can perform a good handstand, she or he should be able to learn the more difficult skills involved in tumbling.

EQUIPMENT TIPS

1. Mats must be firm, padded, nonslippery, and clean.

2. Have students take shoes and socks off. Socks tend to make the skills more difficult by making contact with the mat difficult, and may cause one to slip.

3. There is a wide variety of tumbling surfaces available: spring tumbling floor, tumble tramp, ski tumble floor, and rod tumbling floor, to name a few.

TEACHING IDEAS

1. Flexibility and muscle-warming exercises are essential before practicing skills. Some suggested flexibility exercises for tumbling might include butterfly sit (two sets of 10 seconds), pike sit (hold for 30 seconds), straddle sit (hold each side for 30 seconds to 1 minute), and back bends (three sets, hold for 30 seconds to 1 minute). Also stretch wrists, ankles, shoulders, and neck.

2. Safety is a major concern for those who teach tumbling. The purpose of spotting is to aid students in practicing a skill safely and to prevent possible injury caused by landing incorrectly. The following list presents four safety and spotting suggestions:

   a. Know what the student is going to perform.

   b. Identify likely mishaps, and know when they might occur.

   c. Know what to spot and when the spot must occur.

   d. Have enough strength to assist if needed.

3. Once a student can confidently perform a single skill, other skills can be added to it. This progression can be followed with all tumbling skills. For example, the forward roll progression is as follows:

   a. Forward roll, stretch up

   b. Forward roll, tuck jump

   c. Forward roll, jump, half turn

   d. Forward roll, jump, full twist

   e. Forward roll, jump, straddle toe touch

   Students can perform more advanced skills once they feel comfortable performing a forward/backward roll and handstand (Masser, 1993). These skills help students improve their balance, coordination, and form when finishing a skill.

4. Have students design a routine with five to eight skills they feel comfortable performing.

FYI

For further information and special help, consult the following organization and resource.

ORGANIZATION

USA Gymnastics
Pan American Plaza, Suite 300
201 South Capital Avenue
Indianapolis, IN 46225
Phone: (317) 237-5050
Fax: (317) 237-5069
Website: www.usa-gymnastics.org

PUBLICATION

Weiss, M., Ebbeck, V., & Rose, D. (1992). "Show and tell" in the gymnasium revisited: Developmental differences in modeling and verbal rehearsal effects on motor skill learning and performance. *Research quarterly for exercise and sport*, 63(3), 292–301.

BASIC STARTING POSITIONS AND RULES

SKILL	CUE	WHY	COMMON ERROR
Basic Start Position	Ankles together, stand tall, arms reach toward ceiling		Legs apart, slumping
			Elbows bent
Lunge Position	Lunge position arms reach for ceiling		
	Front leg bent slightly, rear leg straight		
Rules	Tumble longer than your body	Puts less stress and force on the wrists and elbows; also gives the tumbler more power	
	Wherever hands go, body follows		
	For every action, there is an equal and opposite reaction—as if the body is a teeter-totter		
	Finish tall, reach for ceiling		

FORWARD ROLL

SKILL	CUE	WHY	COMMON ERROR
Technique	Hips above head		
	Hands close to feet		Hands away from feet
	Put hands flat on mat		
	Forehead on knees	Gives the back the proper rounded position	Not rounding back
	Look at chest		

continued

FORWARD ROLL, continued

SKILL	CUE	WHY	COMMON ERROR
Technique, *continued*	Push off both feet and roll as if feet are tied together and cannot come apart		Pushing off ground 1 foot at a time
			Pushing into headstand instead of rolling forward
	Lower back down to mat using arms		Putting knees down on mat/rollover open
	Feel back stretching		
	Stand tall, reach for ceiling		Standing up using knees instead of feet
	Squeeze stomach in, as if squeezing an orange		

FRONT ROLL STRADDLE

SKILL	CUE	WHY	COMMON ERROR
Technique	Legs apart, knees locked in straddle position		Knees bent
	Put hands flat on mat		
	Head down, tuck chin, round back		Head up
	Look at chest or belly button		
	Push evenly off both feet and roll	Push through the toes to avoid bending legs	Pushing with 1 foot
	Hands push hard between legs		Hands out to side, bending and unlocking knees
	Move shoulders forward quickly and forcefully		
	Stand tall, arms reach for ceiling		

BACKWARD ROLL

SKILL	CUE	WHY	COMMON ERROR
Technique	Forehead on knees with hands on shoulders, palms up		Head comes up as backward motion is started
	Put hands on mat next to ears, push with hands, as if you are smashing something on ground next to ears		
	Push off feet evenly, as if feet are tied together and cannot come apart		Not pushing evenly with hands when rolling over head
	Roll back fast, keeping forehead on knees		Knees go up above head rather than past head
	Knees glued to chest		
	Keep feet moving backward to find mat		
	When palms touch mat, push to force knees over and past head	Pushing with the arms will take all the pressure off the neck	
	Reach for ceiling		

BACKWARD ROLL STRADDLE

SKILL	CUE	WHY	COMMON ERROR
Technique	Legs apart, knees locked in straddle position		
	Bend forward		
	Place hands between legs and behind buttocks		
	Tuck chin, round back		
	Lean and roll, quickly placing hands on mat beside ears		Not making quick transition of hands between legs to beside ears
	Push hard with hands, moving feet in straddle position to find mat	Helps take weight and pressure off neck	Not pushing evenly with hands when rolling over head
	Stand tall, reach for ceiling, legs in straddle position		

HANDSTAND

SKILL	CUE	WHY	COMMON ERROR
Hands Starting on Mat			
Ready Position	Dominant leg back, palm on mat		
	Shoulder over knuckles into mat	Also extends the shoulders, straightening and strengthening the handstand	Shoulder over the heel of hand
	Swing dominant leg up, lift other leg up to meet it		Switching legs in air
	Bring nondominant leg back down close to hands		Lifting leg when swinging leg up
	Keep head still throughout	The head must remain neutral; if it moves back, it will cause the handstand to arch; if it moves forward, it will cause the handstand to become off balance and tip forward into a forward roll	Dropping head once legs are up
Standing			
Ready Position	Lunge position, reach for ceiling		
Motion	Kick rear leg forcefully upward and backward with body stretched as if body is a teeter-totter		Body too loose
	1. Legs come together upside down, squeeze stomach, legs tight, knees locked	These 3 actions will help maintain balance and will strengthen the handstand; the tighter and taller the hand-stand is, the longer it will balance	Bending arms
	2. Touch toes to ceiling		
	3. Push through shoulders to maintain handstand position		

continued

SKILL	CUE	WHY	COMMON ERROR
Standing, *continued*	Step 1 leg down at a time to lunge position, arms reach toward ceiling	Stepping down or rolling out of a hand-stand are the proper ways to finish	
Forward Roll from Handstand	Do a lunge and kick to handstand		Missing handstand, doing a forward roll
	Bend arms	Bending the arms and lowering the body to roll on the shoulders and upper back will prevent injury to the neck	Not bending arms, falling back, or falling flat on back, like timber
	Drop down and roll		
	Tuck head	Tucking the head round the back	Not tucking
	Bring knees to chest		
	Back rounded		
	Roll forward, stand tall, arms reach for ceiling		

FIGURE 27.1 Roundoff

ROUND OFF (RIGHT)

SKILL	CUE	WHY	COMMON ERROR
Technique (Figure 27.1)	Begin in lunge position, right leg forward	Land the roundoff standing up straight or leaning back a bit	Not pushing off the hands or snapping the feet down will cause the student to land either crouching down too much or leaning too far forward
	Hands go on mat as in cartwheel		
	Kick left leg over head with right leg meeting left leg in vertical		Feet are not together at top in vertical
	Quickly push off hands and snap feet together on mat		Pushing off hands slowly
	Finish standing tall, arms reaching for sky		

BACK EXTENSION ROLL

SKILL	CUE	WHY	COMMON ERROR
Technique	Bend knees with ankles together and begin a backward roll		
	Forcefully extend hips, knees, and arms (to achieve vertical handstand position)		Not extending hips, knees, and arms at correct time to achieve handstand
	Touch toes to ceiling		
	Step down 1 leg at a time to lunge position		
	Arms reach for ceiling		

SKILL	CUE	WHY	COMMON ERROR
Technique (Figure 27.2)	Stand sideways with legs shoulder-width apart, arms reaching for ceiling		Not keeping arms over head
	Step with right foot to side and do a sideways lunge		Lunging with right foot and placing the left hand first
	Place right hand, then left hand on mat, while kicking left leg up and over head, with right leg following		Arms and legs collapse
	Rhythm of hand, hand, foot, foot (1, 2, 3, 4, even rhythm)		
	Throw hips high over hands		Hips not high enough
	Bring first foot down close to hands		Feet landing away from hands
	Land left leg then right leg, body remaining sideways throughout; end sideways		Not passing through vertical
	Hands reaching toward ceiling		Bending at hips
	Stretch body through vertical		

Hand, hand, foot, foot—even rhythm

Kick legs up over head like a handstand

Throw hips high over hands

FIGURE 27.2 Cartwheel

28

Ultimate Frisbee

INTRODUCTION

Ultimate Frisbee originated in Maplewood, New Jersey, in 1968. It uniquely combines high competition with the spirit of the game. "Spirit of the game" means no referees, honest playing, and positive spirits on and off the field. "Spirit" means ultimate athletes need not waste time faking out officials. Instead, efforts focus on high performance and going all out. Combining skills from sports ranging from soccer and Frisbee to basketball, ultimate Frisbee is a fast-paced, highly energetic noncontact sport that isn't for the lazy or pessimistic. In all other sports, players are allowed to do anything until an official informs them that an activity is illegal. (In basketball it isn't a foul unless it is called as such.)

SKILLS LISTED WITH CUES

The cues in this chapter include the following skills: rules, backhand throw, forehand throw (sidearm), and catching.

TIPS

1. A certain level of maturity, trust, and honesty are required for the spirit of the game.
2. Seven players per team.
   a. *Handlers* (three players) are the first players to take a "pull" (similar to the kickoff in football). Generally these players are the most accurate throwers of the seven players on the field.
   b. *Mids* (two players) are players who generally have good cutting and maneuvering skills. They provide constant "flow" of the disk downfield with back or side cuts.
   c. *Longs* (two players) are players who have the ability to run fast,

long back cuts into the end zone or at least downfield. Longs should have field sense and accurate catching skills.

3. Sub out when players get tired; keep a "fresh crew." Only when one team scores can a substitution be made.

4. You can only stand one Frisbee width from the player with the disk, and you count stalling "1, 2, . . . 8, 9, 10." If the thrower still has the disk after 10 is announced by the marker, it then becomes a turnover, and the other team gains possession of the disk.

EQUIPMENT TIPS

1. Lots of Frisbees (175 grams official weight).
2. Rubber cleats, if available.
3. Cones, lines, or flags to mark end zones and boundaries.
4. Field dimensions: 40 yards wide × 70 yards long, with 25-yard-long end zones.
5. Colored vests.
6. Scoreboard.

TEACHING IDEAS

1. Play to 21, victory margin 2 points. Informal games can be played to other point totals or for a certain time period.

2. The game is started by both teams standing on opposite end lines. The disk is thrown to the other team as a kickoff. Players move the disk down the field by throwing it to one another. If the Frisbee hits the ground or goes out of bounds, the other team gains possession. Once a player catches the disk in the end zone, a point is scored and the opposing team must walk to the far goal line and await the pull or throw-off from the scoring team.

3. The game can be played with as few as four players to a team on any flat open space available that has a fairly well marked end zone.

FYI

For further information and special help, consult the following organization.

ORGANIZATION

Items include the following teaching materials, videos, disks, publications, rules, how to start teams or leagues, college starter kit, how to teach ultimate frisbee.Ultimate Players Association

741 Pearl Street
Side Suite
Boulder, CO 80302
Phone: (800) UPA-GetH
Website: www.upa.org

SKILL	CUE	WHY	COMMON ERROR
Basic Guidelines	The disk may never be handed—it must always be thrown		
	No player may move while in possession of the disk		
	Player may pivot on 1 foot in any direction, as in basketball		
	The disk may be thrown in any direction		
	No more than 1 player may guard a thrower		Double guarding equals a free pass on the spot
	Use both legs and hands to guard or knock down the disk		
	The defensive team gains possession of the disk whenever the offensive team's pass is incomplete, intercepted, knocked down, or goes out of bounds		
	Out-of-bounds throws are taken over by the opposing team at the point where the disk went out of bounds	If a disk goes out of bounds after crossing goal line, opposing team may throw in from either corner of end zone at goal line	
	No hand-slapping to knock the disk down or out of the hand of the passer		
	If disk is passed to you, must stop within 3 steps	No running with the disk	
Myths	Played with dogs		
	Don't get a workout		

SKILL	CUE	WHY	COMMON ERROR
Backhand (Figure 28.1)			
Grip	Stand sideways		
	Pinch disk's edge with thumb and forefinger	To control the flight of the disk	
Throw	Wipe table with back of hand, disk flat	Disk will go farther	Releasing with disk at too much of an angle
	Release, like snapping a towel	Accuracy and specific target to focus on	
	Pivot, windup, step, snap, release	Power on the disk	Using too much arm motion
	Point finger at target after follow-through		
	Step at target		
Pull (Full Throw— same as kickoff in football)	Same as backhand except preparatory steps		Incorrect release angle
			Misreading wind
Forehand (Sidearm)			
Grip (Figure 28.2a)	Thumb holds inside of disk	To generate a spinning disk	
	Middle finger is pivot finger		Incorrect grip
Throw (Figure 28.2b)	Outside rim of disk lower than inside	Keeps disk flat while in the air	Too much arm motion
	Step (same side) to target, snap towel	Throw further	Incorrect release angle will cause disk to dive into ground
	Elbow on hip—wrist snap		Throwing like a baseball
	Try not to use arm for strength on this toss		
	All wrist action		

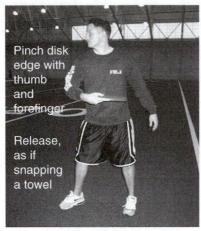

Pinch disk edge with thumb and forefinger

Release, as if snapping a towel

FIGURE 28.1 Backhand Grip and Throw

Middle finger is pivot point

Roll off middle finger

FIGURE 28.2a Forehand Grip (Sidearm)

Elbow on hip—wrist snap

Snap towel

Step to target

FIGURE 28.2b Forehand Throw (Sidearm)

CATCHING

SKILL	CUE	WHY	COMMON ERROR
Sandwich Catching	Watch disk come to hands	Keeps eyes focused on target	Looking away, incorrect timing
	1 big hand on top of disk, 1 big hand on bottom	Big hands gives bigger surface to hang onto the disk	Not using both hands
	Clap before you catch		
	Hands like a clam	More surface area on the disk for better control	
	Spread fingers		

OFFENSE

SKILL	CUE	WHY	COMMON ERROR
Movement	Cut, circle away, cut, circle—keep moving!	Avoids same speed movements	Same speed movements
	Fake and sharp cut	Keep the defensive players guessing	
	Look while pivoting, fake, pivot, fake, anticipate!	The goal is to get open	No faking movements, standing still
	Lead teammate with throw	Better option to catch the disk	
	Throw to area, not to person, on long throw		Not giving player enough lead on throw

SKILL	CUE	WHY	COMMON ERROR
Marking (Figure 28.3)	Stick like glue	Not letting an opposing player get open for a throw	Lack of conditioning
			Going for steal and losing opponent
	Play the unwanted little brother—opponent cannot get rid of you		
	Watch midsection		Watching head and feet—getting faked out
			Overrunning opponent
	Keep hands low		
	Count to 10 slowly; thrower has only 10 seconds to throw before a violation is called		

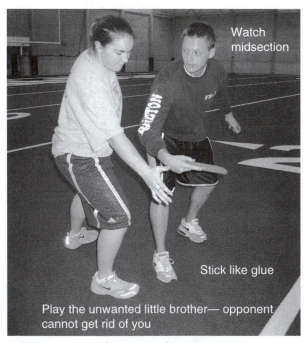

FIGURE 28.3 Defensive Marking

29

Volleyball

INTRODUCTION

Teachers and coaches face a monumental task when preparing instructional methods for teaching motor skills. They must make many decisions regarding content, method, class organization and control, evaluation, and methods of grading. When planning for content and method, one should be able to answer the following questions: Why did you teach that skill the way you did? Why was the instruction sequenced as it was? Why did the group practice like that? Why did you have them use instructional aids? Why did you say what you said to them?

Most, if not all, of these answers should be based on empirical evidence rather than on opinion, tradition, or the teacher's whim. Researchers have found that modeling facilitates motor-skill learning. Magill (1985) states, "Selecting the correct cues is one of the most important elements that an instructor includes in the teaching process."

In addition to focusing a student's attention on essential elements of the model, meaningful cues reduce the amount of information that is given. Because students attend to a limited amount of new material for a limited time, such a routine will enhance learning. For example, when teaching the block, the two cues are "Hands up" and "Make Mickey Mouse ears." These cues provide "hooks" on which to hang memories of the instruction. We find that our students can tell us many of the cues they received in their volleyball classes years later.

SKILLS LISTED WITH CUES

This chapter presents the cues for the following skills: ready position for forearm pass, forearm pass, overhead pass, setter's position and signals, serves (underhand and overhand), spiking, blocking, preparation for dig, forearm pass dig, dig (sprawl, pancake, overhead, fist), team strategies (offensive and defensive), and individual strategies (offensive and defensive).

The cues are listed in a recommended teaching sequence. A list of alternative cues is provided to benefit students who have difficulty linking the first cue with the desired performance. The alternate cues will suggest similar mental images that students may connect to more familiar motor patterns. Teachers should experiment with the cues and match the most helpful cue to each student's need.

TIP

After each drill, have players perform a set number of push-ups and sit-ups. Strength gains happen very quickly, and time is utilized efficiently.

EQUIPMENT TIPS

1. Use a light ball to teach the basic skills (for example, a lightweight plastic ball found at most discount department stores).
2. Leather balls are better than rubber balls in preventing the arms from being hurt.
3. Lower the nets, or have students work back to the baseline on serving drills.
4. Use blackboard and chalk to record competitive drills and the like.

TEACHING IDEAS

1. When possible, perform drills that contain the playing sequence—that is, "pass, set"; "serve, pass, set, hit"; "dig, set, hit"; and so on.
2. Drills should always have a specific goal (i.e., targets, scores, hit a certain number in a row perfectly, create competition with score 13–13, hit until you lose, etc.).
3. Always end drills on a positive note.
4. Games take 20 to 40 minutes to play. Some drills need to be as long as game time.
5. If court space is available, play two-on-two, three-on-three, or four-on-four games.

TEACHING PROGRESSIONS

Forearm Pass

1. *Throw, hit, catch:* A player tosses the ball to a partner, and the partner passes back. The ball is caught and tossed again. Repeat 10 times.
2. *Toss, pass, pass:* Two players start with a toss and keep passing back and forth until 20 passes have been tossed (see Figure 29.1).
3. *In a line of three:* Player A passes to player B, who passes behind his or her head to player C, who passes long to player A. Rotate after 10 passes. Switch the person in the middle to give each player a chance to pass the ball backward over his or her head.
4. *Triangle:* Three players pass the ball in a triangle. This allows the passer to practice facing the ball and angling the arms. Switch after 12 passes.

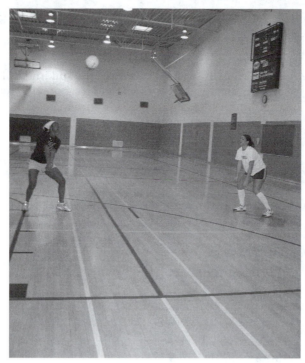

FIGURE 29.1   Forearm Pass Drill, Toss-Pass-Pass Drill

Overhead Pass

1. *Throw, hit, catch:* A player tosses the ball to a partner, and the partner passes back. The ball is caught and tossed again. Repeat 10 times.

2. *Toss, pass, pass:* Two players start with a toss and keep passing back and forth until 20 passes have been tossed.

3. *In a line of three:* Player A passes to player B, who passes behind his or her head to player C, who passes long to player A. Rotate after 10 passes. Switch the person in the middle to give each player a chance to pass the ball backward over his or her head.

4. *Triangle:* Three players pass the ball in a triangle. This allows the passer to practice facing the ball. Switch direction of the pass after 12 passes.

Overhead Serve

1. Serve at the wall.

2. Serve from the attack line with a partner and move back.

3. Serve and chase the ball.

4. Serve to opponents, who try to catch the ball.

5. Serve in a game situation, 3-on-3 games, played on half-courts.

Spike

1. "You Go, I Throw": Players begin their approach and you toss the ball as if they have performed the proper approach. The players need to come to you. Toss the ball as they jump, a couple of feet from the net and directly in front of you.

2. "I Throw, You Go": You toss the ball to the outside. The hitters start off the court and behind the line.

Block

1. Have players practice the two-step move with an opposing partner across the net.
2. Have blocking against hitters in the spiking drill. Be careful of spikers who run under the net. Blockers tend to come down on spikers' feet and sprain their ankles. Encourage setters to set the ball off the net (not tight). This decreases the possibility of injury.

FYI

For further information and special help, consult the following organizations and resource.

ORGANIZATIONS

Provides information about volleyball coaching clinics.

Canyon Volleyball
c/o Carl McGown
3815 Riverwood Drive
Provo, UT 84604
Phone: (801) 225-9271
Fax: (801) 225-9273

USA Volleyball
715 S. Circle Drive
Colorado Springs, CO 80910
Phone: (888) 786-5539, (719) 228-6800
Fax: (719) 228-6899
Website:www.usavolleyball.org

American Volleyball Coaches Association
1227 Lake Plaza Drive, Suite B
Colorado Springs, CO 80906
Phone: (719) 576-7777
Fax: (719) 575-7778
Website: www.avca.org

PUBLICATION

McGown, C., Fronske, H., & Moser, L. (2001). *Coaching volleyball: Building a winning team.* Boston: Allyn & Bacon.

SKILL	CUE	WHY	COMMON ERROR
Forearm			
Ready Position	Hands on knees	By placing hands down by your knees, you are low and ready to come up and pass the ball when it comes to you	Weight on heels instead of balls of feet
			Knees locked straight
Execution	Wrists and hands together		
	Lifelines together	Makes a nice flat and strong surface for the ball to contact	Elbows held at sides, arms too close to body
	Forearm contact with ball		
	Hide your chest		Hitting ball on wrists
	Fat part of arms hits ball		Hitting ball on wrists
	Elbows straight and simple	This provides a smooth surface to bounce the ball off straight	
(Figure 29.2)	Make a flat surface with the forearms		Bending elbows, moving arms up and down to add power
(Figure 29.3)	Face ball, angle arms		
	Shuffle		

continued

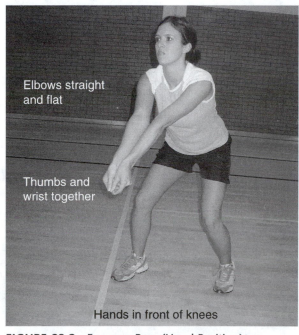

Elbows straight and flat

Thumbs and wrist together

Hands in front of knees

FIGURE 29.2 Forearm Pass (Hand Position)

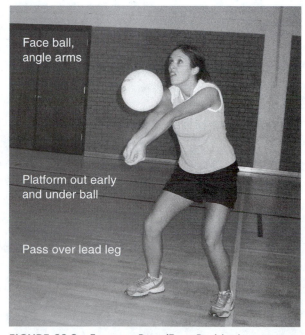

Face ball, angle arms

Platform out early and under ball

Pass over lead leg

FIGURE 29.3 Forearm Pass (Foot Position)

SKILL	CUE	WHY	COMMON ERROR
Forearm *Execution, continued*	Pass over lead leg		Facing target
	Beat ball to the spot		
	See the server, see the ball		
Overhead (Figure 29.4)	Big hands	Big hands allow you to cover a wide surface area of the ball, which gives you more control and accuracy	
	As if looking at the bottom of a full bowl of cereal		
Execution (Figure 29.5)	Shape early	Gives you more time to prepare to receive the ball. This is a key for correct performance. Not shaping early is the biggest cause of failure of this skill. Over-emphasize to your players to have their hands up extra early	
	Hands up at hairline		
	Extend		
	Like a basketball chest pass, elbows straighten		Ball staying in contact with hands too long—violation
			Only using arms to push ball
	Face target		
	Over lead leg		Setting over right or left shoulder, sideways

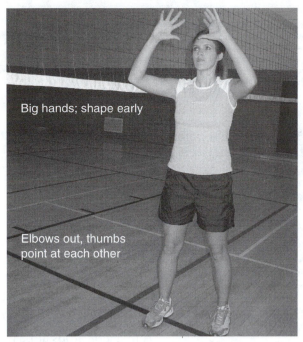

Big hands; shape early

Elbows out, thumbs
point at each other

FIGURE 29.4 Overhead Pass (Ready Position)

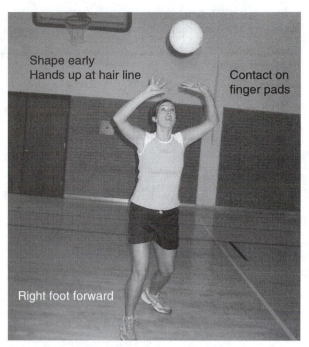

Shape early
Hands up at hair line

Contact on
finger pads

Right foot forward

FIGURE 29.5 Overhead Pass

		SETTER'S POSITION	
SKILL	**CUE**	**WHY**	**COMMON ERROR**
Technique	Right shoulder to net	For consistent sets to spike	Not looking at pass early enough
	Stand next to or as close as possible to the net	Helps control ball	Trying to pass a serve
	Right side of court, front row		
	Shape early	Helps set the ball at hairline—not chin or chest	
	Extend	More power	
	Face target	More accuracy	
Back Set	Hips forward		
	See setter's signals		

SKILL	CUE	WHY	COMMON ERROR
Underhand			
Leg Action	Step toward net with foot opposite to throwing arm	More power to the ball	Stepping forward with same leg as stepping arm
Hand Position	Palm up, make a fist	Bigger surface area for ball to contact; better control of ball	
	Thumb rests on side of index finger		
	Arm close to body, brush shorts	Better efficiency	
	Elbow straight	Helps with the follow-through	Elbow bent
	Hit ball out of hand	Greater control of ball	Tossing ball into air
	Like pitching horseshoes		Arm action stops at ball contact
	Follow-through toward target		
Ready Position (Figure 29.6)	Bow and arrow action	Keeps elbow high and ready to hit ball	
	Stand sideways; left foot points at target	More power to serve the ball	
		Weight transfer from back to front foot	
	Hold ball in 1 hand	Simplifies the serve	
	Ball in left hand and up in front of hitting shoulder	Eliminates extra movement and allows accurate and consistent contact with the ball	
	Hitting elbow up	Timing to contact ball is more efficient	
Toss (Figure 29.7)	Precise toss	Simplifies timing and decreases decision making	
	Toss it (step, toss, hit)		Rotating shoulder forward, elbow stays back
	Toss in front of serving shoulder		
	Heel to target		Hitting behind or on top of ball

continued

FIGURE 29.6 Overhead Serve
(Ready Position)

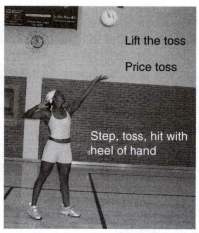

FIGURE 29.7 Overhead Serve Toss

FIGURE 29.8 Overhead Serve
(Contact)

SERVES, continued			
SKILL	**CUE**	**WHY**	**COMMON ERROR**
Toss, *continued* (Figure 29.8)	Contact ball at top of toss		
	Have a routine you do each time, like basket-ball free-throw routines		
Floater Serve	1. Toss in front of right side		
	2. Strike ball with flat hand		
	3. Hit straight through the ball		
	4. No follow-though		
Top Spin Serve	1. Toss ball closer to body		
	2. Step under ball		
	3. Hit the ball and carry your hand over top of ball		
	4. Follow-through		

SKILL	CUE	WHY	COMMON ERROR
Used for Balls Off of Net (Figure 29.9)	Elbow back, hand above head, rotate elbow forward, and reach up with an open hand	Rotation increases torque and equates into a faster, harder hit	
	Hit ball at highest point of reach with the heel of the hand and follow through after contact at the intended target	Increases control of the direction of the ball	
	Similar to a throwing action, with the hand above the head		
	Contact ball on bottom third	A higher contact increases the prob-ability of the ball going over the net	
	Watch the ball hit hand	Decreases the proba-bility of missing the ball	
		Increases the chance of a solid hit.	
Hitting Action	Step under the ball, with the foot opposite of hitting arm	More power in the hit, and lining up the hitting arm with the ball is critical for the ball hitting the hand squarely or solidly	
	The hitting arm should be lined up directly under the ball		

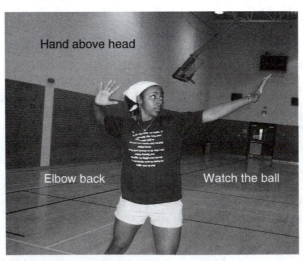

FIGURE 29.9 Offensive Hit (Ready Position)

SKILL	CUE	WHY	COMMON ERROR
Execution	4-step approach: R-L-R-L if right-handed; L-R-L-R if left-handed		No approach, starting approach too close to net
(Figure 29.10)	Arms forward-back-forward		Jumping off only 1 leg like a basketball lay-up
	Bow and arrow action	Increases power and speed of the hitting arm	
	Fingers apart		Fist
	Hand open and firm		
	Hand in shape of ball		Hand is flat, or fist, or Jell-O
	Wrist somewhat stiff		
Timing	First step when ball is set		Running too far forward; ball goes over attacker's head
	Stepping and setting		
	Trust eyes; do not guess		
(Figure 29.11)	Contact ball high and in front of you		Contacting ball too low or behind head
	Powerful wrist snap	Controls the ball and puts spin on ball so it will go down into the court	No wrist snap
	Fast arm swing		

FIGURE 29.10 Spike

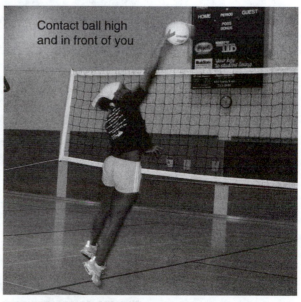

FIGURE 29.11 Hitting Execution

SKILL	CUE	WHY	COMMON ERROR
Set-Up (Figure 29.12)	Keep hands up at eye level		Bringing hands and arms below net, straight legs
	Knees bent, ready to jump		
	Seal the net with body		Body too far from net
	Chin down for peripheral vision		
Arm Action	Hands up as if playing a piano		
	Fingers are firm and spread—Mickey Mouse ears		Fingers close together and not firm
Timing	Ball, setter, ball, hitter		Hands down at sides
			Watching only the ball
	Lead step		
	3-step move		Moving with hands down at waist
	Get over		
	Penetrate		
	Angle hands into opponent's court as if diving into a swimming pool		Being too far away from net
	Reach over		

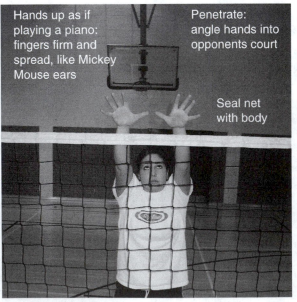

Hands up as if playing a piano: fingers firm and spread, like Mickey Mouse ears

Penetrate: angle hands into opponents court

Seal net with body

FIGURE 29.12 The Block

SKILL	CUE	WHY	COMMON ERROR
Preparation	Anticipate spike		
	Feet apart, arms ready		Weight back on heels, standing straight up
	Ball, setter, ball, hitter; watch hitter's shoulders and head		Watching ball, not hitter
	Knees bent		
Forearm Pass	Arms like a wall; don't swing arms		Swinging arms
	Absorb shock of spike; like a sponge		
	Platform underneath ball		Arms too close to body
Sprawling	Anticipate spike; be stopped when hitter contacts ball		Still moving when hitter contacts ball
	Big step		No tennis hop
	Close to floor, chin up		
	Hit ball, then sprawl	First things first	Falling over instead of moving feet
	Helping hand		
	Turn knee out		
Pancake	Big step		Not moving feet fast enough
	Close to floor		
	Helping hand		
	Turn knee out		
	Slide hand on floor		
Overhead	Tomahawk action		Contact between ball and hands is too long to be legal
	Deflection or rebound back toward net		
Fist	Flat surface		

SKILL	CUE	WHY	COMMON ERROR
Setter	Quarterback of team signals with fingers to spiker and team		Other players call the signal
	Calls the set signal by using a hand signal to notify players of type of play		
Height of Set; Spiker on the Court	4 3 3 2 ————— 1 ——— net 5 4 3 2 1 A B C Setter		
Spiker's Court Position on Net	Setter signals for first number or letter Examples: 1–1 short set 5–1 long short set		Not listening or looking for signal from setter
Height of Ball Number	Setter signals for second number Examples: 5–4 high set C–4 high back set		Confusing the numbers
Short Sets *1–1, 3–1, A–1, C–1*	"You go, I throw"		
	Spiker watches ball go over shoulder		Not watching ball, moving too late or too early
	Correct timing takes practice		
	As soon as ball passes shoulder, chase the ball to net; stay with it		Becoming frustrated and quitting
Medium Sets *1–2, 3–2*	When the ball leaves setter's hands, go!		
High Sets *5–4, C–4*	"I throw, you go"		Leaving too soon
	Watch where ball is set		
	Go when the ball leaves the setter's hands		Not watching the ball leave the setter's hands

SKILL	CUE	WHY	COMMON ERROR
End of Play			
Setter's Responsibility	Setter gives signal before ball is served	Setter gives signal at side of leg to prevent opponent from seeing it	
Hitters' Responsibility	Hitters look for setter's signal as soon as play is over		Forgetting to look for setter's hand signals
	Move with setter on calls net S S H H		Not looking for setter's hand signals
	Everybody watch pass, move accordingly		
During Rally			
Hitters' Responsibility	Hitters can call signals 1–5–C	Communication critical between hitter and setter	
Front Sets	Thumb, index, and middle fingers used for front sets		
Short Set	Index finger = 1–1		
	Index and middle finger = 1–2		
Middle Front Set	Thumb, index, and middle finger = 3–2		
	Four fingers = 4–4		
Long Set	Five fingers = 5–4		
Back Sets	Pinkie and ring finger used for back sets		
Short Back Set	Pinkie finger = A1		
Middle Back Set	Pinkie finger and ring finger = B2		
High Back Set	Make letter C = C4		

SKILL	CUE	WHY	COMMON ERROR
Offense	Stress passing and serving over all other skills	A good pass means the setter can hit and can spike the ball	
	Use all 3 contacts if possible, or other team will		
	Only attempt technically what players can do physically; do not do too much		
	Setter is the most athletic player on team, most important		
	Sets must be high in order to attack		
	Talk to each other when passing, hitting, and so forth	Communication a key to good team play	
Defense	Funnel attack to back-row players		
	First do offense, then defense		
	Front-row players stay close to net		
	Stay low, with good center of gravity		
	Front-row attackers never reach back for a dig; someone will be punched in the face		

SKILL	CUE	WHY	COMMON ERROR
Offense	Front-row hitters, stay away from net	Gives the hitter 3 and 4 step approach, more time to get to ball and hit hard	
	When hitting, keep ball in front of you		
	Try to anticipate what will happen before it happens		
	Hit around the blockers, even if ball cannot be hit it as hard by doing it		
Defense	Be ready for anything, all the time	Communication key to good team play	
	Weight on balls of feet, not heels		
	Try to anticipate attacks		
	If you intend to pass or dig a ball, call for it: "I go," "Mine"		
	Talk!		

30

The Practice of Yoga Exercises

We offer people something very important when we teach yoga in this day and age. Although yoga today is often taught and practiced as a pursuit for health and fitness in a changing world, the spiritual roots still nourish authentic yoga teachings. We have Americanized it and turned it into a workout, so it is important that we as teachers make it restorative and rejuvenating, not miserable!

Yoga can be defined as "mindfulness," or the process of directing the attention toward whatever we are doing at the moment. Through the practice of various yoga techniques or postures, we are continually directed toward the present moment using the breath. In doing so we learn to feel the action from the postures, or *asanas,* from deep within.

The practice of yoga is teaching the mind to steady or to become calm, without distraction, fixed on the sound and quality of our breath. As we improve our ability to control the senses from wandering during the practice, the subtle quality of concentration deepens. Learning to pay attention is critical. Patience may be one of our greatest tools. Each practice session is a journey. Endeavor to move with awareness and enjoy the experience. There is no benefit in hurrying. Yoga grows with time. Some days are easy and the mind is calm and the physical body is light and responsive; other days you may find that the mind is very busy and the body feels like heavy sand.

Why is yoga becoming so popular? Because our life is so fast, we are always multitasking and we aren't making decisions that are simple and one at a time. The practice of yoga can benefit all types of people. From children to adults and from athletes to couch potatoes. Yoga tones the muscles, sculpts the body, improves flexibility, builds muscular strength and endurance, increases lung capacity, and calms the nervous system and mind. It creates the range of motion needed to therapeutically work and heal all areas of the body. It heals, detoxifies, electrifies, and regenerates both body and mind at the deepest levels. One of yoga's greatest advantages is to assist in eliminating injury. It is a helpful tool for recovering from injury, and restoring loss of mobility or range of movement and loss of strength. Another advantage is that yoga clarifies what it is like to support one's own body weight.

We as teachers must create a safe environment for learning yoga. We ask students to wear tighter clothing, to be barefoot, and to get into funny positions. We ask them to look at themselves, and at what they feel—also to create boundaries so that they can relax. Teach everyone as if they have back pain so they won't! The hallmark of a yoga practitioner is moderation. So therefore, a teacher should never allow the pose/posture to take precedence over the person. Yoga is generally safe, and often healing. Practicing with common sense and a little basic knowledge can keep it that way.

SKILLS LISTED WITH CUES

This chapter presents cues for the following: Sun Salutations A and B, standing postures/asanas, seated postures/asanas, and modified closing sequence.

EQUIPMENT TIPS

1. Play yoga music during instruction.
2. Wear clothing that is comfortable and fitted; avoid baggy clothing.
3. Practice barefoot, no socks.
4. Use a clean yoga sticky mat.
5. Have available props for modifications such as blocks, blankets, straps, chairs, wall.

TEACHING IDEAS

1. Stomach and bowels should be empty; practice 2 to 3 hours after a meal.
2. Do not force the body beyond its capacity to avoid injury. Weaknesses come to the forefront during the practice. Discomfort that is felt in a posture should disappear once the pose is released. Try a less strenuous pose until strengthened.
3. If there is any persistent pain, it is a sign of incorrect practice or some physical problem. Consult with a qualified teacher.
4. Hold the postures only as long as the proper alignment can be maintained. The length of time spent in each pose will increase along with strength, flexibility, and endurance.
5. Elongate the spine before bending to maximize disk space. Normal curves keep the spine healthy. The spine bends forward and backward most easily in the lumbar region, so we tend to overwork the lower back. Forcing the spine into forward bends is one of the most dangerous things you can do in all of yoga. It is important to always return the spine to neutral.
6. Alignment principles:
   a. Scoop the tailbone under and lift the chest (telescope the ribs) to create space in the vertebrae.
   b. Draw the shoulders back, in, and down with the lower portion of the blades curling under toward the heart. (A good visual is having the arms lifted shoulder height and bent at a 90-degree angle. Draw just the elbows forward and feel how the blades curl under toward the heart).

7. Address the internal locks, or *bandhas,* every minute.

    a. *Mula bandha,* or root lock, located at the perineum approximately ½ inch in from anus. Drawing the pelvic floor up will help the tailbone scoop under.

    b. *Uddiyana bandha,* or navel lock, is performed by exhaling fully and then drawing the lower belly inward and upward while simultaneously lifting the diaphragm.

8. No *bandhas* for children 4 to13 years of age.

9. Do not force the knees; always ease into poses. Forcing knees into hyperextension can overstretch ligaments.

10. Find a *drishti,* or focal point. Keep eyes focused on this gazing point while practicing; may be off the fingers, toes, nose, or middle of the forehead.

11. Breathing techniques, or the *Pranayama:*

    a. Full expansion of the lungs as you inhale, contraction on the exhale. Pay attention to the exhale as you begin and allow the inhale to happen.

    b. Only nose breathing.

    c. Audible sound of the breath similar to Darth Vader. Inhale with a "hssss" sound and exhale with "haammm" sound.

    d. Feel the breath and its higher velocity in the back of the throat.

    e. Never hold or suspend the breath while practicing.

    f. Keep the breath smooth, fluid, and continuous. If breath becomes choppy, back off of the pose and restore the continuity to the breath.

12. Balance strength and flexibility. Lengthen and strengthen the body. For example, strengthen the arms and legs so the poses will have an effect on the back and spine as in Downward Facing Dog.

13. Value students' opinions; praise and encourage them. Teach respect and compassion through example. Give them options or choices, and help them to see possibilities. Teach them to accept their limitations and where they are at this moment in time. Be playful and loving.

14. According to Sri K. Patthabi Jois, Master Yogi, the Primary Series in Astanga Yoga may be taught to ages 9 to 11. Those over 12 can begin a more serious study of this type of power yoga. Younger children generally can only concentrate for up to 40 minutes, while older ages can practice up to 60 minutes. *Do not overwork* children.

TEACHING PROGRESSIONS

1. Breath: *pranayama* (life current/life force)
2. Internal locks: *Mula bandha, Uddiyana bandha*
3. Alignment principles
4. Sun Salutations A and B
5. Postures
6. *Vinyasa*: a unique linking of one posture to the next in a dynamic flow
7. Closing sequence
8. Final relaxation: *Savasana*
9. Breathe 3 to 5 times while performing each posture, unless otherwise noted.

GAMES

1. Breathing with a sound similar to Darth Vader. Bring hand to mouth and act as if you are steaming up a mirror to get the effect of abdominal breathing. Be playful and do not force students to participate; have fun with this.

2. Use animals and nature to portray the postures. For example: Eagle, Down-dog, Cat/Cow, Stork, Frog, Bug, Cobra, Mountain, Half moon, Tree, etc. Be playful and creative.

FYI

For further information and special help, consult the following organization and resource.

ORGANIZATION

Yoga Journal
2054 University Avenue
Berkeley, CA 94704
Phone: (510) 841-9200
Fax: (510) 644-3101
www.yogajournal.com

PUBLICATIONS

Iyengar, B. K. S. (1989). *The tree of yoga,* Boston: Shambhala Publications, 1989.
Feuerstein, G. & Payne, L. (1999). *Yoga for dummies,* IDG Books Worldwide.

This sequence is designed to produce heat in the body so that muscles and joints are prepared for the physical work to follow.

SKILL	CUE	WHY	COMMON ERROR
Mountain Posture (*Tadasana*)	Stand with both feet together, legs active, spine long; engage the *bandhas*; breathe deep	Awareness of feet, ankles, alignment of spine; strengthens feet, ankles, quads, hams, core, and back	
Upward Hand Pose (*Urdhva Hastasana*)	Inhale, raising both arms, lungs should be full just as the hands touch; gaze at the thumbs; chest upward	Stretches spine, shoulders, and arms; strengthens hips, legs, and feet	
Full Forward Fold (*Uttanasana*)	Exhale, fold forward, taking the chest toward the knees; look toward toes. Note: Every full forward fold *must* be done with bent knees	Lengthens hams and back and strengthens quads and abs	
Look Forward	Inhale, lengthen the spine, draw the chest away from belly; lengthen back of neck, look forward	Lengthens spine, neck and hams; strengthens quads and abs	
4-Limb Stick (*Chaturanga Dandasana*)	Exhale, step back, lower from plank to 4-limb stick while gazing forward Modification: Drop knees, uncurl toes; elbows beside ribs; hover or lay flat on the floor	Total core stability, increases strength in wrists, shoulders, triceps, quads, and hams	
Upward Facing Dog or Cobra (*Urdhva Mukha Svanasana*) (Figure 30.1)	Inhale, straighten the arms or slightly bend at the elbows and roll onto the tops of the feet; knees lifted or dropped to floor; toes pointed	Increases strength in upper body; increases flexibility of chest and abs	
Downward Facing Dog (*Adho Mukha Svcanasana*)	Exhale as you push hips up, lengthen the spine from your sacrum through the top of your head; press heels toward the floor and lift the kneecaps; gaze at navel; engage the *bandhas;* remain here for 3–5 breaths	Increases arm, shoulder, quad, and ankle strength; increases flexibility in spine, hams, calves, and achilles	

continued

FIGURE 30.1 Upward Facing Dog

SUN SALUTATION A SEQUENCE/WARM UP, continued

SKILL	CUE	WHY	COMMON ERROR
Walk or Jump Forward	Inhale as you walk or jump the feet forward in between hands; lengthen the spine, take gaze forward	Strengthens core, arms, and stretches spine	
Full Forward Fold (*Uttanasana*)	Exhale, taking chest toward the knees and gaze at toes.	Lengthens, strengthens hamstrings, core	
Upward Hand Pose (*Urdhva Hastasana*)	Inhale, raising both arms high over head until palms touch; gaze at the thumbs	Stretches spine, arms, and shoulders; increases strength in hips, legs, and feet	
Mountain Posture (*Tadasana*)	Exhale lower arms in preparation for next Sun Salutation A or Vinyasa	Returns the body to a neutral alignment	

SUN SALUTATION B SEQUENCE/WARM UP

SKILL	CUE	WHY	COMMON ERROR
Mountain Posture (*Tadasana*)	Stand with feet together, legs active, spine long, engage *bandhas*, breathe deep	Awareness of feet, ankles alignment of spine, strengthens feet, ankles, quads, hams, core, back	
Fierce Posture (*Utkatasana*)	Inhale as you bend knees and raise both arms to the sky, fill lungs fully; gaze toward thumbs	Stretches shoulders, arms, and spine; strengthens quads, hams, abs, and chest	
Full Forward Fold (*Uttanasana*)	Exhale as you fold forward, chest toward knees as you press the knees back	Lengthen hamstrings and back; strengthens quads, and abs	

continued

SKILL	CUE	WHY	COMMON ERROR
Look Forward	Inhale, lengthen the spine as you look forward, neck long, and draw the chest away from the belly	Lengthens spine, neck, and hams; strengthens quads and core	
4-Limb Stick (*Chaturanga Dandasana*)	Exhale, step back; shift body slightly forward, elbows stay beside ribcage; lower body so 1–2 inches off ground.	Total core stability; increases strength in wrists, triceps, shoulders, quads, and hams	
Upward Facing Dog or Cobra *Dandasana) Svanasana)*	Inhale, straighten arms or slightly bend the elbows back along side ribcage; roll onto the tops of the feet; engage all muscles of the legs; lift chest high; scoop tailbone	Strengthens upper body and increases flexbility in chest and abs	
Downward Facing Dog (*Adho Mukha Svanasana*)	Exhale as you push hip back and up; lengthen spine from your sacrum through to the top of your head; bend knees for modifications then lengthen the spine, strengthen the arms; hands are parallel and symmetrical, as are feet, with fingers spread and gripping; maintain for 3 to 5 breaths	Increases arm, shoulder, quad, and ankle strength; increases flexibility in the spine, ham, calves, achilles	
Warrior I, Right Side (*Virabhadrasana I*) (Figure 30.2)	Inhale as you bring right foot forward between hands and flatten back foot in 30° angle, heel away from little toe. Bend forward knee, knee above ankle; raise hands over head with arms straight until palms touch; gaze at thumbs (this should be done in 1 inhale)	Increases strength in gluteals, legs, core, back, shoulders, arms ankles, and feet	
4-Limb Stick (*Chaturanga Dandasana*)	Exhale; see above	See above	

continued

SKILL	CUE	WHY	COMMON ERROR
Upward Facing Dog or Cobra (*Urdhva Mukha Svanasana*)	Inhale; see cues on page 390	See page 390	
Downward Facing Dog (*Adho Mukha Svanasana*)	Exhale; see cues on page 390	See page 390	
Warrior I, Left Side (*Virabhadrasana I*)	Same as Warrior I, Right Side, but use left side	Increases strength in gluteals, legs, core, back, shoulders, arms ankles, and feet	
4-Limb Stick (*Chaturanga Dandasana*)	Exhale; see cues on page 390	See page 390	
Upward Facing Dog or Cobra *Urdhva*) *Mukha Svanasana*)	Inhale; see cues on page 390	See page 390	
Downward Facing Dog (*Adho Mukha Svanasana*)	Exhale; see page 390; remain here for 3–5 complete breaths	See page 390	
Walk or Jump Forward	Inhale as you walk or jump feet toward hands; lengthen the spine as while gazing forward	Core stabilization, increases strength in arms, stretches spine	
Full Forward Fold (*Uttanasana*)	Exhale; see cues on page 389	See page 389	

continued

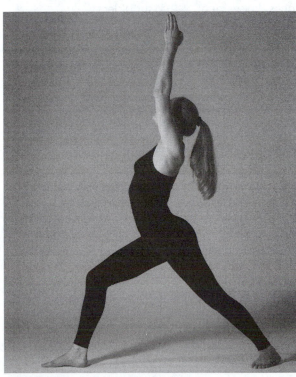

FIGURE 30.2 Warrior I Pose

SKILL	CUE	WHY	COMMON ERROR
Fierce Posture (*Utkatasana*)	Inhale; see cues on page 389	See page 389	
Mountain Posture (*Tadasana*)	Exhale, lower your arms and straighten the legs in preparation for the next Sun Salutation B; gaze straight ahead	Brings spine back into neutral alignment	

STANDING POSTURES SEQUENCE

Hold all standing postures for 3 to 5 minutes.

SKILL	CUE	WHY	COMMON ERROR
Big Toe Posture (*Padangusthasana*)	Feet hip-width apart, inhale, lift gaze toward sky, exhale, forward fold, clasp the big toes with middle and index fingers of each hand. Modification: Hands clasp ankles, bend knees, ribs on thighs	Strengthen quads, shoulders, increases flexibility in hamstrings	
Hand Under Foot Pose (*Padahastasana*)	Exhale, place hand under foot with toes to wrist. Modification: Only fingers to toes or blocks, knees bent	Counterstretch for wrists, increase flexibility in hams, strengthen quads and shoulders	
Extended Triangle Pose (*Utthita Trikonasana*) (Figure 30.3, page 394)	Inhale, walk feet 1-leg length apart; exhale, turn right foot out and left toes in slightly, arms outstretched; lengthen and descend to shin, foot, or block; inhale, come up slowly; repeat other side	Strengthens quads, hams, calves, back, and abs; lengthens concurrently ribs, intercostals, waistline, hips, shins, and inner thighs	
Revolved Triangle Pose (*Parivritta Trikonansana*)	Feet 1-leg length apart; exhale, turn right foot out, left toes in; square hips to the right, place right hand on sacrum; reach left arm forward, descend to shin or outside of right little toe; spiral around, open left shoulder to sky, reach up; repeat other side	Stretches hams, hips, and spine; strengthens quads, shoulders, arms	

continued

SKILL	CUE	WHY	COMMON ERROR
Extended Side Angle Pose (*Uttihita Parsvahonasana*)	Inhale, walk or jump feet 3–4 feet apart, arms outstretched; exhale, turn right foot open and left foot in, bend right knee directly above heel, lower right hand to the floor outside the right foot (inside of foot for beginners); extend left hand up to sky. Modification: Right forearm on right thigh, left hand on sacrum. Repeat other side	Lengthen torso, outer side leg, and ribs. Strengthens hams quads, calves, shins.	
Prayer Twist (*Parivritta Parsvakonasana*)	Exhale, turn right foot out, stay up on left toes, bend right leg, knee above heel, left elbow to outside of right knee; keep back foot flat or up on toes; place left and right hand into prayer; release. Modification: Drop knee to floor. Repeat other side	Rotation of torso; lengthens spine, groins, inner thighs; strengthens hams, quads, shins, calf	
Expanded Leg Pose (*Prasarita Padottanasana*)	Inhale, jump or walk feet so 3–4 feet apart; outer edges of feet parallel, hands on hips, drawing elbows back toward each other; scoop tailbone, contract quads, telescope ribs, lift chest, and look up; exhale, fold forward, hands stay on hips, keep legs active. Modification: Hand on thighs, knees bent	Increases flexibility in inner thighs and outer shins; strengthens back and abs	
Hand to Big Toe Pose (*Utthita Hasta Padangusthasana*)	Inhale, raise right knee; grab big toe with index and middle fingers; straighten leg; hold for 3–5 breaths; open to right side; hold for 3–5 breaths. Modification: Hold bent knee; option is to open bent knee to right side. Repeat other side	Strengthens hips, feet, and knees; stretches hams and opens groins; increases balance	

continued

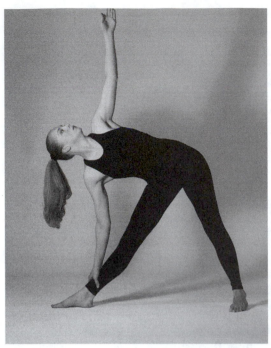

FIGURE 30.3 Extended Triangle Pose

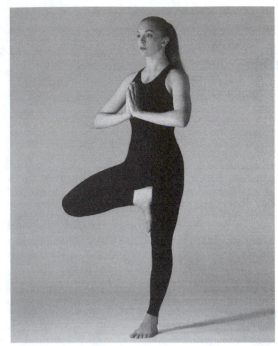

FIGURE 30.4 Tree Posture

STANDING POSTURES SEQUENCE, continued			
SKILL	**CUE**	**WHY**	**COMMON ERROR**
Tree Posture (*Vrksasana*) (Figure 30.4)	Inhale, lift right foot with both hands, exhale, place foot on upper-left thigh, bring hands to prayer position	Strengthens hips, legs and core, hip opener, increases balance	
Warrior I (*Virabhadrasana*)	Inhale, bring right foot forward between hands, flatten left foot in 30° angle, heel away from little toe; bend forward knee, knee above heel; raise hands over head with arms straight until palms touch; gaze at thumbs; keep spine long; repeat other side	Increases strength in legs, gluteals, core, back, shoulders; flexibility in hips and groins	
Warrior II (*Virabhadrasana II*)	Exhale from Warrior I, open arms parallel to floor and in line with legs; left leg should remain in 90° angle, right foot flat at a 30° angle; left knee over heel; gaze over the left middle finger	Strengthens feet, ankles, knees, quads, spine, shoulders. Increases flexibility in groins, legs, feet.	

continued

Hold all standing postures for 3 to 5 minues

SKILL	CUE	WHY	COMMON ERROR
Staff Posture (*Dandasana*)	Seated, exhale, drop chin to chest, legs active, spine long, arms straight, hands pressing down with palms flat, back of knees pressing down; do not lift heels	Stretches the spine, strengthens the shoulders, arms, hands, and chest lifts and opens	
Intense West Posture (*Paschimottansasana*) (Figure 30.5)	Inhale, arms raised up, telescope ribs, tailbone scoop; exhale, fold forward, clasp big toes with middle and index fingers, gaze at toes; keep feet and knees together; contract quads. Modification: Hold shins or ankles with legs straight and spine long	Increases flexibility in the hamstrings and the back; increases strength in the biceps and chest	
Intense East Posture (*Purvottanasana*)	Exhale, place hands flat on the floor behind hips, pointing fingers toward toes; inhale, drop head back; push hips up to sky, keep both legs straight and active with feet touching and soles of feet on the floor; arms straight and fully engaged. Modification: Bent knees with feet halfway in to buttocks, feet hip-width apart and then lift	Increases flexibility in the front of the body; increases strength in the back body, opens anterior shoulder.	
Single Leg Forward Bend A (*Janu Sirasana A*)	Exhale, with left leg straight, bring right foot to inner left thigh, right knee should be at 90° angle; clasp left foot with both hands; repeat other side	Increases flexibility in hams; opens hips	

continued

FIGURE 30.5 Intense West Posture

FIGURE 30.6 Boat Posture

SEATED POSTURES SEQUENCE, continued			
SKILL	**CUE**	**WHY**	**COMMON ERROR**
Seated Twist (*Marichyasana C*)	Exhale, bend right knee, right foot flat near right sitting bone. Place left outside elbow on outside right knee, hand up, fingers spread; place right hand on floor behind; hold right knee with left hand, place right hand on the floor behind you; inhale, lengthen spine and spiral around starting at belly, chest, shoulders, head and neck; repeat other side	Increases flexibility in back and increases range of movement in torso	
Boat Posture (*Navasana*) (Figure 30.6)	Inhale, lift and straighten both legs with feet together, toes spread at eye level; gaze at toes; arms straight, parallel to floor with palms facing each other. Modification: Hold behind the knees and bend them	Core strength	

continued

SKILL	CUE	WHY	COMMON ERROR
Bound Angle Posture (*Baddha Konasasa*)	Exhale, draw both feet into groins; hold feet with fingers on top of foot, thumbs on the soles; open feet, lower knees toward floor. Modification: Use block to elevate hips; knees lower than hips	Increases flexibility in adductors	
Hero Posture (*Virasana*)	Kneel on floor; bring knees and feet together, then sit on your feet. Modification: Place rolled up blanket on calves and sit back	Stretches quads and outer front shin	
Seated Angle Posture	Exhale, open feet wide, legs straight; hold feet with hands; inhale, lengthen the spine and gaze forward; exhale, deepen pose Modification: Use straps around feet or just place hand on shins or floor in front	Increases flexibility in adductors	
Child's Posture (*Balasana*)	On all fours, knees apart, big toes together, fall back into haunches, lengthen arms over head, forehead down on mat, abdomen between thighs; breathe deeply	Restorative and rejuvenating pose; increases flexibility in back of hips	
Spinal Twist	Lay flat on back; draw left knee into chest, extend right leg out; hook left toes on right quad, upper right hand on outside of left knee, open left shoulder, extend arm with palms down on floor; roll to right side, looking over left shoulder	Increases flexibility in ribcage, intercostals, gluteals, lower back	

You must end your workout with this sequence for a minimum of 5 minutes to return the spine to neutral and the body to its basal metabolic rate.

SKILL	CUE	WHY	COMMON ERROR
Knees into Chest (Figure 30.7)	With steady breathing, draw both knees into chest, wrap the arms around the knees and gently roll in a circular motion	Releases lower back, gently massages back; preparation for final relaxation	
Knees into Chest Twist	Open arms to side with palms facing down; draw shoulders down into sockets, drop both knees to right side, look over left shoulder; continuous breathing	Release any residual tension in the lower back, spine, gluteals, intercostals, and lats	
Final Relaxation/ Corpse Posture (*Savasana*)	Gently slide the legs out to laying down flat on your back; release all muscles, dissolve all tension, close your eyes and completely relax	Stay until the heart rate slows down and your breath finds a natural soothing rhythm; you will experience revitalization, rejuvenating effects in this posture	

When coming out of this sequence, wiggle fingers and toes to return to awareness. Then roll on to your right side in a fetal position. When prepared, place both hands on the floor and push yourself up to seated lotus or any comfortable position to maintain a tall spine. Take three slow breaths in and out. *Breathe in slow breaths.* Now the body has been cleansed and the mind relaxed, ready to carry us into the rest of the day with energy and vitality!

Namaste everyone! (My light salutes your light!)

FIGURE 30.7   Knees into Chest

References

Allsen, P. E., Harrison, J. M., & Vance, B. (1993). *Fitness for life. An individualized approach* (5th ed.). Madison, WI: WCB Brown Benchmark.

Blakemore, C. (1995). *Methods of designing cues.* Provo, UT: Brigham Young University.

Christiansen, R. (1995, August 22). [Cues for teaching]. Unpublished interview.

Christina, R. W., & Corcos, D. M. (1988). *Coaches guide to teaching sport skills.* Champaign, IL: Human Kinetics.

Coker, C. (1998, January/February). Performance excellence: Making the most of natural speed. *Strategies, 11*(3), 10–12.

Darst, P. W., Zakrajsek, D. B., & Mancini, V. H. (1989). *Analyzing physical education and sport instruction.* Champaign, IL: Human Kinetics.

Docheff, D. M. (1990). The feedback sandwich. *Journal of Physical Education, Recreation and Dance, 64,* 17–18.

Fronske, H., Abendroth-Smith, J., & Blakemore, C. (1997). Critical overhand throwing cues help 3rd, 4th, and 5th grade students achieve efficient throwing patterns and increase their distance. *The Physical Educator, 54*(2), 88–95.

Fronske, H., & Birch, N. (1995). Overcoming road blocks to communication. *Strategies, 8*(8), 22–25.

Fronske, H., & Collier, C. (1993, September). Cueing your athletes on good jumping events. *Journal of Physical Education, Recreation, and Dance, 64*(7), 7–9.

Fronske, H., Collier, C., & Orr, D. (1993, February). Cueing your participants in on track events. *Journal of Physical Education, Recreation, and Dance, 64*(2), 9–10.

Fronske, H., & McGown, C. (1992, October). Visual teaching cues for volleyball skills. *Journal of Physical Education, Recreation, and Dance, 63*(8), 10–11.

Fronske, H. & Wilson, R. (2002). *Teaching cues for basic sport skills for elementary and middle school students.* San Francisco, CA: Benjamin Cummings.

Lacrosse Foundation. (1994). *The Lacrosse Foundation's parent's guide to the sport of lacrosse.* Baltimore, MD: Lacrosse Foundation, Inc.

Lawther, J. D. (1968). *The learning of physical skills.* Englewood Cliffs, NJ: Prentice-Hall.

Lockhart, A. (1966, May). Communicating with the learner. *Quest, VI,* 57–67.

Magill, R. (1985). *Motor learning: Concepts and applications.* Dubuque, IA: Wm. C. Brown.

Masser, L. (1993). Critical cues help first grade students' achievement in handstands and forward rolls. *Journal of Teaching in Physical Education, 12,* 301–312.

McGown, C. (1988). [Motor learning]. Unpublished lecture notes. Provo, UT: Brigham Young University.

Parker, D., & Bars, J. (1994). *On target for fun* [video]. Palm Beach, FL: The Athletic Institute.

Pfaff, D., Myers, B., Light, R., Freeman, W., & Winkler, G. (1991). *USA Track & Field Level II. Coaching education program: The jumps.* Indianapolis, IN: The Athletic Congress, TAC, USA.

President's Council on Physical Fitness and Sports. (2004). *The president's challenge physical activity and fitness awards.* Bloomington, IN: President's Council on Physical Fitness and sports.

Rink, J. (1993). *Teaching physical education for learning* (2nd ed.). St. Louis, MO: Mosby.

Select Marketing Groups of America. (2000). *The super study of sports participation* [print]. American Sports Data. Available: www.sgma.com/research/marketplace/ superstudy_sports_participation.html.

Strand, B., Reeder, S., Scantling, E., & Johnson, M. (1997). *Fitness education: Teaching concepts-based fitness in schools.* Scottsdale, AZ: Gorsuch Scarisbrick.

U.S. Department of Health and Human Services. (1996). *Physical activity and health: A report of the Surgeon General.* Atlanta, GA: Centers for Disease Control and Prevention.

Winkler, G., & Schexnayder, I. (1998, July). *Level three coaching seminar.* Baton Rouge, LA: United States of America Track & Field.

Winkler, G., Seagrave, L., Gambetta, V., Orognen, J., Jolly, S., & Rogers, J. (1986). *Coaching Certification Level II: Sprints and hurdles.* Indianapolis, IN: The Athletic Congress, TAC, USA.

Index

Page references followed by f indicate figure.